DATE DUE

~~OCT 1 98~~		
~~AP2 6 01~~		
~~FE 19 02~~		
~~NO 28 03~~		

CONSTRUCTION PRODUCTIVITY MANAGEMENT

CONSTRUCTION PRODUCTIVITY MANAGEMENT

PAUL O. OLOMOLAIYE
University of Wolverhampton, UK

ANANDA K.W. JAYAWARDANE
University of Moratuwa, Sri Lanka

FRANK C. HARRIS
University of Wolverhampton, UK

The CHARTERED
INSTITUTE OF
BUILDING

LONGMAN

ite of Building through

and Associated Companies throughout the World.

Illustrations by Pantek Arts, Maidstone and TAS, Hertfordshire
Typeset by 57
Typeset in 10/12 Times
Produced by Addison Wesley Longman Singapore (Pte) Ltd.,
Printed in Singapore

First printed 1998

ISBN 0–582–096030

British Library Cataloguing-in-Publication Data
A catalogue record for this book is available from the British Library

CONTENTS

ACKNOWLEDGEMENTS

We are grateful to the following for permission to use material in these tables: Table 1.1, The Construction Confederation; Table 4.1, The International Labour Office; Tables 4.2, 4.3 and 8.24, The Chartered Institute of Building; Tables 5.4, 5.5, 8.18 and 8.19 Routledge; Tables 7.2, 7.3, 7.4, 8.1, 8.2, 8.3, 8.4, 8.5, 8.6, 8.9, 8.10, 8.11, 8.13, 8.14 and 8.15, The American Society of Civil Engineers; Tables 8.16, 8.17, 8.20, 8.21, 8.22, The Institution of Civil Engineers; Tables 8.7 and 8.8, MCB University Press; Tables 9.1, 9.2, 9.3, 9.4, Elsevier Science.

We also acknowledge the following for permission to use material in these figures: Figure 2.2, copyright International Labour Organisation 1987; Figures 4.10, 8.33, 8.34, 8.35, The Chartered Institute of Building; Figures 5.13, 8.16, 8.17, 8.18, 8.3, 8.4, 8.5, 8.6, 8.7, 8.8, 8.9, 8.10, The American Society of Civil Engineers; Figure 7.1, *The Psychological Review*, American Psychological Association; Figures 8.14 and 8.15, MCB University Press; Figures 8.26, 8.27, 8.29, 8.30, 8.31, The Institution of Civil Engineers; Figures 8.11, 8.12, 8.13, 8.22, 8.23, 8.24, 8.25, Routledge; Figures 8.32, *The International Journal for Construction Management and Technology*.

We have been unable to obtain permission from the Institution of Civil Engineers for Figures 8.19. 8.20 and 8.21 and Table 8.12, and from F. J. Drewin for the contribution contained in Figure 2.2, and would be grateful for any information that will enable us to do so.

PREFACE

Building and civil engineering turnover involving design services, contracting and materials manufacture represents around 10% of GNP for most nations, yet, disturbingly, annual growth in construction productivity generally falls below that achieved by the economy as a whole and is disconcertingly less than that of more technologically advanced industrial sectors. Here the benefits of capital investment through the application of modern machinery and equipment coupled with limited use of labour can be clearly observed in the real wage levels enjoyed.

The poorer record of construction in this respect has tended towards inflationary wage increases, causing fewer and reduced commissions than might otherwise be the case. Indeed, the attractions of other industries are clearly manifest in the drift of the construction workforce to seek better conditions elsewhere during recessions and the lack of recruits when economic activity becomes more buoyant.

Clearly, if this disturbing pattern is to be checked – and hopefully reversed – the amount of output per input needs to be increased. The measures required, however, are complex and linked to many factors, some outside the industry itself, such as national economic demand for construction, capital and labour availability and competition for resources, while others can be influenced more directly through the levels of training and education of the construction workforce, quality of design and construction achieved, higher standards of management and better companies in general. Importantly, these latter aspects form the subject of this book; effective production management methods lie at the root of improving labour productivity irrespective of the other factors necessary to induce growth conditions. The core of the approach has been developed over a period of some twenty years in teaching students and research work covering a wide variety of construction projects involving national research organisations and companies alike.

Each chapter is designed to present technical information coupled with managerial techniques to aid decision making on the choice of construction methods and processes, all directed towards achieving productivity improvement through more efficient use of labour resources and the application of modern machinery. In particular, many of the worked examples are based on realistic case studies modelled and solved on the computer to illustrate the potential contribution this modern form of technology can make towards better production management.

The book is therefore written to cater for the needs of both students and practitioners involved in planning and managing field construction for building and civil engineering projects. Specifically, it will find a market among working contractors, engineers, builders, quantity surveyors, equipment and materials manufacturers, designers and specification writers. Students on diploma, degree and postgraduate programmes will also find the contents essential reading in understanding the principles and practices of production management. Consequently, a special effort has been made to augment the text with diagrams, tables and performance data, which together with the worked examples should help the reader to prepare construction plans and estimates and ensure timely and successful completion of projects to the satisfaction of all parties involved in the process.

To this end the chapters are set out in a logical sequence beginning in Chapter 1 with definitions, importance, trends, measuring problems and factors influencing construction productivity. Chapter 2 provides symptoms of failing productivity and tools for its identification, classifies construction activities and discusses aspects of the construction workforce, common production problems and constituent elements of operation time to set the foundation for subsequent chapters. Chapter 3 describes methods for improving construction operations, beginning with the benefits of method study, constraints inhibiting its application, basic principles and procedures, and various method study techniques, followed by realistic examples highlighting potential benefits. Chapter 4 describes the merits of work measurement, work measurement techniques, and methods of calculating standard times and planning times, finally covering the industry situation with regard to its application and future trends.

Chapter 5 describes several other methods and techniques that can be used to record production data, diagnose poor productivity, analyse production and measure productivity levels. Techniques such as activity sampling, learning curves, video and time-lapse photography, supervisor delay surveys, worker questionnaires and worker questionnaire sampling are all explained. Chapter 6 deals with the principles and approaches to construction planning from enquiry to completion of a project, including CPM, precedence and line of balance techniques, integration of planning with estimating, budgetary control and costing together with a summary of the application of computer systems. Chapter 7 discusses theories of workforce motivation, their application to construction operatives, the results of empirical studies on workforce motivation, motivation and demotivation variables, their significance and financial incentives. Chapter 8 embraces computer modelling in determining suitable methods for construction tasks in conjunction with appropriate operational research techniques in deciding the best from alternatives. Finally, Chapter 9 describes several other approaches for overall performance improvement towards long-term excellence. To this end, it discusses goal setting, quality management, including quality control, quality assurance and total quality management, followed by benchmarking (a performance comparison technique), breakthrough approaches for overcoming productivity barriers and lean construction (a new production philosophy), culminating in a global productivity improvement system integrating all of the related productivity enhancement approaches.

P.O. Olomolaiye, A.K.W. Jayawardane, F.C. Harris

1

CONSTRUCTION PRODUCTIVITY: DEFINITION AND IMPORTANCE

1.1 INTRODUCTION

Necessary reconstruction after the Second World War resulted in a surge in construction activities, requiring new production techniques and incentive schemes, especially to quantify output per input as the basis for paying workers. Hence, Work Study and Bonus departments were set up and time studies conducted to evaluate construction tasks for improved performance. Being payment driven, the various incentive schemes devised to 'tease' out more output from construction workers were not entirely effective, or functioned at best when newly introduced. They have been described by Herzberg (1968) as mere 'kicks in the ass' in the productivity improvement process.

Construction industry fortunes tend to fluctuate with the general economy, and organisational patterns change with time, reflecting the socio-economic environment and sometimes becoming almost incomprehensible. For example, new procurement systems and management techniques are constantly being tested, with management contracting and partnering being the most novel to date. Furthermore, many other management techniques are practised, few of which demonstrate a grasp of sound management philosophy. However, irrespective of the situation, the construction manager must consciously drive resources to higher productivity and profit in a very competitive business environment. Indeed, with more sophisticated and knowledgeable clients, combined with increased competition and low profit margins, the difference between survival and failure is largely a question of productivity.

Even when industry is buoyant demand is accompanied by skills shortages, particularly when boom is followed by recession. In the UK for example, an exodus of construction craftspeople during the recession of the early 1990s was followed by a shortage in 1997 when the workload increased (Table 1.1). Clearly, the challenge facing the modern construction manager is to maintain on-site productivity with better management and modern technology.

Productivity remains an intriguing subject and a dominant issue in construction

Table 1.1 Percentage of firms experiencing skills shortages.

Type of labour	Demand as at June 1997 (%)
Skilled civil engineering operatives	52
General civil engineering operatives	20
General building operatives	15
Electricians	34
Steel benders and fixers	35
Painters and decorators	20
Plant operators	26
Plasterers	42
Plumbers	40
Carpenters and joiners	54
Roofers	38

Source: Construction Confederation Construction Trends Survey, July 1997.

management, promising efficient usage of resources and cost savings and ultimately affecting the bottom line of every effort in the construction process. The concept of productivity is therefore stressed in this chapter, together with the importance of measurement issues, as a prelude to detailed explanations of productivity management issues in subsequent chapters.

1.2 THE PRODUCTIVITY CONCEPT

Improving *productivity* is a major concern of any profit-orientated organisation as representing the effective and efficient conversion of resources into marketable products and determining business profitability. Consequently, considerable effort has been directed to understanding the productivity concept, with the different approaches taken by researchers resulting in a wide variety of definitions, measurements and applications.

1.2.1 Issues in defining productivity

Most people understand 'peace' or 'love' but would offer different definitions depending on their personality and situation at the time they are asked. Defining such concepts does not lead to a consistent set of words as expected in definitions, but explanations of the main characteristics of the subject. Productivity faces the same definition problems in the construction industry context.

The *Concise Oxford Dictionary* (9th edn) defines productivity as the 'capacity to produce, the state of being productive; effectiveness of productive effort, especially in industry; production per unit of effort'. While providing a good starting point, this definition uses the word 'productive' in defining productivity but, importantly, three distinct productivity concepts are brought out: (i) the *capacity to produce*, that is the force behind production itself,

(ii) *effectiveness of productive effort* as a measure of how well the resources are utilised and (iii) the *production per unit of effort* (or rate) to measure output of the factors of production over a defined period of time.

Definitions offered by different authors are commonly limited to only one or two of these three. For example, economists often define productivity as the ratio of physical output to physical input, thereby reflecting only the third component, rate. English and Marchione (1983), however, argued that output involves not only quantity but also quality, and attempted to define the true input dimensions to embrace raw materials, capital and wages together with management, organisation, ingenuity, creativity and attitudes. Indeed, the managerial input into the production process, while often invisible, obviously has a great influence on productivity levels.

The argument of English and Marchione was further buttressed by Fenske (1985), in an analysis of the meanings of fifteen different definitions of productivity. He agreed that productivity is a 'tangible reality', but instead of limiting it to physical outputs and physical inputs, suggested including invisible *services*. He thus defined productivity as 'the amount of goods and services produced by *a* productive factor in a unit of time'. Levitt (1982) went further and defined productivity as 'the ratio between the value of a unit of output and the cost of *all* of the inputs' as a better alternative. However, the definition in Davis (1951) – 'the degree to which the power to make or provide goods or services having exchange value is utilised as measured by the output from the resources utilised' – seems to occupy the 'centre ground', incorporating the three main characteristics of the productivity concept, and consequently is adopted as the working definition in this book.

1.2.2 Measuring productivity

Although productivity is not the same as performance (some workers perform strenuously but have low productivity owing to ineffective methods), two performance measures feature prominently in productivity discussions: *effectiveness* and *efficiency*. Both generally work together but have entirely different meanings, with effectiveness measuring whether goals such as profit or market share are met and whether the approaches, methods and tools used are correct, while efficiency is a measure of productivity. Indeed, the expressions for efficiency in engineering applications and productivity are the same:

$$\text{Efficiency} = \frac{\text{Output}}{\text{Input}}$$

Measuring productivity in this manner is straightforward in concept until the input part is considered – Manpower, Management, Materials, Money and Machines, some of which are particularly difficult to quantify. Productivity expressed in relation to all of these factors is termed *total-factor productivity* and is a gauge of the overall efficiency of an industry or organisation. Other measures consider the relationships between output and a particular input or an incomplete combination of inputs. These are referred to as *single-factor productivity* (when only one factor is involved, for example labour) or *partial productivity* (when more than one, but not all, factors are involved) and can be expressed as:

$$\text{Total-factor productivity} = \frac{\text{Total output}}{\text{Total input}}$$

$$\text{Partial productivity} = \frac{\text{Total output}}{\text{Partial input(s)}}$$

Measuring total-factor productivity involves an aggregation problem because output and all inputs have to be expressed in monetary terms as the common base of expression. The resultant productivity index, *economic productivity*, suitably assesses the overall productivity of the industry, where improvements reduce the cost of constructed facilities. However, *physical productivity* is more meaningful to the construction setting, with the emphasis being on labour input, but such partial measures are really derivatives of the multivariate function – total productivity – and quantify the effect of a single variable by assuming that all other variables are constant. Because other variables are rarely constant, partial productivity measures become dubious expressions of true productivity.

While total productivity potentially provides the best measure, 'labour' has traditionally dominated, especially in establishing indices for inter-firm comparison and measures of overall efficiency of an industry. Even though 'capital' is more precise, it become meaningless, however, in job sequencing, determining the number of operatives to employ and in day to day job planning on construction sites and would also require details in monetary terms of the value of land, machinery and equipment as well as the rate of any depreciation. All of these details are less readily available, especially in the required form. In contrast, labour, being easily quantifiable, constituting a large part of construction costs and being more susceptible to management decisions than other resources, is considered the predominant measure of construction productivity. Consequently, the emphasis in this book is on labour, meaning both managers and operatives.

The difficulty of determining productivity in the construction industry context is further compounded by problems in measuring and comparing the value of outputs over a long period since the price of a given input or output varies due to such factors as:

(1) Changes in the general level of prices; that is, inflation.
(2) Changes in the supply–demand equilibrium for a given resource, causing its price to rise faster or slower than prices in general.
(3) Changes in the quality of the output; for example, a detached bungalow built in 1997 may be more aesthetically pleasing and more functional than a similar house built in 1967.

Other problems include identifying outputs, there being no single and common physical term to measure output in construction. Houses, roads, power plants, office buildings and so on are all outputs but often without any similarity. Thus, for national level productivity estimates, output is usually established by two methods: (i) the total monetary value, which has the advantage of combining all forms of output, and (ii) functional units such as number of residential units, other buildings in terms of floor area, power plants in terms of kilowatts and so on.

Output for the construction site manager, however, is required in terms of a particular task such as volume of concrete placed, area plastered or number of bricks laid, and is difficult to establish when output is in several forms. For example, a trade may contribute to several operations, such as joiners making windows, doors or form work. Even each distinct operation can be further divided into several minor operations, the very nature of the operations posing problems in deciding whether output should be calculated per day, month or year or in relation to the completion of a specific assignment. Some, however, are not too inhibiting, typically bricklaying and concreting where partial productivity measurement in physical terms is possible.

Despite these shortcomings, various measurement techniques have evolved but with no standard or universally acceptable method of measurement yet. Some measures are more appropriate to evaluating workers' efficiency; others are suitable for manpower planning and utilisation; some are applicable only to certain types of operations.

1.3 TRENDS IN CONSTRUCTION PRODUCTIVITY

Governments and construction firms now appear more aware of construction productivity and the associated effects on the standard of living. For example, the Latham review suggested that productivity improvements of up to 30% by the year 2000 are necessary to face the challenges of the next millennium (Latham 1994). Similarly, in the USA a series of reports has been published by Business Roundtable Publications based on a comprehensive study carried out to address declining US productivity through a Construction Industry Cost Effectiveness Project (Business Roundtable Publications 1991). This growing concern with productivity levels in the construction industry is justified when its growth rate is compared with that of manufacturing industry (Figure 1.1). Furthermore, the industry's sizeable contribution to the gross national product (GNP) – ranging from 6–8% in the UK and the USA to 9% or more in some developing countries – has contributed to concern and awareness about productivity in the construction industry.

Nevertheless, both the definitional and measurement problems highlighted earlier pose difficulties in establishing accurate trends since data sources are rare, and in some cases non-existent. Where data sources are available, they are often haphazardly arranged. Indeed, until Fleming (1980) was commissioned by the Department of the Environment (DoE) no readable data was compiled for the UK industry, and despite the enormity of the task, some data are still not usable because a little analysis would reveal basic flaws. Also, comparative analysis of data from different sources often gives contradictory views. For example, Betts (1987)

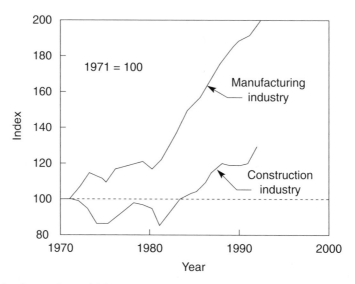

Figure 1.1 Comparison of labour output trends in the UK, 1972–1992.

compared data on public expenditure as a measure of construction output with contractors' output (in monetary terms) only to discover a gulf between the two output measures.

In order to impose some coherence, the following three main sources for measuring and comparing construction productivity per worker were identified by Hillebrandt (1984):

(1) Monetary value of work done by the industry divided by the corresponding labour figures.
(2) Census of Industrial Production data giving gross value added at factor cost per head.
(3) The National Income Expenditure Accounts data giving the net GDP in construction divided by the number employed in the industry.

Detailed statistics on the first are published on a quarterly basis in the UK Housing and Construction Statistics and cited in various publications, but, as highlighted by Fleming (1980), may be ambiguous due to such factors as:

(1) Resource inputs often form a large proportion of total output and the eventual productivity index so derived thus critically depends on the proportions of these other inputs.
(2) Because of the different types of construction work – for example, roads, residential buildings and industrial buildings – an index derived by this method may reflect only the mix of work rather than a change in construction productivity.

(3)   The DoE data are limited, deficient in coverage and do not take account of all workers, especially self-employed workers.
(4)   The price index base for discounting prices to constant levels still has significant errors of accuracy.

These arguments, although reasonable, have to be largely discounted in the absence of any other reliable data for measuring overall construction productivity, and the data can be considered reasonably accurate, especially in establishing trends. Figure 1.2 illustrates UK construction productivity trends for 1980–1996 in terms of the value of construction output per thousand employees, based on Housing and Construction Statistics (1996). Although the trend shows a relatively steady growth, this may be due to increased mechanisation and improved tools and methods rather than to significant improvements in labour utilisation.

   Although these results may be helpful, the efficiency of a particular resource input in the construction process would be a more useful indicator for contract management. Here the Building Research Establishment in the UK and Harris *et al.* (1985) conducted a number of studies to determine productivity levels in physical terms, for example labour hours per house, cubic metres of concrete placed per hour and so on. Although the method of construction affected labour resources, the distribution of work between trades and skills remained fairly constant over the years, with labour content declining with increasing prefabrication.

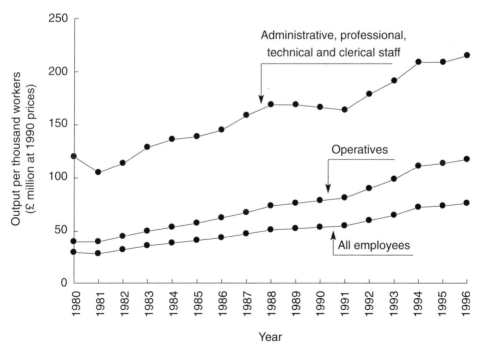

Figure 1.2   Variation in construction output per employed worker in the UK, 1980–1996.

1.4 FACTORS INFLUENCING CONSTRUCTION PRODUCTIVITY

The difficulties of establishing productivity levels and comparing on-site productivity with established values are compounded by the existence of a large number of influencing factors with no particular limit – in other words, everything affects productivity. Since these factors are rarely constant and may vary from country to country, from project to project, and even on the same project depending on the circumstances, anything influencing them can subsequently affect productivity. Only the more important factors are discussed here, divided into two categories, *external* and *internal*, representing those outside the control of the firm's management and those originating within the firm, respectively.

1.4.1 External factors

NATURE OF THE INDUSTRY

The traditional separation of the design and construction functions has affected construction productivity through waiting for drawings, design changes and subsequent rework. A more rational and economic use of construction resources could be enhanced with the two processes 'under one roof' as in manufacturing industry so that the buildability of the designed structure can be correctly evaluated at the sketch design stage, preventing time wastage. Fortunately, this traditional separation is now being bridged to some extent with new forms of contract, for example design and build, management contracting, fast-track construction, concurrent engineering, partnering and so forth.

THE CONSTRUCTION CLIENT

Construction clients have sometimes been impediments to construction productivity because of their lack of, or too little, knowledge of construction procedures and hence employment of project managers, architects, engineers and quantity surveyors. Changes still occur during the course of projects because of variations in owner requirements or insistence on materials not easily available in the market. Furthermore, clients often have negative leverage on labour situations on sites, where irrational and unpredictable attitudes increase uncertainty during construction, with negative effects on job sequencing and execution (Holt 1995).

WEATHER

Being an outdoor industry, construction experiences various climatic conditions affecting labour productivity. As reported by Markham (1942) the workforce functions most efficiently at ambient temperatures between 60 and 76°F with a moderate 40–70% humidity. Hot and wet climates are far less conducive to mental and physical energy, and tropical climates do not favour muscular activity generating much body heat and discomfort. Baldwin and Monthei (1971) ranked weather highest in the causes of construction delays in the US, while Harris (1979) developed a model to evaluate effects of weather on construction projects in the UK to help avert the negative effect of the British climate on the country's construction productivity.

LEVEL OF ECONOMIC DEVELOPMENT

Global construction industry productivity depends greatly on the general level of economic development and buoyancy. If the economy booms with money available to carry out developmental projects, construction industry productivity should increase, while productivity suffers most during recession or a downturn in economic fortunes; these factors are all intermingled with political stability in determining to a great extent the level of investment.

In addition to the factors discussed above, health and safety legislation, procurement policies, codes of practice and so forth are further external factors influencing site practice and productivity.

1.4.2   Internal factors

MANAGEMENT

In Taylor's (1961) advocation of scientific management, responsibility for employing, training and equipping workers for the job in order to achieve optimum productivity belongs to management through proper plans, control and coordination of resources. With increased project size and complexity this responsibility has become even more important; management inadequacies can result in a waste of resources with consequent losses in productivity.

Sadly, managers often attempt to pass the blame to somebody else, typically construction workers, when things go wrong, but quickly claim the praise for their 'ingenuity' when goals are met. English and Marchione (1983) reported that this hypocrisy mainly arises because management sees workers as a means to an end, explaining further that when autocratic management puts pressure on employees without removing the causes of low production the result is more absenteeism, staff turnover, sabotage or strikes. On the other hand, democratic management that attempts to change worker attitudes without fulfilling its own functions may result in negligible improvement, therefore the need to perform management duties properly should be addressed before any attempts to unlock the latent abilities of workers are introduced.

TECHNOLOGY

Clearly, productivity improves with the proper use of plant and tools; for example, digging with an excavator will produce more than manual digging. Apart from quantity, quality also generally improves when suitable machines are used. New technology is constantly being introduced to the construction industry, perhaps to cope with current skills shortages. Also, there seems to be a gradual shift in training towards more formal education to acquire new technological skills, with traditional apprenticeships failing to cope with the rapid developments in technology. However, the 'big bang' approach to increasing productivity, whereby management seeks to improve productivity through large capital expenditure, is naive because more investment in technology is not necessarily a cure for low productivity. With advances in technology, construction managers should be better equipped with new developments and operatives should be better trained to use new equipment and tools to maximise the advantages.

LABOUR

With labour being a major influential factor in construction productivity, Maloney (1983) showed that the level of productivity is directly related to the 'driving, induced and restraining forces acting upon workers' – that is, their motivation. Although the direct influence of labour cannot be seen clearly when productivity is perceived globally, as far as on-site productivity is concerned labour acts as the hub for other resources and hence is a major controlling variable in construction productivity.

The personal attributes of the worker can also affect productivity in a particular trade, craft or operation through: (i) skills, qualifications, training and experience, (ii) innate ability – both physical and mental energy – and (iii) the intensity of the application of both skills and innate ability to the production process. Although construction might appear to a simple or untrained person as mere physical exertion, the skill comes only through proper training and experience. It is therefore of great importance to train workers and to employ trained workers if higher productivity is to be achieved.

UNIONS

Unions are commonly seen by management as having negative influences on workers' productivity and in certain instances can be very influential. Unions are alleged to be against productivity growth because they perceive it as a threat to job security, and are therefore often accused of working against the interest of the society. For example, Ortega (1931) reported that 'the mob goes in search of bread, and the means it employs is generally to wreak the bakeries'. Kellog et al. (1981) also reported about the US that 'improvement of productivity is often beyond the control of management of the nation's contractors and subcontractors – it is effected more by restrictive union work practices on the one extreme'.

Construction unions are not so powerful in the UK, with membership consisting of 40–50% of direct labour, and generally less than 30% of all operatives due to the casual nature of employment (Hillebrandt 1984). What influence they do possess is now being further eroded by the individualism being promoted by subcontracting.

1.5 SUMMARY

A productivity concept relevant to the construction industry was described, with a detailed discussion of definition and measurement issues. The importance of construction productivity, productivity trends in the industry, and the shortcomings of available data were highlighted and productivity growth compared to highlight the present level of achievement. Finally, both external and internal factors affecting productivity were explained as a prelude to detailed explanations of productivity management in later chapters.

REFERENCES AND BIBLIOGRAPHY

Adrian J. (1987). *Construction Productivity Improvement*. New York: Elsevier

Baldwin J.R. and Monthei J.M. (1971). Causes of delay in the construction industry. *Journal of the Construction Division ASCE,* **97**(2)

Benes J. (1984). The possibilities of the measurement of productivity in the building industry. In *3rd International Symposium on Building Economics*, 24–32

Betts M. (1987). British public expenditure on construction less than claimed? *Construction Management and Economics*, **5**(1), 13–20

Business Roundtable Publications (1991a). Measuring productivity in construction. In *Construction Industry Cost Effectiveness Report A1*. New York.

Business Roundtable Publications (1991b). More Construction for the Money: Summary Report of the Construction Industry Cost Effectiveness Project, October. New York

Chau R.W. and Lai L.W.C. (1994). A comparison between growth in labour productivity in the construction industry and the economy. *Construction Management and Economics*, **12**(2), 183–185

Construction Confederation (1997). Construction Trends Survey

Davis H.S. (1951). The meaning and measurement of productivity. In *Industrial Productivity*. Madison, WI: Wisconsin Industrial Relations Research Association

Department of the Environment (1996). *Housing and Construction Statistics*. London: HMSO.

English J. and Marchione A.R. (1983). Productivity: a new perspective. *California Management Review*, **XXV**(2)

Fenske R.W. (1985). An analysis of the meanings of productivity. *Productivity Measurement Review*, August

Fleming M.C. (1980). Statistics collected by the Ministry of Works 1941–1956, 2 vols. London: Department of the Environment

Holt G.D. (1995). A methodology for predicting the performance of construction contractors. *PhD thesis*, University of Wolverhampton, UK

Harris F.C. (1979). A model for evaluating the effects of weather on construction projects. *PhD thesis*, Loughborough University of Technology, UK

Harris F.C., Price A.D.F. and Emsley M. (1985). An evaluation of production output for construction labour and plant. *SERC GR/B 55138*

Herbsman Z. and Ellis R. (1990). Research of factors influencing construction productivity. *Construction Management and Economics*, **8**, 49–61

Herzberg F. (1968). One more time – how do you motivate employees? *Harvard Business Review*, **46**(1)

Hillebrandt P. (1984). *Analysis of the British Construction Industry* pp.221-236. London: Macmillan

Horner R.M.W. and Talhouni B.T. (1995). *Effects of Accelerated Working, Delays and Destruction on Labour Productivity*. London: CIOB

Kellog J.C., Howell G.E. and Taylor D.C. (1981). Hierarchy model of construction productivity. *Journal of the Construction Division ASCE*, **107**(CO1), 137–152

Koch J.A. and Moavenzadeh F. (1979). Productivity and technology in construction. *Journal of the Construction Division ASCE*, **105**(CO4), 351–366

Latham, M. (1994). *Constructing the Team – Joint Review of Procurement and Contractual Arrangement in the UK Construction Industry*. London: HMSO

Lema N.M. and Price A.D.F. (1995). Benchmarking: performance improvement toward competitive advantage. *Journal of Management in Engineering ASCE*, **11**(1), 28–37

Levitt E.R. (1982). Defining and measuring productivity in construction. In *Proceedings of the Spring Conference of the American Society of Civil Engineers*, April

Logcher R.D. and Collins W.W. (1978). Management impacts on labour productivity. *Journal of the Construction Division ASCE*, **104**(CO4), 447–461

Lowe J.G. (1986). Alternative approaches to the definition of productivity in the construction industry. In *Translating Research into Practice, CIB 86: Advancing Building Technology*, vol. 9, pp. 3786–4304

Lowe J.G. (1987). The measurement of productivity in the construction industry. *Construction Management and Economics*, **5**, 101–113

Maloney W.F. (1983). Productivity improvement: the influence of labour. *Journal of Construction Engineering and Management ASCE*, **109**(3)

Markham S.F. (1942). *Climate and Energy of Nations*. Oxford: Oxford University Press

Olomolaiye P.O., Wahab K.A. and Price A.D.F. (1987). Problems influencing craftsmen's productivity in Nigeria. *Building and Environment*, **22**(4), 317–323

Ortega Y.G. (1931). *Jose–Revolt of the Masses*, annotated translation, p. 60. New York: W.W. Norton

Price A. (1992). Factors influencing construction productivity, ECI document

Prokopenko J. (1987). *Productivity Management – A Practical Handbook*. Geneva: ILO

Sozen Z. and Girtilli H. (1987). Factors affecting construction productivity – a survey. *International Journal of Construction Management and Technology*, **2**(1), 49–61

Suite W.H.E. (1987). Measurement of productivity in the construction sector. In *Managing Construction World-wide*, Vol 2: *Productivity and Human Factors in Construction*, pp. 856–867, Proceedings of CIB W-65 Symposium London: CIOB

Taylor F.W. (1961). *The Principles of Scientific Management*. New York: Harper & Row

Thomas H.R. (1992). Effects of scheduled overtime on labour productivity. *Journal of Construction Engineering and Management*, **118**(1), 60–76

Thomas H.R. and Mathews C.T. (1986). *An Analysis of the Methods of Measuring Construction Productivity*. Construction Industry Institute, University of Texas, May

2

FAILING PRODUCTIVITY DIAGNOSIS

2.1 INTRODUCTION

Having discussed the definitions, the importance of construction productivity and factors influencing productivity in Chapter 1, this chapter provides the basic understanding necessary to decide on the implementation of productivity improvement attempts using the tools and techniques given in subsequent chapters.

The first part of the chapter provides a discussion of the symptoms of failing productivity to help identify which site and which operations need improvement. It also classifies construction operations into productive, contributory and unproductive activities, with an example from bricklaying to show that construction operations very often include a significant proportion of contributory and unproductive activities that can be eliminated or reduced. The personality of construction workers, their perception of management, how they spend a typical working day and problems causing unproductive time are explained using actual case studies. Finally, the time taken to carry out a construction operation is broken down into constituent elements, exposing additional work contents and ineffective times contained in the total time, to provide an indication of the potential for productivity improvement in construction operations.

2.2 SYMPTOMS OF FAILING PRODUCTIVITY

Professionals involved in managing construction projects should be able to identify quickly the symptoms of failing productivity in order to take timely corrective action. In this respect, off-site managers operating from the head office, who generally supervise several sites, should have formal means for constantly monitoring performance and quickly identifying the projects falling behind or ahead of the planned schedule and cost budgets. On-site managers should, in addition, identify the operations needing attention to bring the project back on track. Clearly, timely identification of problematic sites and specific operations needing closer attention is the first and most important step in any productivity improvement programme.

2.2.1 How to identify which site needs improvement

Cost monitoring reports, progress monitoring reports and formal site meetings that provide feedback information from sites are the three formal assessment tools available for off-site managers to monitor project performance. Indeed, these tools, which are discussed briefly below, are effective and useful only if appropriate data from schedules and cost systems are available, workable and accurate, and if feedback information is received by managers at the proper level at the proper times.

COST MONITORING

This is a part of cost control involving observation and evaluation of cost data, comparison of observed cost data with cost targets and reporting to appropriate managers. If the reported project costs overrun the budgeted costs then management is alerted for closer scrutiny and subsequent corrective action. Cost monitoring through a paper process is generally routine for most contractors, but cost control that additionally involves taking decisions on corrective action and actual implementation of those decisions to bring the project expenditure back on track is the difficult part and hence is often treated less rigorously than the monitoring aspects.

There are several cost control methods that can be adopted by contractors, including overall profit or loss, profit or loss on each contract at valuation period, unit costing, standard costing, the programme evaluation and review technique (PERT)/cost, and integrated cost/schedule. The *overall profit or loss* system is at one extreme. As the name implies, it is intended to compare the overall profit or loss at the end of a contract, which clearly is too late for any corrective action on the project. The *unit costing* method at the other extreme can be used to obtain each resource variance for each activity or bill item; for example, the difference between the budgeted quantity of cement for concreting the ground floor and the actual quantity of cement used for this purpose. Clearly, this kind of detailed system helps cost monitoring of individual operations to find out which specific operations need improvement.

A cost effective system may lie between these two extremes and the contractor should select a suitable degree of sophistication depending on such factors as the size of the company, the type of work undertaken, the type of contract, how much information is needed from the system for effective management, how quickly the information is required and how much money the contractor is willing to spend. See Pilcher (1994) and Oxley and Poskitt (1986) for more details on this aspect.

It is, however, very important to identify the weaknesses and, sometimes, dangers in relying completely on these reports since there can be numerous shortcomings in their implementation unless this is carried out properly. Some notable ones are:

- The reported cost data may be inaccurate if, for example, work supervisors are assigned to report the costs at the end of each work shift, perhaps resulting in misallocation or wrong allocation of resources due to negligence or carelessness.
- The detailed cost codes may be too ambitious in the light of the site resources available to compile and compare information, leading to misallocation or multiple allocation of resources and resulting in understating or overstating of the true situation.
- The reported data are vulnerable to deliberate falsification if work supervisors are assigned to report the resources utilised and the work achieved, and the same report is used by management to direct criticisms or evaluate rewards.

Thus, off-site managers should be aware of these shortcomings and guard against them if the reports are to be used to capture project performance signals.

PROGRESS MONITORING

Progress monitoring is a part of progress control involving comparison of actual physical progress with planned progress. If important operations take considerably longer than the time allocated in the schedule then management should be alerted. Planning future tasks to get the project progress back on schedule or modification of the schedule for this purpose is called updating. Progress monitoring, taking corrective actions and updating are collectively called progress control. Here several tools are available for planning, preparation of schedules and progress monitoring, such as critical path methods, bar charts, line of balance, PERT, S-curve and operational research techniques. Some of these techniques are described in Chapters 6 and 8.

As with cost control systems, management should guard against the possible shortcomings of progress reporting; for example, work schedules improperly prepared without a detailed consideration of resources and method of operation during the preplanning stage. Furthermore, the schedules would not have incorporated subsequent changes in scope due to variation orders or unforeseen conditions, thus making the base plan inaccurate or unrealistic for comparison. Moreover, many contractors prepare pre-tender plans and schedules as a contractual requirement but once the project is awarded and under way the efforts devoted to this all-important aspect of preplanning are diminished. Even when detailed pre-construct planning is done, some contractors tend to neglect effective progress control throughout the project due to such factors as unrealistic, *ad hoc* or arbitrary preplanning in the first instance making it too difficult to adhere to the schedules thereafter; schedules quickly becoming outdated due to the large number of variables affecting construction, and other unforeseen delays. The common excuse then given is that there is insufficient time to carry out proper planning under the pressure of day-to-day problems, which are often created by yesterday's mistakes. Today, a range of project planning and control software packages is available, with varying degrees of sophistication. Such packages can greatly assist the process.

FORMAL SITE MEETINGS

Site meetings are one of the main channels of communication between parties during project execution. Except for contractors' internal meetings with their subcontractors, they are mainly aimed at external project control by clients or their representatives but indirectly help the contractor in project control and problem identification in two ways. First, the fact that the contractors have to present the project progress to the client, consultant or project manager, together with sound justifications for failure to meet the planned progress, compels them to make a detailed study of their own problems. Second, the opportunity given to the contractors to present reasons, justify constraints and point out requirements to be met by other parties enables them to reduce costs.

In addition to the above three formal tools, off-site construction managers can also obtain information on project performance from other project records such as safety reports, quality reports, information contained in site diaries and so forth, if these are well maintained. Furthermore, other project-specific factors, such as profit and overhead allocated for the project and the extent of liquidated damages, are considered by contractors for closer monitoring of specific projects.

2.2.2   How to identify which operations need improvement

Irrespective of whether the directive comes from the off-site manager, after scrutiny of performance data such as cost and progress reports, or alternatively initiated by site management itself, the specific operations needing improvement should be carefully identified to obtain the maximum benefits. Some of the notable symptoms of failing productivity are:

- excessive use of labour overtime to complete a unit quantity of work;
- bottlenecks in material flow due to poor site layout, interference with other operations or as a result of poor material supply methods;
- high material wastage due to faulty storage, delivery at the wrong place requiring multiple handling, or carelessness of workers;
- frequent plant breakdowns due to excessive use, lack of inspection, lack of maintenance, or operation by unskilled or unauthorised people;
- work fatigue due to unsuitable methods or working under poor conditions;
- late programme as reported by progress reports;
- poor quality of workmanship due to lack of skill, carelessness of workers and poor quality of materials;
- delays to and delays by subcontractors;
- excessive errors and mistakes, resulting in repetitive work;
- insufficient information to proceed with work;
- poor site organisation resulting in ineffective time and extra work;
- cost overrun as reported by a detailed cost monitoring system;
- poor design of temporary work resulting in safety risks, inefficient methods and wastage;

- constant employee complaints on certain aspects of operation, facilities, tools or working conditions;
- site congestion resulting in obstructions, accidents and waste of resources;
- safety risks resulting in slowing down of work or accidents.

Most of these signals are interdependent, implying that a particular operation needing improvement most likely will have more than one signal; for example, excessive errors and mistakes will frequently have excessive labour, material waste, late programme and cost overrun. These signals can be picked up by site management through the following means:

- casual observation;
- cost reports;
- progress reports;
- internal meetings;
- scientific observations;
- site records.

CASUAL OBSERVATION

Symptoms such as poor quality of workmanship, poor design of temporary work and site congestion are readily seen by casual observation. However, such casual approaches can miss other signals that do not persist all the time, requiring longer observation periods to know in detail what was going on at the work face. Unfortunately, except for supervisory level management, top-level managers can rarely devote time to detailed scrutiny of ongoing operations by asking questions such as 'Are materials and tools available and suitable?', 'Is the work procedure efficient?', 'Is the required equipment available and in working order?', 'Is the gang of suitable size and make up?' and so forth, since they are often busy with either crisis management or planning future activities. Answers to these questions can be realistically obtained only by someone specifically assigned to that task carrying out systematic observation.

COST REPORTS

Proper implementation of a detailed cost control system may also identify signals on cost overruns for each and every activity. Analysis is generally carried out at the head office, if carried out at all, based on information provided by the sites. Any operations having significant deviations are then reported to the site manager for necessary corrective action. As mentioned earlier, the site management should bear in mind the possible errors in cost reporting and guard against reporting erroneous cost information.

PROGRESS REPORTS

The maximum benefits of progress monitoring reports that indicate any deviation of the actual physical progress from that of the base plan for each and every operation can only be obtained if they are supported by suitable project management computer software. Software tools readily provide all schedule details, including starting and completion time for each activity, actual starting time and actual completion time for completed activities, actual starting time, percentage completion and predicted actual completion for all activities in progress if continued as at present, overall effect of any delays in activity durations on subsequent activities and the entire project and so on. These tools are invaluable for site managers to take prompt corrective action. They are discussed further in Chapter 6.

SITE MEETINGS

Internal site meetings with in-house supervisors and subcontractors are specifically aimed at progress evaluation. The participants have the opportunity to present activity progress, problems such as bottlenecks in material flow, problems in equipment, fatiguing work, delays to and by subcontractors, insufficient information, employee constant complaints, safety risks and so on. These presentations provide ample information to identify which operations need attention, and in obvious cases decisions are taken immediately to improve the situation.

SCIENTIFIC OBSERVATION

These techniques include *field count*, *productivity rating* and *activity sampling* and can be used to identify activity inefficiencies quickly and reliably. These techniques are described in detail in Chapter 5.

In addition to the above tools there are other ways by which a site manager can identify operations needing attention, including informal discussions with supervisors and workers and day-to-day site records such as site diary, and labour, plant and material returns.

All of the means identified above will provide signals for clear identification of activities requiring productivity improvement and obvious constraints can be rectified without a detailed study. They are, however, incapable of pinpointing the exact causes of poor productivity, which often need detailed analysis requiring financial commitment, depending on the nature of the problem and the selected analytical technique. This is dealt with more specifically in Chapter 3.

2.3 CLASSIFICATION OF CONSTRUCTION ACTIVITIES

The proportion of time spent carrying out active work on site undoubtedly affects the productivity levels of individuals, gangs and sites. This, however, may not reflect the true state of productivity because of variations in skill, poor working conditions and bad site layout introducing unnecessary work elements or increasing the time spent on unproductive work. To incorporate this factor in productivity improvement, it is therefore necessary to have a clear understanding of associated work elements, categorised as *productive, contributory* and *unproductive*:

- **Productive activities** are work elements directly involved in the actual process of construction or putting together or adding to a unit being constructed. For example, pouring concrete, vibrating concrete, loading a truck and travel with a load in earthmoving operations are considered to be productive since they contribute directly to output.
- **Contributory activities** are work elements that do not directly add to output but are generally required and sometimes essential in carrying out an operation. These include handling material at the work face, receiving instructions, reading drawings, cleaning up the workplace, ancillary work and so on.
- **Unproductive activities** include either being idle or doing something that is unrelated to the operation being carried out or in no way necessary to complete that operation. These include walking empty handed, work carried out using the wrong tools or the wrong procedures, rectifying mistakes and so on.

It is important to note that there is no right way of classifying the multitude of work elements involved in construction activities into productive, contributory and unproductive. What is necessary is to identify involved work elements and realistically classify into these categories so that they can be used in any productivity improvement effort.

Let us consider the bricklaying operation as an example. A suitable classification of bricklaying elements into productive, contributory and unproductive is shown in Tables 2.1, 2.2 and 2.3, respectively. The work elements given in Table 2.1 are the main activities in bricklaying that are directly contributory to the output. These productive work elements do not receive much attention during any productivity improvement attempt since they are, in any case, productive.

Table 2.1 Productive activities in bricklaying.

Productive activities	Description
Spreading mortar	Spreading mortar on the wall in preparation for laying bricks
Fetching mortar	Taking mortar with trowel for spreading or buttering bricks to be laid
Fetching brick	Taking brick from the stack for buttering, cutting or laying
Cutting brick	Cutting bricks to required size using a trowel or chisel
Laying brick	Positioning and pressing the brick on the course, including tapping
Filling joints	Placing and compacting mortar into vertical gaps between bricks
Setting and checking	Setting line for the next course and checking verticality and horizontally using spirit level or other device
Raking and pointing	Removing excess mortar from joints using a trowel or pointing (depending on design) using pointing bars

The work elements given in Table 2.2 include essential contributory elements such as distribution of bricks and mortar to workplaces and non-essential elements such as instruction, inspection and ancillary work. Distribution of bricks and mortar, although essential for bricklaying, may be considered as contributory since it does not directly add to the output. Any savings in time spent on it by improved material handling or having effective site layouts would clearly improve productivity. To classify this element as productive would direct attention away from that possibility. Thus, management should attempt to plan working arrangements so that these contributory elements and the time spent on them are minimised.

Clearly, all of the elements given in Table 2.3 are either unrelated to bricklaying or idle time. Every attempt should be made to avoid such elements by proper preplanning and by using effective methods.

Once the activities involved in a construction operation are suitably classified into productive, contributory and unproductive activities, a labour utilisation factor (LUF) can be established using the following formula:

$$LUF = \frac{\text{Time spent on productive activities} + P \text{ (time spent on contributary activities)}}{\text{Total time spent on all activities}}$$

The constant P is a factor representing the proportion of contributory activities required to carry out a particular operation and often depends on the amount of essential contributory activities required. It is often helpful for contractors to keep a

Table 2.2 Contributory activities in bricklaying.

Contributory activities	Description
Measuring	Checking distances in line with drawings using tape or other device
Instruction and inspection	Taking instructions from supervisor or interruptions during supervisor's inspection
Ancillary work	Work relevant to bricklaying such as fixing lintels, windows, doors, anchors, thermal insulators, setting platform and so on
Driving dumper	Usually by the labourer for collection and distribution of materials
Operating mixer	Mixing mortar, including loading the mixer with constituent materials
Distributing bricks or mortar	Distribution of mortar onto mortar boards and bricks into stacks on the platform for laying bricks
Fetching	Fetching bricks or mortar from depot or mixer for distribution and fetching tools by operatives
Cleaning	Washing the mixer, removing excess mortar and broken bricks at the end of working day
Reading drawings	Checking drawings for necessary details before or during setting

Table 2.3 Unproductive activities in bricklaying.

Unproductive activities	Description
Idle and away	Operative not working while work is available or not on plot for no obvious reason
Relaxation	Apparent relaxation for necessary physiological fatigue
Waiting	Waiting by the operative for materials or tools, or due to interference by another gang
Searching	Looking for misplaced tools or any other necessary equipment for implementing a task at hand
Rework	Removing and replacing already completed work due to operative's fault or management fault
Confused	Undecided or abrupt stoppage of work sometimes followed by consultation
Other work	Doing work not directly related to bricklaying

record of LUFs for various common construction operations both by completely avoiding contributory activities (where $P = 0$) and by partially considering contributory activities with a suitable value of P. It is then possible to compare actual LUFs established on the basis of field observation (using techniques described in Chapter 5) with these established standards. Indeed, site managers should strive to obtain the maximum LUF with only productive activities for true productivity improvement.

2.4   THE CONSTRUCTION WORKFORCE

The human element as represented by the construction workforce is the main catalyst/determinant of construction efficiency or productivity. The efficiency of the workforce in converting resources into a built product is largely dependent on both technology and the sociological environment of the contracting organisation and the construction site. The ability of the manager to make the working environment conducive to optimum productivity will determine how successful the project is in meeting time, cost and quality targets. That is the main task in getting the best from the workforce. This is made easier by understanding the workers and how they perceive their working environment, then the motivating principles discussed in Chapter 7 can be applied effectively to improve labour productivity.

The construction working environment is a product of the organisational response to providing adequate production resources and the workers' assessment of this response reflected in their motivation and productivity. The manager's problem in identifying the variables in the working environment that directly or indirectly affect operatives' output could be partially resolved through a structured approach such as worker questionnaire survey or a more scientific approach like activity sampling, discussed in Chapter 5. In order to explain the construction environment in more detail as a prelude to proper understanding of subsequent chapters, this section provides the results of an investigation carried out using the worker questionnaire survey technique and activity sampling on a sample of bricklayers in the UK.

2.4.1 The personality of construction workers

Personality reflects worker qualities, knowledge, attitudes and characteristics; for example, training, experience, age, perception and so on. Clearly, personality changes with time (such parameters not being static), needing management's constant monitoring and alertness for changes impacting productivity. The results of the investigation related to the personality of construction workers are summarised in Table 2.4.

Table 2.5 provides a ranking of factors influencing workers' decisions to stick to or quit a particular place of work. Earnings-related issues were the most significant factor influencing bricklayers' decisions to quit a particular site for another or quit the trade altogether. Working conditions and overall management of the sites were ranked second and third. These results are in line with what may be expected from workers in other industries.

Interpretation of the results given in Tables 2.4 and 2.5 provides insight into certain aspects of workers' personality, such as type of employer, pattern of employment, loyalty to employer, age structure, training, experience, skill levels, how workers perceive their work and their associated problems. This information

Table 2.4 Characteristics of construction workers.

Characteristic	Classes				
Type of employer	Labour only subcontractor 53%	Main subcontractor 12%	Main contractor 34%	Other 1%	
Length of stay with employer	0–2 years 46%	2–5 years 19%	5–10 years 18%	10–20 years 11%	>20 years 6%
Age structure	15–20 years 16%	21–30 years 35%	31–40 years 15%	41–50 years 23%	>50 years 11%
Mode of training	Apprenticeship 49%	Trade school 0%	CITB 8%	On-site 36%	Combination 7%
Experience by type of job	Housing 53%	Public building 19%	Industrial 20%	Commercial 8%	
Experience in years	0–2 3%	2–5 16%	5–10 18%	10–20 23%	>20 40%
Energy output	Very strenuous 38%	Strenuous 46%	Adequate 16%		
Remuneration level	Excellent 0%	Very good 0%	Good 30%	Fair 42%	Bad 28%

Table 2.5 Factors influencing bricklayers' decisions to leave sites.

Factor	Rank
Earnings-related	1
Working conditions	2
Management/supervision	3
Workmanship	4
Distance from home	4
Workmates	6
Better design	7
Do not want to work	8
Dismissal	8
Transfer to other trades	10
Transfer to other sites	11

can then be used by management in setting up programmes for increased output from workers.

These results relating to UK-based bricklayers provide a typical example of construction operatives' identity. However, some of the discussed characteristics can and will vary from country to country and trade to trade depending on several factors, such as level of economic development, education level, training policies, social status and so on. The interested reader may refer to similar studies carried out in the USA (Rowings *et al*. 1996), Iran (Zakeri *et al*. 1996), Indonesia (Kaming *et al*. 1997), Nigeria (Olomolaiye *et al*. 1987) and Sri Lanka (Jayawardane and Gunawardane 1998) to study their variation.

2.4.2 Workers' perception of management

In addition to workers' identity or personality, discussed above, management should be aware of workers' perception of management itself in order to effectively direct the workforce to higher productivity while at the same time maintaining a trouble-free, satisfied workforce with good team spirit. This perception will depend on management's contribution to the working environment in terms of work organisation, supervision, efforts to progress on site, participation by management and operatives' awareness of management's efforts.

The operatives' assessment of the overall organisation of their sites in terms of work organisation, work supervision and conditions of work environment obtained using the worker questionnaire survey technique are shown in Table 2.6. The general opinion of the sites was requested in three forms to test the consistency of response. From these consistent responses, the working environment was judged to be fair by the operatives although this judgement depended on the circumstances under which they were working.

The results also revealed that approximately 60% of the operatives believed that their management was well aware and concerned about the progress they were

Table 2.6 Workers' perception of management.

Function	Excellent (%)	Very good (%)	Good (%)	Fair (%)	Bad (%)	Very bad (%)
Work organisation	12	12	33	35	6	3
Work supervision	12	15	39	28	6	0
Working environment	5	20	34	30	5	6

making on their jobs but 15% indicated that management was not aware of anything about their work – an indication of some distance between management and operatives. Construction workers have an aversion to being asked by management about job progress when materials or other production essentials are not available. Only 25% of the workers saw management as being ready to identify sources of delays and rectify them.

Furthermore, 72% of the operatives were not aware of the project's costs and the profit being made on it but only knew the prices for their work and the progress rate expected from them, indicating the extent of the distance between management and operatives when it comes to more sensitive issues like costs and profits.

Here again Table 2.6 provides a typical example based on the views of a sample of UK bricklayers. Applied to a specific situation, this type of information provides valuable insight into the effectiveness of production management.

2.4.3   How construction workers spend a typical working day

To decipher some of the expected subjectivity often generated in opinion surveys, a more scientific and objective technique – activity sampling (see Chapter 5) – was adopted to survey how production time is actually spent by workers.

The data were analysed considering only the working time and the results are shown in Figure 2.1.

On average, workers spend 55.5% of their working time (excluding official break times) on productive activities, 2.1% on supervision-related activities, 13% on 'extra breaks' and 29.4% unproductively. The extra breaks consist of early quits and late starts; clearly, a loss of 13% is considerable for a typical construction site. The observed supervision time – that is, time spent taking instruction and inspection – varies depending on the type of work, available details such as drawings and also on the skill and knowledge of the operatives, and can be considered unavoidable given a particular situation.

Unproductive time as classified in Section 2.3 consists of approximately 29% of working time – clearly, more than any construction manager would like to observe. Detailed studies using some of the techniques described later in the book will often be necessary to identify the root causes of each unproductive activity in the evaluation of the construction environment.

Overall, Figure 2.1 provides a warning for any construction manager and

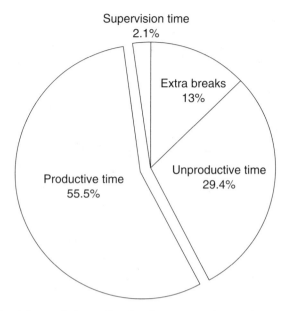

Figure 2.1 Breakdown of time utilisation by construction workers.

indicates ample opportunities for significant improvements in labour productivity using the approaches described later in this book.

2.5 PROBLEMS CAUSING UNPRODUCTIVE TIME

In addition to having an understanding of the nature of the construction workforce for effective deployment of workers, a further understanding, which is even more important for a construction manager, involves awareness of common production problems and their relative impact on productivity. One effective way to identify such problems is by asking the operatives themselves using a technique such as the worker questionnaire survey, as described in the previous section. This section reports the results of an investigation carried out using this technique to provide a typical example of common production problems faced by construction workers in the UK, as an aid to better understanding of the chapters that follow.

Construction workers were requested to rate a general list of probable problems on their respective sites on a three-point scale, Very Important, Important and Just Important, which were subsequently scored 3, 2 and 1, respectively. The total scores by all bricklayers for each problem were then converted to relative indices using the relative rank index technique (Table 2.7). Furthermore, the operatives were asked to estimate time losses per problem area and the sources of the problems (Tables 2.8–2.10). These four tables form the basis of the following discussion of the problems contributing to unproductive time.

Table 2.7 Ranks of problems influencing bricklayers' productivity.

Problem	Rank point total	Relative index	Overall rank
Lack of materials	111	0.36	1
Gang interference	105	0.34	2
Repeat work	53	0.17	3
Supervision	22	0.07	4
Lack of equipment/tools	19	0.06	5
Absenteeism	6	0.02	6

Table 2.8 Estimated time loss per problem in a 40-hour week.

Problem	Estimated time loss (hr/week)
Lack of materials	3
Gang interference	2
Repeat work	2.5
Supervision	2
Lack of equipment/tools	2
Absenteeism	0.5

Table 2.9 Rank of causes of lack of materials.

Problem	Rank
Lack of planning	1
Transport within site	2
Improper materials	3
Interference	3
Paper work	5

Table 2.10 Rank of causes of rework.

Problem	Rank
Change of instructions	1
Unclear instructions	2
Complex specifications	3
Poor workmanship	4

LACK OF MATERIALS

This causes the greatest hindrance to operatives' productivity, with an average estimated loss of 3 hours per 40-hour week. Detailed analysis indicated lack of planning, in terms of inadequate job sequencing and site planning, as the main source of the problem. The major causes were found to be transport difficulties within the site, improper materials delivered to sites and interference by other gangs (for example, material prepared for a particular gang being used by another gang).

GANG INTERFERENCE

This ranks as the second most important factor influencing bricklayers' productivity, wasting up to 2 hours per 40-hour week. This loss is mainly caused by having to wait until the workplace is ready to continue working; for example, waiting for the scaffolder to fix scaffolds for the next stage of work and sometimes interference by joiners, concretors or even equipment. Clearly, such delays could be solved or reduced with adequate planning of jobs on sites.

REPEAT WORK

This was ranked third, with an average estimated loss of 2.5 hours per 40-hour week. It was found to be caused mainly by changes in instructions or unclear instructions, matters that are obviously related to supervision.

SUPERVISION DELAYS

While time spent taking instruction or inspection is an essential part of construction, the study revealed that there are times when the supervisor disturbs the production process unnecessarily. This was identified as the fourth most important problem, with an estimated loss of 2 hours per week, and could be avoided if clearer instructions were given in the first instance and by avoiding mere repetition or stating the obvious. (See Table 2.11 for an example of workers' assessment of their direct supervisor.) The problem list continues depending on the situation and the significance attached to each production problem.

Table 2.11 Workers' assessment of their direct supervisors.

Criteria	Agree (%)
Around when needed	37
Friendly and approachable	35
Very skilled	16
Keeps information	5
Does not listen	5
Does not know their work	3

It is, however, important to note that the above example is just one attempt to identify production problems and their relative impact on productivity. Indeed, there can be variations in the ranking and time loss for each problem area depending on the circumstances under which operatives work, especially depending on the efficiency of management. For example, Table 2.12 provides an international comparison of these findings with results from the USA, Indonesia and Nigeria using a similar approach. Although the studies may have had different foci and it is therefore risky to use them for serious comparative analysis, it is possible to draw some inferences from these figures using the reported indices as measures of the importance attached to the problems in different countries. One notable similarity is that lack of materials at the workplace is the worst problem in all four countries.

It has been argued (Business Roundtable Publications 1982) that where these problems exist in significant proportions, it will be useless trying to motivate or even study motivation in workers because even a highly motivated worker cannot be productive in an environment where basic construction resources are lacking and other production problems linger. Thus, construction managers should attempt to resolve their site production problems before any attempt is made to improve worker motivation.

2.6 ASSEMBLING OPERATION TIME ELEMENTS

Having treated the symptoms of failing productivity, the means to capture these symptoms, the different types of activity involved in construction operations and some aspects of the construction workforce, further understanding of the causes contributing to the total time of a construction operation and their relative influence on the operation time is necessary (Figure 2.2). The basic work content (A) in Figure 2.2 is the amount of work *contained in* the operation in terms of total labour hours and/or equipment hours if the operation is carried out under perfect conditions (other than legitimate rest periods for the operatives), which is never achieved in practice. The actual total operation time thus consists of the following additional time elements:

- *Work content added by unavoidable externalities (B)*. This includes additional time spent due to causes outside the control of the contractor such as weather,

Table 2.12 Comparative ranking of productivity problems in different countries.

Problem	UK	Nigeria	Indonesia	USA
Lack of materials	1	1	1	1
Gang interference	2	6	3	5
Repeat work	3	2	2	3
Supervision	4	4	6	4
Lack of equipment/tools	5	3	5	2
Absenteeism	6	5	4	6

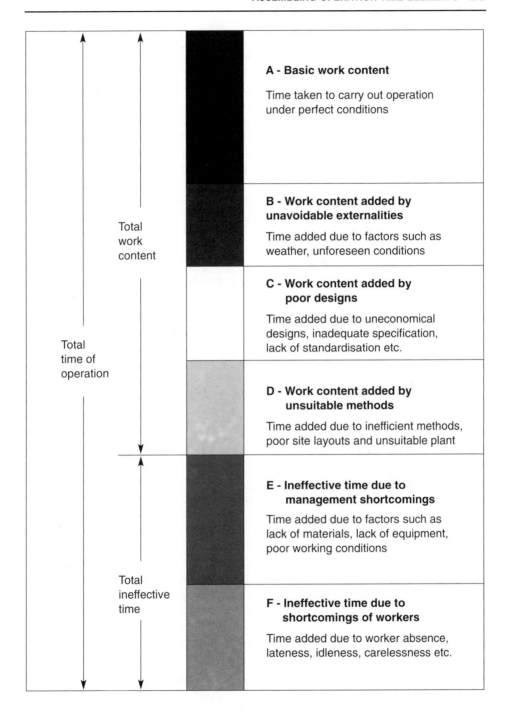

A - Basic work content

Time taken to carry out operation under perfect conditions

B - Work content added by unavoidable externalities

Time added due to factors such as weather, unforeseen conditions

C - Work content added by poor designs

Time added due to uneconomical designs, inadequate specification, lack of standardisation etc.

D - Work content added by unsuitable methods

Time added due to inefficient methods, poor site layouts and unsuitable plant

E - Ineffective time due to management shortcomings

Time added due to factors such as lack of materials, lack of equipment, poor working conditions

F - Ineffective time due to shortcomings of workers

Time added due to worker absence, lateness, idleness, carelessness etc.

Total work content

Total time of operation

Total ineffective time

Figure 2.2 Assembling operation time elements. (Adapted from ILO 1979; Drewin 1982.)

unforeseen ground conditions and material shortages in the market. This time cannot be reduced or avoided. The ultimate aim should therefore be to reduce the actual operation time to 'A + B'.

- *Work content added by poor designs (C)*. This includes additional time spent due to reasons such as changing the design after work has started, over-design, inadequate specification and lack of standardisation; for example, too much reinforcement in a concrete slab resulting in more fixing time or too many sizes and varieties of beams and columns requiring additional time for fabrication of form work. Clearly, these also involve additional material costs, which directly affect the productivity.
- *Work content added by unsuitable methods (D)*. Additional time spent due to factors such as use of unsuitable plant, equipment and tools, poor layout and working conditions involving multiple handling of materials, unnecessary movements and so forth are also inherent in typical construction operations.
- *Ineffective time due to management shortcomings (E)*. This includes additional time caused by delays in providing necessary working drawings or instructions, delays in supplying necessary materials, plant, equipment and tools, poor planning of work operations resulting in interference and waiting time, and failure to ensure safe working practices.
- *Ineffective time due to shortcomings of workers (F)*. This includes additional time taken by workers due to factors such as time off without good cause, lateness, idleness, deliberate slowdown, carelessness resulting in accidents and rework, and failure to use proper tools and so forth (see also Figure 2.1).

The relative sizes of the time elements shown in Figure 2.2 have no special significance and can vary from operation to operation due to their specific nature, but as a rule of thumb the actual time spent to carry out a construction operation in practice can be more than double that required if it were carried out under proper conditions. As far as the contractor is concerned the time components A, B and C in Figure 2.2 are unavoidable but D, E and F can be controlled.

2.7 SUMMARY

Symptoms of failing productivity and the tools available to capture these symptoms were discussed for timely identification of sites and operations needing corrective action. As an aid to maximising the benefits from any productivity improvement attempt, activities involved in construction operations were classified as productive, contributory and unproductive and illustrated using an example in bricklaying. Aspects of the construction workforce and common production problems on site were discussed using actual case studies. Finally, the time taken to carry out a typical construction operation was broken down into its constituent time elements, exposing additional time spent on unnecessary work contents and due to the shortcomings of management and workers alike, to highlight the productivity improvement potential in construction operations.

REFERENCES AND BIBLIOGRAPHY

Alfred E.L. (1988). *Construction Productivity: On-Site Measurement and Management.* New York: McGraw-Hill

Bresnen M.J. (1984). Effective construction site management: a review. *Journal of Construction Engineering and Management,* **110**(4), 420–436

Business Roundtable Publications (1982). Construction Labour Motivation. A Construction Industry Cost Effectiveness Project. *Report A-2,* August. New York.

Drewin F.J. (1982). *Construction Productivity.* New York: Elsevier

ECI (1994). *Total Productivity Management: Guidelines for the Construction Phase.* Productivity Task Force, European Construction Institute

Harris F.C. and McCaffer R. (1995). *Modern Construction Management* 4th edn. London: Blackwell Science

International Labour Organisation (1979). *Introduction to Work Study* 3rd (revised) edn. Geneva: ILO

Ireland J. (1994). Improving construction site productivity. *Construction Industry Computing Association (UK) Bulletin,* 7 September

Jayawardane A.K.W. and Gunawardene N.D. (1998). Construction workers in developing countries–a case study in Sri Lanka. *Construction Management and Economics* submitted

Kaming P.F., Olomolaiye P.O., Holt G.D. and Harris F.C. (1997). Factors influencing craftsmen's productivity in Indonesia. *International Journal of Project Management,* **15**(1), 21–30

Mawdesley M., Askew W. and O'Reilly, M. (1997). *Planning and Controlling of Construction Projects.* London: Longman

National Economic Development Organisation (1989). *Promoting Productivity in the Construction Industry.* London: NEDO

Olomolaiye P.O., Wahab K.A. and Price A.D.F. (1987). Problems influencing craftsmen's productivity in Nigeria, *Building and Environment,* **22**(4), 835–845

Oxley R. and Poskitt J. (1986). *Management Techniques Applied to the Construction Industry* 4th edn. London: BSP Professional Books

Pilcher R. (1994). *Project Cost Control in Construction,* 2nd edition, Blackwell Science, Oxford

Rowings J.E., Federle M.O. and Birkland S.A. (1996). Characteristics of the craft work force. *Journal of Construction Engineering and Management ASCE,* **122**(1), 83–90

Zakeri M., Olomolaiye P.O., Holt G.D. and Harris F.C. (1996). A survey of constraints on Iranian construction operatives' productivity. *Construction Management and Economics,* **14**, 417–426

3

METHOD IMPROVEMENT IN CONSTRUCTION OPERATIONS

3.1 INTRODUCTION

Construction is becoming increasingly challenging, with modern-day clients' intricate requirements for complex construction, high quality products and shorter completion times. Moreover, there seems to be a never-ending stream of new plant, equipment, materials, components and regulations, all compounded by the notoriously competitive environment compelling contractors to carry out business at low profit margins, with the attendant risk.

Thus, the successful contractor constructs projects by methods that ensure the maximum rate of production at the minimum cost, with *method study* providing the framework of factual data to assist decision making. This enables resource optimisation by applying a systematic approach to problems rather than intuitive guesswork.

Following the discussion of the symptoms of failing productivity, their diagnostic tools, different types of construction activity, characteristics of the workforce, common site problems and the constituent time elements of a construction operation in Chapter 2, this chapter describes means of improving methods of construction operations. The benefits of method study and the constraints inhibiting its application in the construction industry are first discussed. The basic principles and the procedure in carrying out a method study on-site are then presented, followed by explanations of the use of the various techniques that are available. Finally, realistic examples are detailed, exemplifying the suitability of the approach and highlighting the potential benefits that can be obtained.

3.2 THE BENEFITS AND THE PRESENT STATUS

The objective of method study is to examine the ways of doing work in order to develop easier and more effective methods of construction or operation by determining the optimum layouts, selecting the most suitable construction teams (both equipment and labour) and balancing work gangs for the most efficient use of resources. In other words, the benefits of method study are: (i) improved: site layout, traffic and pedestrian flow around the site, material handling methods, use of materials, storage methods of materials, use of plant, use of manpower, working methods, working conditions, and organisational structure, (ii) simplified tasks by introducing standard methods and by reducing the variety of work and (iii) reduced: fatigue, unnecessary work, and idle or wasted time.

Unfortunately, a cursory observation of most construction sites shows many instances of failing productivity due to poor construction methods, inefficient material handling and disorganised workplaces and sites, indicating lack of application of systematic method improvement. The common reasons for this are:

(1) The inherent characteristics of the construction industry, such as the unique nature of construction projects, short activity times, the fact that most operations are not performed in a predetermined sequence, the non-repetitive nature of activities and the presence of a large number of uncontrollable variables (for example, weather), make practitioners reluctant to apply work study techniques on a widespread scale.

(2) The senior management of contractors is usually busy with strategy in securing future projects while site management is tackling day-to-day problems and emergencies often created by yesterday's mistakes due to lack of preplanning. Thus, there is insufficient time or financial commitment for work study, reflected in the failure to employ staff for this purpose in order to keep overheads low due to competition.

(3) Construction operations, especially those of long duration, often require expensive items of plant which are often on-site before any study is carried out, since preplanning for construction is often hurried. As on-site costs can be very high, decisions behind plant selection are unlikely to be changed even if a more effective method is later found; indeed, the benefits that could be applied to similar future projects are usually ignored.

(4) There are no proper work study data banks readily available to the construction industry. Firms practising work study, and having benefited from it, have started from scratch with significant financial commitments. Moreover, the competitive nature of construction compels confidentiality, thereby contributing to the diverse presentation and application of work study existing today.

(5) While work study had its roots in the building industry, since Gilbreth it has been developed and used extensively in manufacturing industry. Consequently, most of the available work study terminology and techniques evolved in that industry and only after reconsideration can these techniques be revised or adapted to meet the requirements of the construction industry. In this respect research publications and textbooks (Geary 1970; Parker and Oglesby 1972; Drewin 1982; Adrian 1987; Heap 1987; Oglesby *et al.* 1989) have contributed to this end but without a significant impact. Furthermore, attempts at direct adoption of manufacturing work study techniques, combined with the lack of a

construction background, have curtailed the impact of work study in the industry.

(6) The construction industry has shifted considerably from direct labour to subcontracting, making the main contractor's role managerial and coordinating rather than constructing. Thus, the main contractor's interest in method improvement is limited and the subcontractors do not have the necessary expertise or resources for such attempts.

These factors may have distracted the attention of most practitioners from systematic method improvement. Nevertheless, method improvement is one of the main areas of attention needed to reverse the declining trend in construction productivity.

3.3   METHOD STUDY PROCEDURE

The exact procedure in carrying out a method study on-site varies depending on the purpose of the study and the technique adopted but the basic steps, which are considered in detail in subsequent sections, are:

- Step 1: **Select** the operation, job or site to be method studied, or that is to be set up.
- Step 2: **Record** all the relevant facts about the present or proposed method.
- Step 3: **Examine** those facts critically and systematically.
- Step 4: **Develop** the most practical, economic and effective method.
- Step 5: **Install** the developed method.
- Step 6: **Maintain** the new method by regular routine checks.

This is the classical approach to method study in any industry. In contrast to those techniques requiring substantial modifications for effective application in the construction industry, this approach is broadly applicable to construction method improvement.

3.3.1   Selection of an operation for method study

Although the nature of construction work lends itself to method improvement since in many cases preplanning is hurried and ill-conceived, the construction environment constantly changes due to various factors such as weather, poor ground conditions, subcontract work and material shortages. Therefore, good reasons for adopting a detailed method improvement investigation need to be in evidence. Chapter 2 discussed how to identify site(s) needing improvement together with pointers to failing productivity (as aids in identifying the operations needing improvement) and the tools available to capture these signals. These are all eye openers, but how do we identify which area should be studied first?

Clearly, the first and the most important factor to consider is *economy*, with larger cost savings generally being obtained by a systems approach rather than by considering individual operations first. The systems approach considers overall aspects of the project, which at the site level may include overall layout, working conditions, management, supervision, tool allocation and so forth. Any improvements in these aspects are concurrently passed through to several operations, thereby encouraging properly planned, organised and disciplined sites and resulting in large savings. Thereafter, individual operations can be considered in detail.

Indeed, if the operation is short term or the present working conditions unstable, method improvement is unlikely to produce an economic return and hence should not be started. However, any improvements in the situations listed below always result in significant cost savings and should therefore be considered:

- Operations making up a large proportion of the contract value; for example, concreting in a large reinforced concrete structure.
- Operations of a repetitive nature either on the same site or any other site; for example, hoisting or brickwork.
- Operations of a difficult and complex nature; for example, confined basement excavation and construction.
- Operations involving a large quantity of material; for example, large earthmoving operations, loading a large quantity of bricks on to scaffold.

The second consideration is *human reaction*. Few site managers like to have labour difficulties hence the general rule is first to choose, without risking unrest or conflicts on sites, only those operations that are particularly unpopular; for example, dirty or heavy work such as cleaning out blocked inspection chambers. If studies of such tasks can determine improved working methods then there will be support for productivity improvement in other tasks.

The third consideration should be *safety*. Good and safe practices are often cost saving. If there are known risks, actual or potential, then further study should be carried out to eliminate or reduce such risks, irrespective of cost implications.

In addition, selection will be considered in situations where the plant and equipment items used are new developments, whose performance under real-life conditions is unknown, but are required to optimise resources in terms of providing balanced teams. It will also be helpful in decision making. For example, new form work or false work systems might be studied if time and cost savings in erection, striking and durability can be promised.

Before selecting an operation, one must also consider whether it is really necessary; that is, can the operation be eliminated entirely or can it be done somewhere else? For example, it will be more economic and productive to fabricate door and window frames in the contractor's main workshop rather than on-site.

It is not necessary to consider only existing operations for method study since many of the problems can be foreseen before they actually happen or before it is too late for improvement. Method studies for operations to be set up can be successfully carried out during preplanning using historical work study data, thereby eliminating field data collection.

3.3.2 Recording the relevant facts

Unless the job selected in Step 1 has inefficiencies that are clearly visible, in which case prompt corrective action is taken, it is essential to make a clear and concise record of the proposed or existing activities in order to carry out a detailed analysis for method improvement. Clearly, the success of the whole exercise depends on the accuracy of the recorded facts and the ease with which they can be studied. This fact-finding will depend on whether the selected work is ongoing or proposed.

ONGOING WORK

If the task is not complex, simple recording of the sequence of operations together with associated time involvement, delays, interruptions and their causes would be sufficient. In other situations a systematic procedure is required. The recording techniques (in some cases recording and analytical techniques) are mainly divided into four groups. Of the large number of techniques available under these four groups, Table 3.1 shows those applicable to the construction industry and the situations where they are suitable. Their application together with examples that are discussed in detail in subsequent sections.

Irrespective of the recording technique adopted, it is essential for the person making the study to contact relevant workers, foremen, supervisors, and others concerned to explain the reasons for making the study and to emphasise that everyone's cooperation is sought in improving the job. It is important to point out

Table 3.1 Method study recording techniques.

Group	Technique	Suitable situations
Charts	Outline process chart	To understand the construction process and to find out whether a detailed analysis is required
	Flow process chart	To investigate the construction process and diagnose inefficiencies in material process, worker and equipment utilisation
	Multiple activity chart	To diagnose and quantify idle times, resulting in unbalanced teams, and analyse alternatives
Diagrams	Flow diagrams	To understand the construction process and diagnose inefficiencies in layouts
	String diagrams	To diagnose inefficiencies in worker and equipment movements, site congestion and layout
Models	Three-dimensional models	To visualise completed projects and to solve complicated structural assembly
	Two-dimensional models	To investigate alternative layouts
Photographic methods	Photographs	To obtain a quick appraisal of site layout and working conditions
	Films	A recording technique for any study
	Videos	A recording technique for any study

that no criticism will be implied and no redundancies will occur as a result of the study. Failure to give adequate explanations gives rise to rumours and unrest.

Although there is a possibility of influencing worker behaviour when the workers are being observed, experience suggests that after a little excitement, workers tend to settle down to normal behaviour and very often cooperate.

During observation, workers, foremen and supervisors may come up with good ideas, which should be recorded. If these are incorporated in the proposed method, credit should be given to improve worker morale. Further, people tend to make their own ideas work better than those of someone else.

In addition to the specific information required, depending on the recording technique adopted, the observer should make notes and sketches of the existing method, performances seen, and any instances of obstructions to work flow of operatives and plant which will assist during the critical examination process.

NEW OPERATION

In this case information is required to develop an effective and efficient method for work to be carried out or to be set up. Any previous experience of similar work will be of great help. The facts to be obtained are: (i) the nature of the work, including quantity and quality; time available; contract conditions; specifications; location; weather and ground conditions; access and budgeted costs, and (ii) the resources available in terms of materials, plant and labour.

All of this is part of the development of a method statement, an operation performed by the planning engineer, usually in consultation with the contracts or site manager, during preplanning.

3.3.3 Examination of the facts

Once the necessary information has been recorded the next step is to examine critically the work under investigation, the purpose of this key step in method study being to evaluate the optimum method by carefully considering every aspect of work, eliminating unnecessary work and simplifying other steps. This is normally achieved through the classical questioning process shown in Table 3.2 (International Labour Organisation 1986; Foster 1989).

This questioning process looks at the purpose of the activity, the place occupied, the sequence of operations adopted, the persons or equipment used, and the procedure in carrying out the job. The primary questions detailed in Table 3.2 are meant to enable understanding of aspects of the existing operation and examination of the exact reasons for adopting the present method. The secondary questions examine all the other alternatives and help to select the most economic or efficient option among them. Clearly, not all of the questions given in Table 3.2 are applicable in every situation and the analyst should either avoid or modify these questions to suit the specific situation being studied.

During this examination process it is important that the analyst carefully

Table 3.2 The questioning process.

Criterion	Primary questions		Secondary questions	
	Existing method			
	Description	Reason	Alternatives	Selection
Purpose	What is done?	Is it necessary?	What else could be done?	What should be done?
Place	Where is it done?	Why there?	Where else could it be done?	Where should it be done?
Sequence	When is it done?	Why then?	When else could it be done?	When should it be done?
Person	Who does it?	Why that person?	Who else could do it?	Who should do it?
Means	How is it done?	Why that way?	How else could it be done?	How should it be done?

consider the following aspects:

(1) When discovering the reasons for adopting the existing methods, discussions and interviews with workmen, foremen and supervisors are essential in order to access reliable information, including soliciting their suggestions. It is important to approach them diplomatically without criticising their work.
(2) The analyst should examine the facts as they are and not as they appear to be or ought to be.
(3) Avoid being influenced by preconceived ideas since this may exclude other solutions or colour the existing situation.
(4) Avoid any hasty judgements; note the 'hunches' as they occur but immediately return to the orderly questioning procedure.
(5) The analyst should challenge all aspects of the problem and accept no answer until proved correct.
(6) Do not consider new methods until all of the undesirable features of the existing method have been exposed by systematic examination.

3.3.4 Develop an improved method

After the critical examination process the selected alternative is investigated further to develop the best method by eliminating all unnecessary activities, combining several activities when suitable, rearranging activities for efficient execution and simplifying complicated activities. The ultimate solution may, however, be influenced by the time constraints and cost implications of the various arrangements.

Creative and analytical thinking is necessary during both the examination and the development stages. Indeed, if the examination process has been carried out in this way, development is partly complete since solutions often come to light during this critical phase.

The application of brainstorming techniques can greatly assist the process and is particularly useful when both examination and development are carried out as a systems approach, rather than examining only one aspect or one work item.

Participants for the brainstorming session could comprise higher management, peers and subordinates (supervisors, foremen), with the technique preferably applied in two stages. The first is the creative part where group members contribute ideas and possibly solutions, no one being allowed to criticise ideas or discuss pros and cons at this stage. No idea should be rejected since sometimes silly or impracticable proposals can lead to other creative ideas and solutions. During the second stage the merits and demerits of the proposed ideas are discussed and evaluated, and bad ones are discarded. Subsequently, a list of possible alternative solutions is prepared, analysed and improved, and the best solution selected. See British Institute Management (1981) for further information about creative thinking and brainstorming in general.

Depending on the situation and the degree of improvement necessary, the changes may include:

(1) Rearrangement of site layout: covering relocation of storage points for efficient material handling, reduction of movements and elimination of double handling; improvement of ground conditions and other facilities; and in rare situations even relocation of offices and temporary huts.
(2) Materials: consideration of material substitutions for expensive materials, modification of size/shape for improved handling, fabrication, casting or production of components at some other place and so forth.
(3) Equipment: decision to employ more appropriate machines, plans to reduce downtime and increase site utilisation and so forth.
(4) Workers: use of skilled personnel, use of alternative more suitable tools, balancing of gang sizes, alternative simpler sequences and so forth.
(5) Work environment.
(6) Design changes.
(7) Increased use of mechanisation.

When an improved method has been developed, it should be re-evaluated through the systematic questioning process to ensure that the developed method is practical and economic and cannot be further refined without greater expenditure of resources than that warranted by the job.

3.3.5 Installing the new method

Once an improved method has been developed the actual installation on-site should be carried out in several stages commencing with seeking approval for the new method followed by planning, organising, trial run and finally installation.

SEEKING APPROVAL

If the changes to be introduced are within the control of the analyst, then clearly, approval for the new method need not be sought, except perhaps discussions with union representatives (if deemed necessary) and communicating to higher management for their information purposes. In other situations, the necessary approval should be obtained from management or administration responsible for those parts of the operation to avoid subsequent problems. If higher management were involved during the development phase installation would be relatively straightforward; otherwise, the new method, necessary changes, financial commitments, anticipated benefits and so on may have to be properly documented and organised, including a presentation to higher management if the proposed changes are substantial.

PLANNING

This task should preferably be executed by one person, who may be the site manager, contracts manager, work study engineer, the analyst or the planner depending on the circumstances and the size of the firm. The extent of planning will indeed depend on the scope of the change to be made. However, it is essential that all the stages are carefully thought through before actual installation.

ORGANISING

This involves actual organising for the new method and setting up the operational framework to include:

- checking that all the required plant and equipment is available and in working condition;
- checking that all necessary materials and components are available and ready for use;
- selecting the workforce to be involved in the new method – especially important when establishing a new team;
- providing the necessary tools and training for the selected team;
- agreeing rates of pay for the new method (if deemed necessary);
- ensuring that everyone concerned is aware of what is happening and when the new method will actually be installed.

TRIAL RUN

A trial run may be necessary to provide a further opportunity to iron out any teething problems.

INSTALLATION

After all of the above steps, the new method can be fully installed. However, during the early stages the following should be considered:

- increase supervision until operatives are familiar with the job;

- introduce minor modifications if deemed necessary;
- provide extra training if the operatives find difficulty with their new task;
- use tact and patience until the method is running smoothly.

It is essential to have a 'team' approach and 'team spirit' during installation, with any apathy against the new method by supervisors or operatives resolved immediately by consultation.

3.3.6 Maintaining the new method

After the improved method has been installed, then it is a matter of constant vigilance to keep a regular check on performance to prevent deterioration. Quite often operatives and foremen will make further suggestions for refinement; they should be cultivated and encouraged at all times to instil continuous method improvement.

3.4 OUTLINE PROCESS CHARTS, FLOW PROCESS CHARTS AND FLOW DIAGRAMS

When such techniques are adopted for recording and analysis of construction processes, work sequences are commonly recorded using the five standard symbols shown in Table 3.3, which are called ASME symbols after the American Society of Mechanical Engineers.

The following charting conventions are also adopted during the development of process charts (Currie and Faraday 1977):

(1) Similar symbols are numbered consecutively with a brief description on the right and, if required, time taken or distance travelled on the left.
(2) Materials, components and equipment first introduced to the process are shown as an arrow entering from the left.
(3) The start of the chart is indicated by an arrow to show the entry of the main material or component.
(4) The major process is charted towards the right-hand side of the chart with subsidiary processes to the left, subsidiary processes being joined to each other and to the main trunk at the place of entry of the materials or components (see Figure 3.1a).
(5) Rejects, rejects for reprocessing and repeated cycles are shown as indicated in Figure 3.1b, c and d, respectively.
(6) Separated material receiving different treatment should be charted as shown in Figure 3.1e, the right-hand branch normally representing the major flow.
(7) When the same operation is carried out at more than one place or by more than one worker in order to balance the flow of work, the chart is split into two or more elements as shown in Figure 3.1f.

In addition, notes may be used alongside activities shown on the chart to pinpoint

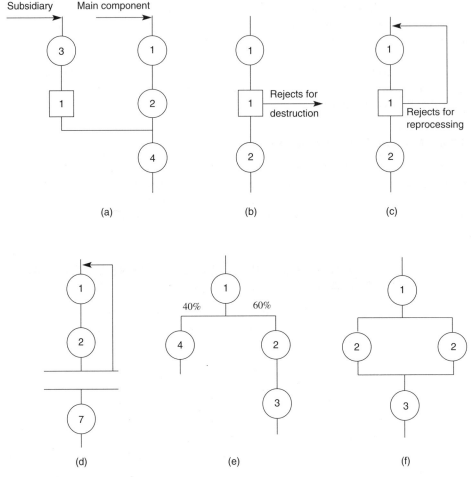

Figure 3.1 Charting conventions.

difficulties or to indicate comments such as awkward operations, distances moved, heavy or bulky loads and working conditions.

3.4.1 Outline process chart

The *outline process chart* is commonly used to obtain an overall view of the total operation before detailed study is undertaken; here, only the main operations and inspections are recorded using the operation and inspection symbols shown in Table 3.3. A simple outline process chart drawn to obtain an overall understanding of a concreting operation is shown in Figure 3.2; being only an outline process chart, additional information need not be provided. Although each of the activities shown

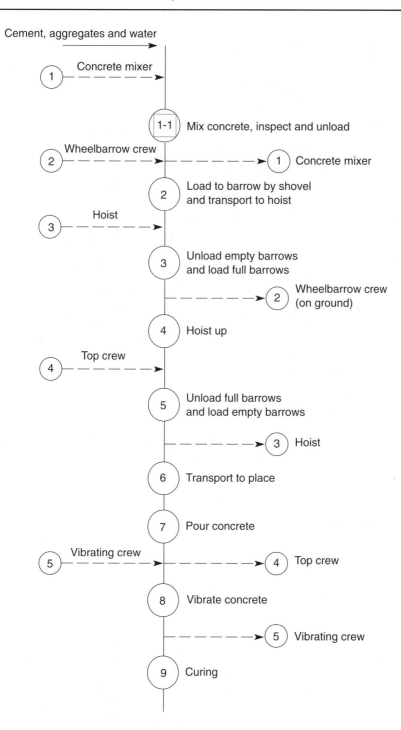

Figure 3.2 Outline process chart of a concreting operation.

Table 3.3 Standard symbols used in process charts and flow diagrams.

Symbol	Meaning	Description	Example
◯	Operation	Something is produced or accomplished. Usually a step further towards completion of operation	Concreting a slab, loading a truck, fixing form work
⇨	Transport	Movement of materials, workers, equipment from place to place, excluding small movements which form part of a single operation	Transport of earth by trucks, movement of processed material for storage
▽	Storage	Controlled storage where an object or product is deliberately kept and protected against unauthorised removal	Equipment stationed at plant yard, material stacks on site
▢	Inspection	Something is inspected for identification, quality or quantity	Inspection of concrete mix for quality
D	Delay	Temporary hold-ups/delays or obstruction or temporary storage until required	Bricklayer waiting without mortar, truck waiting to be loaded in a queue
◖	Combined	When two or more events take place together the appropriate symbols are combined with the predominant event in the outer symbol	Inspection combined with a subsidiary operation

may warrant a separate study, even at this stage, the application of method study principles could lead to elimination of unnecessary work. However, for a detailed analysis, it is usually necessary to record all the activities and illustrate the flow of work in a flow process chart or other suitable technique, depending on the aspect being studied.

3.4.2 Flow process chart

The *flow process chart* provides a detailed account of the sequence of every operation, inspection, delay, transportation or storage activity occurring in a construction process using all five process symbols given in Table 3.3 and combining time involvements and distances travelled in the process, in addition to the activity sequence.

Such charts can be categorised into two types: labour/equipment-type and material-type. The labour/equipment-type chart is normally used to analyse the activities of a worker or a piece of equipment while the material-type chart mostly concerns what happens to material (material process). Unlike an outline process chart, a particular flow process chart, therefore, looks at only one aspect of the problem in greater detail. Hence, these charts are useful in ascertaining the suitability of the work sequence and the presence of unnecessary as well as unproductive work elements.

Flow process charts can be presented in two forms, one being simply an expanded version of the outline process chart to include all of the activity details (Currie and Faraday 1977; Oxley and Poskitt 1986) while the other is more structured (International Labour Organisation 1986). Figure 3.3 shows a

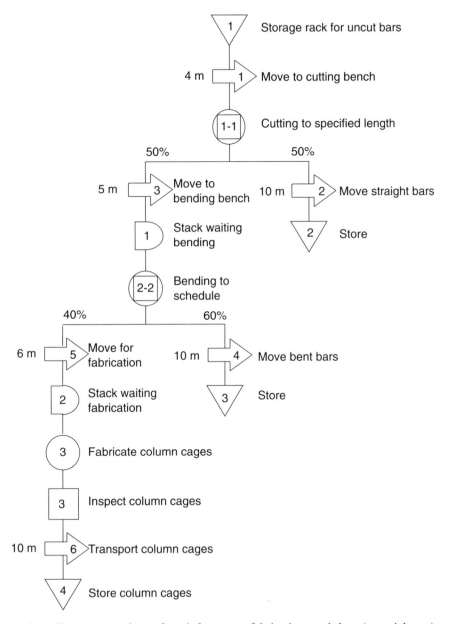

Figure 3.3 Flow process chart of a reinforcement fabrication workshop (material type).

material-type flow process chart developed to illustrate the fabrication process of reinforcement in a bar-bending workshop using the first method.

As can be seen, this method is suitable for obtaining a detailed understanding of the process rather than as an analytical aid to method improvement. Here, the delay elements do not necessarily provide a warning in being material waiting processes. However, a similar chart drawn for labour/equipment would essentially be of cyclical nature and would provide meaningful signals for method improvement, if delay times, distances travelled and so on were accurately recorded on the chart.

Figure 3.4 shows a labour/equipment-type flow process chart recorded to investigate the activities of a person transporting concrete from a mixer to a hoist presented in structured format. As can be seen, the sequence of activities, times taken for each operation and distances involved are provided together with supporting information such as difficulties, tools used and so on to help the analyst to understand the inefficiencies. However, a less clear picture of the process is available compared to the previous method. To overcome this problem, therefore, flow process charts are often used in conjunction with flow diagrams (see below) and are consequently suitable in situations where information on the process and its layout is required in addition to the sequence. An example of a combined flow process chart and a flow diagram is given later in the chapter.

3.4.3 Flow diagram

A *flow diagram* is a scale model prepared on a two-dimensional plan showing the locations of work activities, materials, and worker and equipment movements around the work site, with various movements and activities of workers and machines marked using the process symbols given in Table 3.3.

This recording technique can be used to examine the handling and processing of materials on a work site or to investigate worker or equipment activities. For example, Figure 3.5 shows the steel fabrication process we studied earlier (Figure 3.3) in the form of a flow diagram where the layout of the area being studied and how exactly reinforcement is processed, distances involved, delay points and interferences can be clearly observed. Such information is invaluable for the analyst in improving existing layouts or developing efficient layouts for new operations. An example illustrating how this technique can be applied in investigating worker/equipment activities is presented later in the chapter.

3.5 MULTIPLE ACTIVITY CHARTS

In construction operations productivity is often affected due to internal delays or delays created within the system, such as one member of the team (a worker or a piece of equipment) waiting for other members to complete their part of the work. The labour-type flow process chart described earlier (Figure 3.4) can highlight some of these interferences but fails to give a clear picture of delays and idle times created by interdependencies of team members. In this respect, the *multiple activity chart*, which is both a recording and an analytical tool for method improvement, can

FLOW PROCESS CHART			Type: Labour / Material / Equipment		
			Chart ref:		Sheet No:
			Date:		
Project:		Activity	Present	Proposed	Saving
Operation: *Concreting beam*		Operation	5		
Method : Present / Proposed		Transport	5		
Observer:		Delay	4		
Workers:		Inspection	1		
		Storage	-		
Notes:		Distance	60		
		Time	12.9		

Description	Qty.	Dist. (m)	Time (min)	○	⇨	D	□	▽	Remarks
Waiting for mixing			0.5						
Waiting for inspection			0.2						
Waiting for unload			0.4						
Load to barrow			2.0						*Using shovel*
Wheel barrow		15	0.5						
Wait for hoist			1.0						
Unload barrow and load			0.5						
Wheel empty barrow		15	0.5						
Load barrow			2.0						
Wheel barrow		15	0.6						
Unload and load			0.5						
Wheel empty barrow		7	0.2						
Inspect wheel			2.0						*Wheel stuck*
Wheel empty barrow		8	0.2						
Load barrow			1.8						
Total									

Figure 3.4 Flow process chart of a concrete transport operation (labour/equipment type).

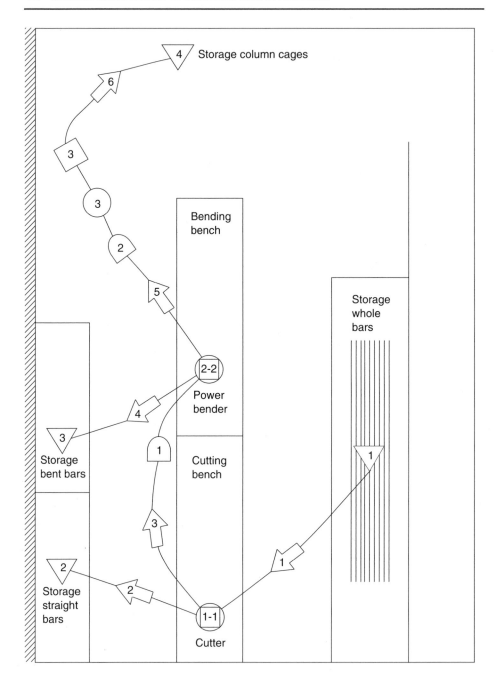

Figure 3.5 Flow diagram of a steel fabrication workshop.

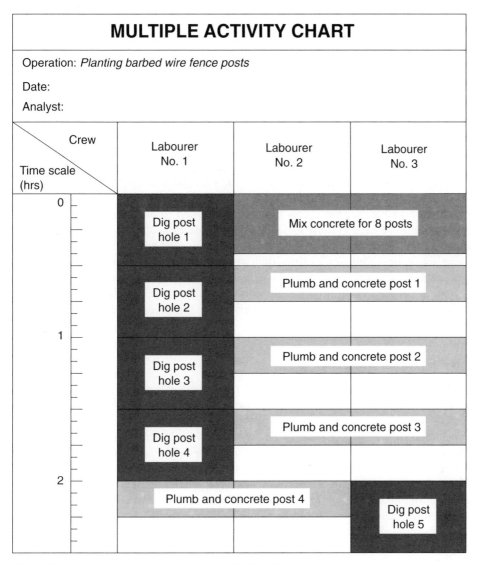

Figure 3.6 Multiple activity chart of a fencing operation.

readily be adopted to identify the effect of these interdependencies, to quantify the resultant idle times and to evaluate various alternatives. It is extremely useful in organising or balancing teams of operatives and equipment on mass production work.

The basic principle in developing a multiple activity chart is to record the activities of all the team members (workers and equipment) in the form of time bars on a common time scale to show their interrelationships, the principal objective being to obtain balanced resource utilisation, hence the alternative name *crew balance charts*, common in the United States (Oglesby *et al.* 1989).

A simple multiple activity chart developed to investigate the efficiency of a labour crew erecting a barbed wire fence around a large construction site is demonstrated in Figure 3.6, where the interdependencies and the resultant idle times are clearly seen, the time scale being either horizontal or vertical to suit the application. A critical examination of the chart often enables rearrangement of the activities to reduce ineffective time or change the team consistency.

First, the activity times need to be determined by either timing and recording (see Figure 3.19) or alternatively from time-lapse film or video recordings (see Chapter 5). Timing using a wrist-watch with a second hand is frequently adequate, particularly for relatively long operations, but stop-watch results are preferred whenever possible. Several cycles should be recorded to obtain a representative average time for each activity element before a multiple activity chart is plotted. Alternatively, several consecutive cycles can be recorded and presented on the chart using actual observed times rather than average activity times. This approach is more suitable in situations where the activities tend to deviate from a purely cyclical nature. A detailed example explaining how a multiple activity chart is used to analyse inefficiencies and develop alternatives for improved productivity is given later in this chapter.

3.6 STRING DIAGRAMS

While flow diagrams indicate the general movement of workers, materials and equipment in a construction process, detailed flows within the work site cannot be achieved easily on a congested site, especially when keeping track of various movements or distances involved – hence the need for a *string diagram* set on a scale plan of the site, workshop or workplace with a thread or string tracing the patterns and distances travelled by the workers, materials and equipment. For example, Figure 3.7 shows a string diagram for distributing concrete in a precast concrete yard. Optimum layouts with minimum movements and reduced congestion can be obtained, especially in situations having long-term repetitive movements such as activities in a precast concrete yard, reinforcement fabrication or joinery workshop or work of a similar nature.

Detours and congestion due to haphazard build-up of materials, waste dumps and so on can also be investigated. Like the flow diagram, a string diagram supplements the flow process charts and when combined provides a clear picture of what is actually happening, exposing problematic situations. Except in simple situations, however, a string diagram cannot be drawn directly and the observer needs to record necessary data systematically using a suitable field data collection format (see Figure 3.11). When the full view is possible recording can be done from one place, otherwise several observers are needed and records must be synchronised and coded. Recording should continue for sufficient time to obtain a representative picture of the whole operation.

When the recording has been completed, an accurate scale layout drawing of the

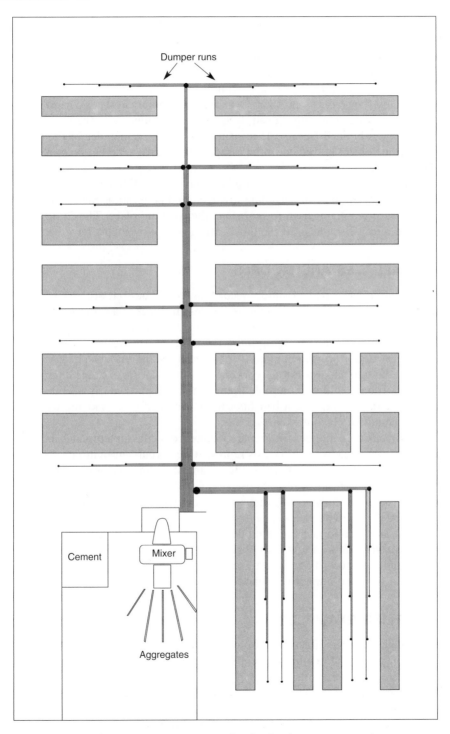

Figure 3.7 String diagram showing concrete distribution in a precast yard.

area studied should be prepared including all the features of the area such as buildings, doorways, walls, material dumps, storage space and so forth. This should be attached to a hard board and pinned at each destination observed and where the direction of movement between points changes.

A measured length of thread tied around the pin at the starting point of movement and then led around the pins at the other points in the order noted in the study sheet provides the path moved, frequency and congestion, the total distance travelled being obtained from scale measurement of the remainder of the string. If more than one object is studied in the same working area different coloured strings can be selected.

Thereafter, comparisons between different layouts or different methods of doing a job in terms of amount of travelling involved and congestion can be simulated with cardboard templates used to rearrange the working place. The routes are re-threaded and measured until the most satisfactory movements have been found.

3.7 TEMPLATES AND MODELS

Templates and *models* are not simply recording techniques but are also effective visualisation and analytical tools. During the design stages of a project they are used by architects and designers in arranging permanent buildings or structures such as houses on a scale-drawn plan to optimise the usage.

For construction work, templates (or two-dimensional models) can be used for efficient site layouts incorporating workers' accommodation, storage compounds, offices, mess rooms, and plant and equipment and are particularly useful when site space is limited. The maximum benefits can be obtained by employing templates before the actual site layout is carried out.

Two-dimensional models are simple to make from cut-out templates at the same scale as the work area, with thin cards representing permanent buildings, temporary huts, offices, storage and waste areas and arranged as observed on the site. Loose templates can be rearranged to optimise site, work space or even room layout. For example, Figure 3.8 shows a two-dimensional model with cut-out templates prepared for the analysis of a site layout.

In contrast, three-dimensional models for site layout are more limited but can provide clear visualisation of the finished product or structure to help foresee problems and plan accordingly and to solve complicated structural assembly, which are not clear in a two-dimensional model or in drawings.

3.8 APPLIED EXAMPLES

The following examples illustrate a potential method improvement for the construction project shown in Figure 3.9 involving construction of a multi-million pound housing complex consisting of 10 three-storey residential flats, a two-storey community centre, a single-storey shopping complex, a playground, a carpark and a booster intz-type water tank, which is also to supply water to an adjacent housing complex. The area covered by the project is approximately 0.9 hectares.

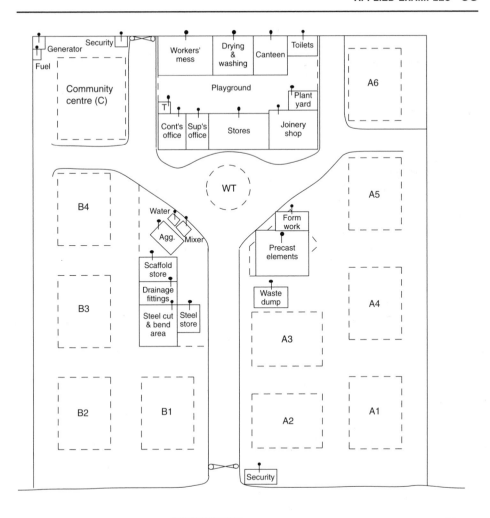

Figure 3.8 Site layout development using cut-out templates held by mapping pins.

The method improvement examples that follow are based on the project characteristics and extracts from the contractor's method statement.

(1) Buildings are mainly of load-bearing brickwork with some parts, particularly the areas with carparks within buildings, requiring reinforced concrete frames. Columns, beams and the majority of slab components for the frames are precast, with occasional *in situ* concrete elements for non-standard structural items. The buildings cannot be covered by a single lifting device, hence the contractor selected a 12 ton mobile telescopic boom crane.

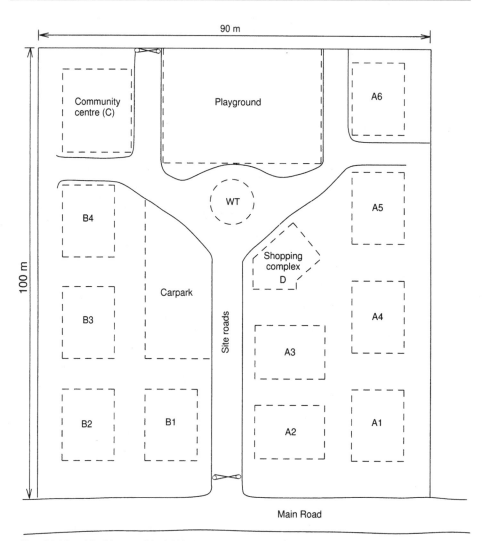

Note: A1-A6 and B1-B6 are residential blocks

Figure 3.9 Layout plan of the housing complex.

(2) Foundations, non-standard structural elements, large span slabs and the entire water tank are constructed in *in situ* concrete. Sufficient site space is available (area reserved for playground and carpark) for site-mixed concrete.

(3) The same mobile crane planned for precast structural elements is used for concreting and form work handling operations of the water tank.

(4) The contractor has a central site mixing facility near the water tank and distributes concrete to various house locations using three 0.5 m^3 dumpers when necessary.

(5) The site works nine hours per day and five days per week.

3.8.1 Site layout

Clearly, layout depends upon the method and sequence of operations to be carried out and the space available, which in turn depend upon the space available, time for completion, relative costs of different methods, and availability of resources and their constraints.

The solution chosen for site layout was arrived at by cut-out templates for various temporary buildings, plant and storage areas, waste dumps and so on as discussed earlier, rather than sketching by trial and error or using wax crayon on clear plastic overlaid on the layout (although this may be satisfactory for simple projects). The advantage is that exact required sizes of building units and other areas can be cut out on templates and rearranged in any orientation or moved to different locations for evaluation. In this way various arrangements can be considered. The site layout adopted for construction is shown in Figure 3.10.

One of the shortcomings noticed is that it does not account for the sequence of operations since all the space required for permanent buildings has been reserved even though some of these buildings are sequenced at different stages. Such space could have been used effectively for temporary siting of equipment or material and hence affected productivity, as illustrated in subsequent sections.

3.8.2 Improvement of material movement and reduction of site congestion

The construction work commenced with the water tank and housing blocks A1 and A2 with the objective of moving to blocks B1 and B2 as well since it was a contractual requirement to hand over these four units first. During the initial stages no precast structural elements or vertical material movements were required, the work being mainly *in situ* concreting of the foundations. Concrete was mixed in the central batching plant near the water tank and three dumpers were used to transport concrete to the required building blocks (initially only to blocks A1 and A2).

The question now arises as to whether the choice of concrete supply from this central location is economic. In fact there are several reasons to argue against it:

- The mixer when supplying concrete for the water tank cannot provide concrete for other applications.
- Excessive dumper movements can be anticipated along the main access road consuming much fuel, creating noise, wasting dumper time and producing congestion to access vehicles.
- When the excavator on foundation work moves to block A3, the soil heaps and the machine operation restrict the main site access, creating further site congestion and delays, and resulting in mixer idling in waiting for dumpers and concreting gangs idling waiting for concrete.
- This situation becomes worse when the mobile crane starts handling and placing precast elements.
- No contingency plan for any downtime in the central batching plant.

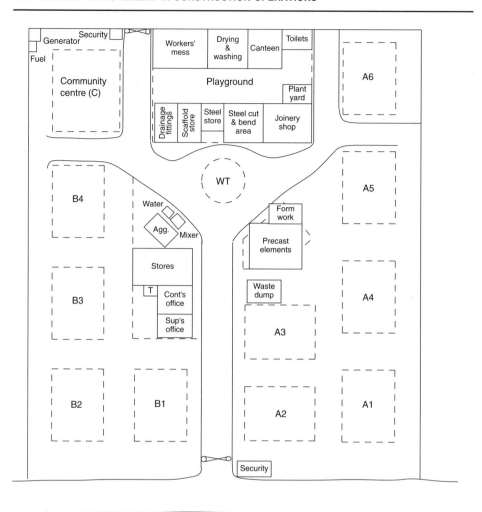

Figure 3.10   Site layout adopted for construction.

POSSIBLE SOLUTION

The contractor could use a small mixer closer to blocks A1 and A2, perhaps within the space taken by block A3, to temporarily accommodate mixer and aggregates thus reducing dumper movements or using wheelbarrows for closer locations. This is analysed as follows using the systematic method study procedure.

Step 1: Selection   The objective is to investigate the excessive movements of dumpers transporting concrete and the resulting congestion and delays where the

string diagram technique, which is not expensive to adopt and can be completed within, say, two days, is a possible tool to use. Any resultant changes very often involve rearrangement of workplaces and perhaps change of transport methods, which are not controversial and do not require much preparation and organising. Thus, the benefits can be quickly harnessed for the operation being studied and when the same operation is carried out in other housing blocks. Selection of this operation for method improvement is therefore justified.

Step 2: Recording   The operation was observed over a half day using the string diagram study form (Figure 3.11) together with a scale plan of the area being studied, with possible dumper paths and code numbers for the possible destinations marked on it for convenient recording of exact paths and destinations. See Figure 3.11 for specimen observations and Figure 3.12 for the developed string diagram.

The observer did not observe all of the movements marked on Figure 3.12 within the half-day period but the paths taken by the dumpers to transport concrete to each foundation pit could be inferred. Indeed, Figure 3.12 shows how dumpers would have travelled to transport one dumper load to each foundation pit in blocks A1 and A2 indicated using a single colour for all three dumpers.

Step 3: Critical examination   The Purpose, Place, Sequence, Person/equipment and Means are now determined by asking primary questions on the existing method and secondary questions to evaluate alternatives and select a possible alternative for development (see Table 3.2).

Purpose   What is done? Supplying *in situ* concrete to foundations of blocks A1 and A2. Is this necessary? Yes, concrete has to be supplied. What else could be done? Nothing else. What should be done? Somehow supply concrete for this purpose.

STRING DIAGRAM STUDY FORM					
Project: *MT housing scheme*				Time started:	Date:
Operation: *Concrete distribution to fdns.*				Time finished:	Observer:
Dumper id	Time departed	Time arrived	Time elapsed (min)	Destination	Path followed and remarks
DP1	8:05	8:10	5	A2(5)	A-B-C-D-E-A2(5)
DP2	8:09	8:15	6	A2(10)	A-B-C-D-F-A2(10)
DP1	8:13	8:18	5	A	A2(5)-E-D-C-B-A

Note: Destination points and paths followed have been indicated using the code numbers given in Figure 3.12.

Figure 3.11   String diagram study sheet used to record dumper movements.

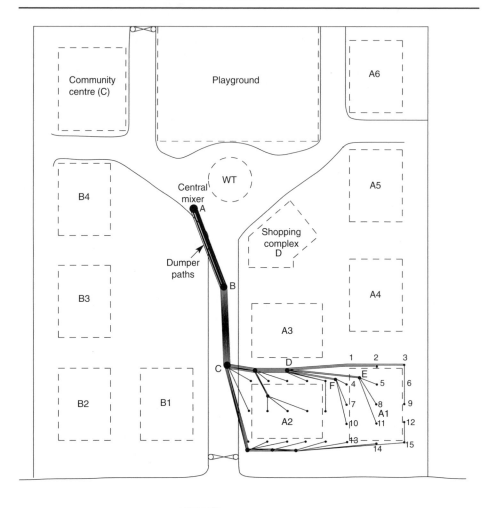

Figure 3.12 String diagram of dumper movements (original method).

Place Where is it done? Mixing at the water tank and placing at foundations of houses. Why there? It is economical to have the mixer at the water tank since a large quantity of concrete is to be supplied to the concrete tank, but there is no reason why another supply source cannot be used for foundations. Where else could it be done? Closer to buildings needing concrete. Where should it be? The above alternative should be considered.

Sequence When is it done? Just after preparation for concreting (after excavation, fixing form work and reinforcements) but before the other buildings. Why then? Work sequence cannot be changed and the client wants these buildings first. When else could it be done? No alternative except perhaps changing the sequence within the four buildings required first. When should it be done? There is no other viable alternative which is more productive.

Person/equipment   Who does it? Mixing by a 0.5 m^3 capacity central batching plant, transporting by three dumpers and placing and vibrating by a labour gang. Why those? Except for the placing and vibrating gang no satisfactory answer could be found. Who else could do it? Mixing can be done either manually or using another mixer and transporting by wheelbarrows. Who should do it? Mixing by another mixer located closer to the works and transporting by dumpers. Wheelbarrows were not considered since large volumes were to be handled.

Means   How is it done? Concrete mixed by mixer at water tank and transported by three dumpers. Why that way? No satisfactory answer can be found. How else could it be done? Another mixer centrally located to the buildings currently needing concrete could be used. The same dumpers could also be used, perhaps reduced in number, and wheelbarrows for close locations in transporting concrete. How should it be done? The above alternative should be considered.

The formal questioning process was adopted so as not to miss any significant point, but with experience the analyst can quickly pass all the questions with relative ease, although in some situations extensive discussions with the people concerned might be required, as previously described.

Step 4: Develop   This is the stage in which the selected alternative by critical examination is further studied to develop an improved method. As identified in Step 3, the possibility of locating another mixer closer to blocks A1 and A2 by temporarily utilising part of the area reserved for block A3 was considered. The string diagram developed for this arrangement to make one dumper load for each foundation pit is shown in Figure 3.13.

Analysis of the two string diagrams reveals that the total distance travelled by the dumpers in the original arrangement to deliver one dumper load for each foundation pit of the two buildings is 4 km while that in the developed arrangement is 1.2 km – a reduction of movement by 70%. Each foundation pit requires 1 m^3 of concrete, that is two dumper loads. Therefore, the total saving of distance is 5.6 km. The reduction of travel distance by 70% also indicates that the new arrangement needs only one dumper instead of three.

How concrete is to be transported to each building in the entire site can now be envisaged and a string diagram developed resulting in a saving of travel distance as follows:

Block no.	Distance savings (km)
A1	2.4
A2	3.2
A3	2.0
A4	2.0
A5	2.3
A6	2.9
B1	2.3
B2	3.1
B3	1.7
B4	1.4
C	2.0
D	1.4
Total	26.7

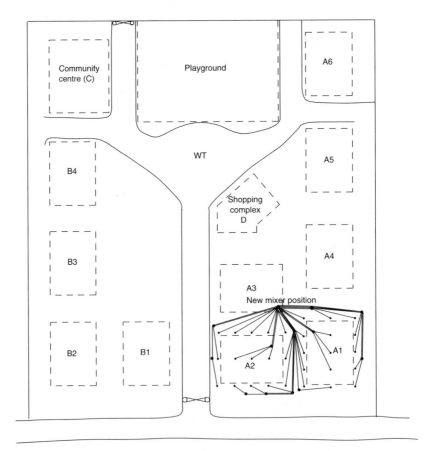

Figure 3.13 String diagram of dumper movements (improved method).

The total duration allocated for concreting of foundations in all the buildings was four weeks and cost comparison of the two methods revealed the following.

Proposed change	Additional cost (£)	Saving (£)
Reduction of two dumpers at £55 per week	–	440.00
Addition of 0.5 m^3 mixer at £50 per week	200.00	–
Fuel saving, say	–	15.00
Total	200.00	455.00

The new method has the following advantages:

- Net cost saving of £255 just from building foundations.
- Additional mixer is available on-site as a back-up facility.
- The operation can continue even when the water tank is concreted by the central batching plant.
- Site congestion is significantly reduced, increasing productivity of other operations.
- Efficiency of foundation operation is increased due to the decentralised system.

Steps 5 and 6: Install and maintain Installation is now relatively easy, arrangements being made to acquire another mixer. Of the two additional dumpers, one is held on-site for a different purpose and the other sent away. Relevant supervisors and foremen are instructed to prepare the site for temporary storage of aggregates and set up the mixer, the arrangement subsequently being used for all the other building blocks.

Although this exercise was carried out after commencement of construction, the planning engineer could have performed the task during the preplanning stage, visualising the real situation in the field using a string diagram.

3.8.3 Improvement of activity sequence and eliminating unnecessary work

When the project was fully under way with work going on in almost every structure, the mobile crane had a difficult task in serving all demand points with precast concrete elements, occasional lifting of concrete to structural elements and also the lifting requirements of the water tank. Casual observations indicated that the crane was needed in all directions by different supervisors without a proper schedule or sequence of operations. Indeed, the crane was in demand even when only a small amount of concrete was to be lifted, causing considerable delays.

This kind of situation, with poor activity sequence and haphazard movements, can be investigated by combined use of flow process charts and flow diagrams, as described previously.

Step 1: Selection Similar to the dumper movement, the study can be completed within a relatively short period of time with potential changes often in the sequence of activities, and the benefits applied to the same project since this activity lasts for a long time. Thus, selection of this operation for method study is justified.

FLOW PROCESS CHART				Type: Labour / Material / Equipment				
				Chart ref:		Sheet No:		
				Date:				
Project: *MT housing complex*				Activity	Present	Proposed	Saving	
Operation: *Concreting beam*				Operation	8			
Method: Present / ~~Proposed~~				Transport	10			
Observer:				Delay	5			
Workers:				Inspection	2			
				Storage	2			
Notes:				Distance	455			
				Time				

Description	Qty. (m3)	Dist. (m)	Time (min)	○	⇨	D	□	▽	Remarks
Crane in plant compound								●	
Crane inspected			10				●		
Travel to Block A2		70			●				
Delay (restricted access)			5			●			
Complete travel to A2		20			●				
Placing precast slab			45	●					
Travel to Block A1		20			●				
Delay (restricted access)			5			●			
Complete travel to A1		30			●				
Handling concrete	0.5		10	●					
Travel to Block A2		24			●				
Placing precast slab			45	●					
Travel to Block B1		72			●				
Placing precast elements			90	●					
Travel to water tank		50			●				
Lifting formwork			60	●					
Delay waiting			5			●			
Lifting formwork			45	●					
Travel to Block B1		70			●				
Waiting for concrete mixing			6			●			
Lift in situ concrete	0.5		10	●					
Travel to water tank		74			●				
Wait for steel fab.			5			●			
Lifting steel			10	●					
Travel to plant yard		25			●				
Inspect			10				●		
Store crane in yard								●	
Total		455							

Figure 3.14 Flow process chart of crane activities (original method).

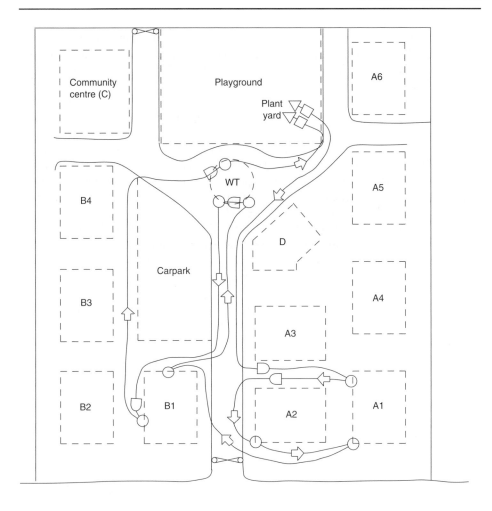

Figure 3.15 Flow diagram of the crane movements (original method).

Step 2: Recording The flow process chart and flow diagram were prepared as shown in Figures 3.14 and 3.15, respectively, after observing the movements of the crane and its activities throughout a typical working day.

Step 3: Critical examination Only the important questions under different criteria are considered here. Clearly, under 'purpose' and 'place' no alternatives are possible, but the 'sequence' can be changed and unproductive movements of the crane throughout the site considerably reduced by preplanning the sequence of precast elements and *in situ* concrete to avoid haphazard crane movements.

Similarly, there is no reason to adhere to the same equipment or means as handling and placing of precast concrete elements require the crane but lifting and placing of *in situ* concrete in most of the cases (except for large span slabs) could have been achieved either manually or using simple block and tackle.

Step 4: Develop   Development can now be completed by improving the sequence of the crane activities and eliminating unnecessary activities. Here a careful look at Figure 3.14 indicates that the use of the crane for *in situ* concrete handling in blocks A1 and B1 could have been eliminated since the quantities are small. Discussions with the supervisors revealed that this is possible and that the main reason for haphazard demand for the crane is lack of proper coordination.

Careful planning suggests that all supervisors should provide details of crane requirements for the following day at the end of the previous day. If this was the case for the part of the operation studied, the flow process chart and the flow diagram would be as shown in Figures 3.16 and 3.17, respectively. As can be seen, the efficiency of the crane operation has increased considerably.

Steps 5 and 6: Install and maintain   The procedure developed in Step 4 would then be mandatory and given to supervisors to inform the planning engineer at the end of the previous day of all the lifting requirements of the following day. The planning engineer then could schedule the crane activities, identifying priorities and eliminating haphazard movements, and could also inform supervisors when the crane was not available for handling small quantities of concrete. This arrangement eliminated the requirement for another crane, thus saving a considerable amount of money.

3.8.4   Improvement of team performance by gang balance

Concreting of the water tank was carried out as preplanned using the following team:

- 0.5 m^3 loading hopper
- 0.5 m^3 concrete mixer and mixer operator
- 0.5 m^3 bottom dump concrete skip
- 12 ton mobile telescopic boom crane and operator
- vibrating gang of four men.

The first lift of wall concreting went fairly satisfactorily although there were some delays in handling concrete by the crane, resulting in idling of the mixer and the concrete vibrating gang. This was not noticed initially because the mixer gang and the vibrating gang adjusted to the slow pace of the operation. However, as the wall went up idling of the mixer gang and the vibrating gang were noticeable due to the increasing cycle time of the crane making the whole operation inefficient. Further, the site management wanted to increase the rate of production to meet high demand for the crane and to prevent other operations waiting for want of the crane.

FLOW PROCESS CHART

Type: ~~Labour~~ / ~~Material~~ / Equipment

Chart ref: Sheet No:

Date:

	Activity	Present	Proposed	Saving
Project: *MT Housing complex*				
Operation: *Concreting beam*	Operation	8	5	
Method : ~~Present~~ / Proposed	Transport	10	6	
Observer:	Delay	5	3	
Workers:	Inspection	2	2	
	Storage	2	2	
Notes:	Distance	455	289	
	Time			

Description	Qty. (m3)	Dist. (m)	Time (min)	○	⇨	D	□	▽	Remarks
Crane in plant compound									
Crane inspected			10						
Travel to water tank		50							
Lifting form work			60						
Delay waiting			5						
Lifting form work			45						
Travel to Block A2		50							
Delay (restricted access)			5						
Complete travel to A2		20							
Placing precast slab			45						
Travel to Block B1		70							
Placing precast elements			90						
Travel to water tank		74							
Wait for steel fab.			5						
Lifting steel			10						
Travel to plant yard		25							
Inspect			10						
Store crane in yard									
Total		289							

Figure 3.16 Flow process chart of the crane activities (improved method).

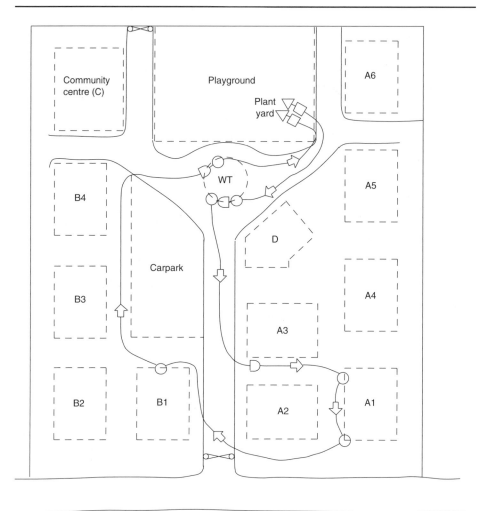

Figure 3.17 Flow diagram of the crane movements (improved method).

Clearly, this is a result of poor team formation or an unbalanced gang and can be investigated using the multiple activity chart. Before the detailed study, consider how exactly this process is carried out and how the various elements of the team interact with each other by studying the outline process chart (Figure 3.18). The reader may find this process obvious, but an outline process chart may be necessary for situations with complex interactions.

Let us now follow the systematic method study procedure.

Step 1: Selection   When symptoms of failing productivity were observed about 90% of the concreting was to be done and productivity was dropping continuously with the increasing crane cycle time. The necessary data collection, plotting, analysis and

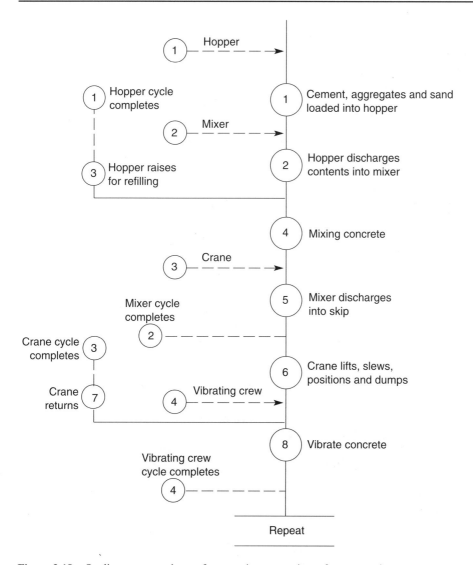

Figure 3.18 Outline process chart of concreting operation of water tank.

development of an improved method using a multiple activity chart for this kind of operation can be completed within a maximum of 2 days. Further, any changes would involve reconstituting the team, which is not drastic or controversial, and the benefits could be harnessed quickly. Thus the selection is justified.

Step 2: Recording Data necessary for plotting a multiple activity chart can be obtained by several means: simple time study, video filming or time-lapse photography. The most convenient and the quickest method is a simple time study

Time Study Sheet for Concreting Operation

Cycle number	Hopper						Mixer				Crane				Vibrating gang	
	Start loading	End loading	Start discharging	End discharging	Start lowering	End lowering	Start mixing	End mixing	Start discharging	End discharging	Start lifting	End lifting	Start returning	End returning	Start vibrating	End vibrating
1	8:10:0	12:0	12:0	12:30	12:30	13:0	12:30	14:30								
2																
3																
4																

Figure 3.19 Data collection format used for multiple activity chart of concreting operation.

with the necessary cycle element times recorded in a standard time study format (see Figure 4.6) or a specifically developed format such as the one shown in Figure 3.19, the latter being convenient for keeping track of different cycles and extracting data. Elemental times for 30 cycles were recorded in the case study using a wrist-watch with a second hand and were considered to be sufficiently accurate to obtain representative cycle element times. The resultant average elemental times were as follows:

Cycle element	Average time (min)
(1) Loading hopper	2.0
(2) Discharging to mixing drum and adding water	0.5
(3) Lowering hopper for refilling	0.5
(4) Mixing concrete immediately after task (2)	2.0
(5) Discharge concrete into skip and attaching crane hook	0.5
(6) Crane lifts, slews, positions and discharges concrete	3.0
(7) Crane returns back to position for refilling	2.0
(8) Vibrating concrete	4.0

The multiple activity chart drawn for the original set-up is shown in Figure 3.20, where the mixer operator has not been considered as a separate team member since a further breakdown over-complicates the chart and makes little contribution to analysis (unless the dependency of equipment and the operator is required).

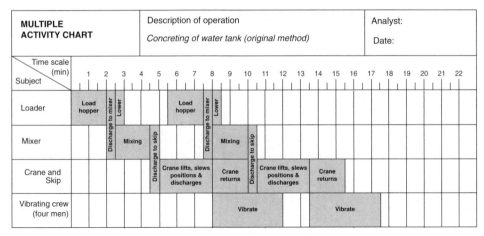

Figure 3.20 Multiple activity chart of the original method.

Step 3: Critical examination Only the necessary arguments of the critical examination process are discussed here as the details were discussed earlier. A cursory examination of Figure 3.20 indicates that the resultant cycle time of the whole team is 5.5 minutes, but if the loader, mixer and vibrating gang could work independently their cycle times would be 3, 3 and 4 minutes, respectively; in other words, the hopper and mixer can produce 0.5 m³ of concrete every 3 minutes and the vibrating gang can vibrate 0.5 m³ every 4 minutes but this rate is not achieved because of dependency on the crane, which can handle only 0.5 m³ every 5.5 minutes. Therefore, for each 5.5 minute cycle the hopper and mixer each idle for 2.5 minutes (45%) and the vibrating gang idles for 1.5 minutes (27%). Thus, any alternative considered should aim to reduce these ineffective times and at the same time increase the production rate significantly.

Step 4: Develop Clearly, the crane is critical and attention should therefore be directed either to reducing the crane cycle time or increasing the skip size or both. Possibilities to reduce the crane cycle time are usually limited. The second alternative is consequently likely to be more favourable since the crane was capable of lifting a 1 m³ skip and the mixer is 45% under-utilised. Selection of a 1 m³ skip together with the existing 0.5 m³ mixer causes the crane to wait for two mixer loads before the skip is lifted and hence further lengthens the crane cycle time. An improved solution would be to have two 1 m³ skips, or perhaps two 0.5 m³ skips or even a 1 m³ skip and a 0.5 m³ skip. Thus, various alternatives can be suggested but it is only after charting that their suitability and efficiency can be evaluated.

The solution attempted was to choose two 1 m³ skips instead of a 0.5 m³ skip, with one skip always at the mixer to unload its content. The concrete vibrating gang

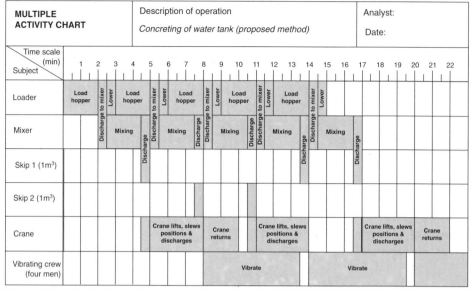

Figure 3.21 Multiple activity chart of the proposed method.

was also increased to six to handle the increased volume. The multiple activity chart of this new arrangement is shown in Figure 3.21.

The following points should help understanding of this chart.

(1) The two skips should be considered as separate items because unlike in the original method, the skips need not always be moving with the crane.
(2) The cycle time for the six-member vibrating gang to vibrate 1 m³ concrete was estimated based on the rate of output of the four-member gang.
(3) The very first skip handled by the crane has only 0.5 m³ concrete; all subsequent skips have 1 m³ concrete.

Figure 3.21 shows that the hopper and mixer are 100% utilised but the crane is idle for 0.5 minutes per cycle. This is considered to be satisfactory since crane cycle time tends to increase with progress of the water tank construction as vertical height increases.

A cost comparison of the contractor's savings can now be performed using the following data:

Total volume of concrete to be placed in the water tank	90 m³
Cost of concrete batching plant	£130 per week
0.5 m³ concrete skip	£10 per week
Mobile telescopic boom crane	£400 per week
1 m³ concrete skip	£15 per week
Labourer	£5 per hour
Compacting equipment	£15 per week

Original method

Cycle time of the operation	5.5 min
Cycles per day: (60/5.5) × 9 (for 9 hour working day)	98
Output per cycle	0.5 m^3
Output per day: 98 × 0.5	49 m^3
Duration required for the operation: (90/49)	2 days (say)

Costs

Cost of the batching plant: (130/6) × 2 (6 day working week)	£43.33
Cost of the crane: (400/6) × 2	£133.33
Cost of skip: (10/6) × 2	£3.33
Cost of compacting equipment: (15/6) × 2	£5.00
Vibrating gang: 5 × 9 × 2 × 4	£360.00
Total	£544.99

Cost per m^3: (544.99/90)	£6.05

Improved method

Cycle time of the operation	6.0 min
Cycles per day: (60/5.5) × 9	90
Output per cycle	1 m^3
Output per day: 90 × 1	90 m^3
Duration required for the operation: (90/90)	1 day

Costs

Cost of the batching plant: (130/6) × 1	£21.67
Cost of the crane: (400/6) × 1	£66.67
Cost of two 1 m^3 skips: (15/6) × 2	£5.00
Cost of compacting equipment: (15/6) × 1	£2.5
Vibrating gang: 5 × 9 × 1 × 6 (for six-member crew)	£270.00
Total	£365.84

Cost per m^3: (365.84/90)	£4.06

Percentage cost saving = (6.05−4.06)/6.05 = 32.9%

The new proposal not only saves money for the concreting operations but also improves availability of the crane, thereby providing more time for the other operations and so facilitating potential productivity improvement.

3.9 SUMMARY

The challenges facing construction contractors require increased efficiency and economy, to be met partially by continuous use of method improvement. In this respect, this chapter highlighted the benefits of method study together with constraints for its application, and the method study procedure to be followed, covering applications of the outline process charts, flow process charts, flow diagrams, multiple activity charts, string diagrams, templates and models. The potential benefits were then exemplified using a case study example of a construction project.

REFERENCES AND BIBLIOGRAPHY

Adrian J.J. (1987). *Construction Productivity Improvement*. New York: Elsevier Science

British Institute of Management (1981). *Introduction to Creative Thinking and Brainstorming*. London: BIM

British Standards Institution (1979). *Glossary of Terms Used in Work Study and Organisation and Methods (BS 3138)*. London: BSI

Calvert R.E. (1981). *Introduction to Building Management* 4th edn. London: Butterworth

Currie R.M. and Faraday J.E. (1977). *Work Study* 4th edn. London: Pitman

Drewin F.J. (1982). *Construction Productivity*. New York: Elsevier

Foster D. (1989). *Construction Site Studies – Production, Administration and Personnel*. London: Longman

Geary R. (1970). *Work Study Applied to Building*. The Builder, 24–59

Harris F.C. and McCaffer R. (1995). *Modern Construction Management* 4th edn. Oxford: Blackwell Science

Heap A. (1987). *Site Productivity in the Construction Industry*. Geneva: ILO

International Labour Organisation (1986). *Introduction to Work Study*. Geneva: ILO

Mundel E.M. (1978). *Motion and Time Study*. Englewood Cliffs, NJ: Prentice Hall

Oglesby C.H., Parker H.W. and Howell G.A. (1989). *Productivity Improvement in Construction*. New York: McGraw-Hill

Oxley R. and Poskitt J. (1986). *Management Techniques Applied to the Construction Industry* 4th edn. Oxford: Blackwell Science

Parker H.W. and Oglesby C.H. (1972). *Method Improvement for Construction Managers*. New York: McGraw-Hill

Pilcher R. (1992). *Principles of Construction Management*. New York: McGraw-Hill

Taylor F.W. (1971). *Scientific Management*. New York: Harper & Row

4

PRODUCTIVITY IMPROVEMENT BY WORK MEASUREMENT

4.1 INTRODUCTION

Timely completion at the minimum cost satisfying quality requirements and specifications is the main objective of any construction project. Consequently, application of the most economic construction methods and appropriate resources in balanced numbers at the right time, with the assistance of proper planning, scheduling and control, is required. This demands an accurate knowledge of realistic times taken to carry out various activities, or in other words 'standard times'.

There are basically two ways to obtain such output figures: (i) experience, assumption and common sense supported by historical records, and (ii) scientific work measurement. The first, while useful in some situations, has certain limitations: (i) data are usually averages of past output values, and do not often incorporate all the circumstances of the particular contract; (ii) data include all ineffective times and do not show what outputs and costs could be achieved if the job were properly managed and the workers properly motivated; (iii) data cannot readily be used for new operations; and (iv) historical data are mostly obtained from the operatives' time sheets, which are commonly inaccurate. The second method, work measurement, is able to overcome these shortcomings and uses a series of scientific techniques to identify ineffective times and set sound time standards for most construction work.

This chapter describes how work measurement can be used for construction productivity improvement commencing with an introduction to work measurement and its uses. Subsequently, the application of work measurement, work measurement techniques followed by the means of calculating standard and planning times and work measurement using feedback are presented, with examples where necessary. Finally, the industry situation with regard to application of work measurement and its future trends is discussed.

4.2 WORK MEASUREMENT AND ITS APPLICATIONS IN PRODUCTIVITY IMPROVEMENT

BS 3138:1979 defines *work measurement* as 'the application of techniques designed to establish the time for a qualified worker to carry out a specified job at a defined level of performance'. The 'qualified worker' in this definition is a worker who is physically fit, and has the required level of education, intelligence, skill and knowledge for the job, and 'defined level of performance' is when the worker is brisk, skilled and motivated.

In other words, the outcome of work measurement is to obtain the realistic time required to complete a clearly specified operation by a 'qualified worker' without waiting and idling except that required for normal rest and relaxation. Naturally, this definition applies not only to single workers but also to gangs including machines, making such data indispensable for estimators, planners and managers in a multitude of situations.

4.2.1 Uses of work measurement data

The application of work measurement data revolves around how time standards are used by management for various management functions. The main uses are:

As planning data

(1) To determine the number of workers to be assigned for a task (given the total quantity of work to be done and the planned duration).
(2) To determine the activity duration (given the total quantity of work to be done and the resources allocated).
(3) To plan balanced gang sizes by comparing standard times taken for various tasks performed by a gang; for example, the number of labourers required to supply materials to two bricklayers to maximise labour utilisation, or the bucket size of a crane or the capacity of a mixer required to optimise resource usage in a concreting operation.
(4) To determine the most economic method from alternatives by working out associated costs using standard times for various alternative methods.

As estimating data   To determine the unit rates for various operations using standard times for unit output together with planned gang sizes and resource costs.

As controlling data

(1) To provide a basis for sound financial incentive targets. For example, assume that a bricklaying gang of two bricklayers and one labourer is capable of laying 400 bricks per eight-hour day at the standard rate of working and the gang cost is £16 a day. In other words, laying cost per brick is 4 pence, or £1 for 25 bricks. Thus, the contractor benefits by setting an incentive target of, say, 75p for each additional 25 bricks laid.
(2) To provide a basis for cost control by fixing standard performance targets. For

instance, in the above example if the bricklaying gang fails to lay at least 400 bricks a day then the management can introduce a cost control measure.

As an integral part of on-site method study During on-site method studies, work measurement techniques, especially time study, may have to be used to reveal ineffective times to analyse various alternatives using techniques such as multiple activity charts and flow process charts, as described in Chapter 3. Thus, work measurement can also be considered as an integral part of method improvement discussed in Chapter 3.

Clearly, work measurement data for planning, estimating and control need to be accurate since they are used repetitively for these purposes. They should therefore be measured in a planned environment, and not obtained from a disorganised site with inefficient working practices. Furthermore, the operatives should be qualified, jobs should be clearly defined and level of performance known. However, if these data are to be used as an integral part of method study the objective is to improve only the ongoing operation; thus the above restrictions need not apply.

In this sense, method study and work measurement cannot, in practice, be completely separated as each is complementary to the other. When developing standard times for work operations for planning, estimating and control, it is necessary to analyse the method used and determine whether or not it is the best. On the other hand, when planning out methods to be used to do a job, the selection of the best from various alternatives is governed by the comparative standard times of each.

4.2.2 Work measurement techniques and outline procedure

Of several techniques available for work measurement, those that are commonly used in the construction industry are:

- time study
- rated activity sampling
- synthesis
- analytical estimating
- comparative estimating.

The first two techniques involve field observation and measurement but the last three are more or less analytical procedures carried out in the office in establishing basic and standard times for various construction operations. These techniques can be used on their own or combined to establish time standards for construction operations. The outline procedure of work measurement, measuring techniques and the parties benefiting by work measurement data are shown in Figure 4.1. These techniques are now discussed in detail.

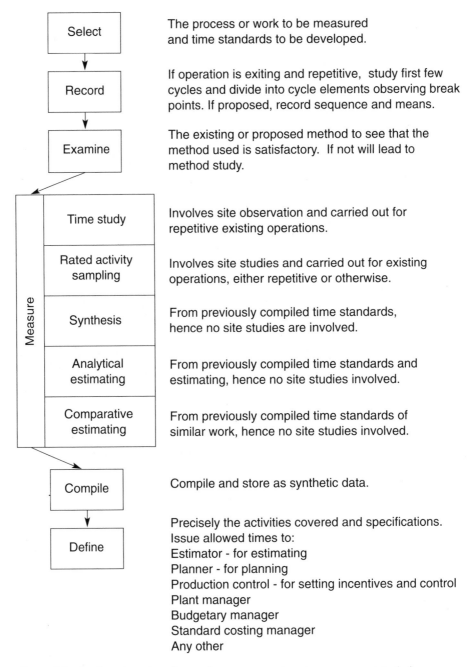

Figure 4.1 Outline procedure for work measurement and measurement techniques.

4.3 TIME STUDY

Time study was the fundamental approach to productivity improvement introduced by Frederick W. Taylor and Frank Gilbreth in the late 19th and early 20th centuries, and it is the principal technique of work measurement even today. In the current usage, it is not simply the timing of an operation but a process designed to develop standard time or standard output for any construction operation irrespective of the rate of work being observed. Time study therefore involves:

(1) Timing, to discover how long various operations are taking;
(2) Rating, to assess the worker being observed against a norm;
(3) Building up of time standards, by allowing for appropriate relaxation and contingency allowances.

4.3.1 Time study terminology and concepts

TIMING

Time studies (stop-watch studies) essentially involve recording of incremental times necessary to complete various activity elements that make up an operation. Unless the timing is carried out as an integral part of method study, in which case a wrist-watch with a second hand is often sufficient, accurate recording of times using a stop-watch is always recommended.

Timing can be obtained in two forms: (i) continuous or cumulative timing where the watch is started at the beginning of the first element and is not stopped until the whole operation is completed; watch readings at the end of each element are recorded and elemental times obtained by subtractions afterwards; and (ii) repetitive or fly-back timing where the watch is simultaneously read and snapped back to zero at the end of each element.

The stop-watch may take several forms. The simplest type, with one hand, is not recommended since it can accumulate an appreciable error if the watch is stopped and read at the end of each cycle element. This shortcoming can be overcome with a fly-back decimal minute stop-watch, in which the large hand completes 1 minute per revolution, graduated in hundredths of a minute, while the small hand records the cumulative time up to 30 minutes in 1-minute graduations. A fly-back mechanism on the large hand allows the timing of the elements to start at zero for each element without affecting the elapsed time shown on the small hand, making this type of watch suitable for either fly-back timing or cumulative timing. The third type of watch used for cumulative timing is a split-hand type or interval timer, which has two hands. One hand runs continuously while an auxiliary travels with it except when stopped for reading. The fourth method, perhaps easier but more expensive, is to use three stop-watches ganged together to a common touch bar so that depressing the touch bar will stop one watch, reset the second and start the third, allowing plenty of time for recording. Computer methods, time-lapse photography and video recordings, discussed later, can be used as alternatives.

RATING

Timing alone does not produce a fair assessment of effort required to complete an operation since the working ability or the efficiency of a worker affects the timing. The rate of working may vary between individuals due to such factors as age and gender. It can also vary for the same individual from time to time during a day. For example, first thing in the morning, after a break, after lunch or perhaps after a physical strain, it takes some time for a worker to adjust to a normal tempo of work, and rate of working can change for various other reasons, reflected in the time taken to complete an operation. A system of rating has therefore been devised so that the performance of the worker can also be measured in addition to timing.

BS 3138 defines rating as 'to assess the worker's rate of working relative to the observer's concept of the rate corresponding to standard rating'. Thus, in addition to timing the observer should also assess the rate of working for each time element. To do this accurately, the time study practitioner must have a correct concept of standard rating, which comes only from practical experience and training in judging different speeds of movement, effort, consistency and dexterity. Constant practice and frequent training checks, which are available in the form of films and tests, are necessary to maintain a reliable rating ability.

The graphical presentation technique shown in Figure 4.2 is one such test. The principle is that for a particular repetitive work element with the same work content in every cycle, the observer records the time against the assessed rating and the best straight line through the points is drawn. The true rating line should pass through the origin, since in theory, infinite rating should take zero time and vice versa. This shows whether the observer is under-rating or over-rating to help tune the concept of standard rating. To assist this process Table 4.1 provides a rating scale divided into five-part graduations, with 100 representing standard rating.

Some practitioners believe that rating is not a fair and a proper way to establish basic times because the observer is the sole arbiter of the operative's rate of working and hence the process can be subject to error. It is true that wide variations in rating would result in inaccurate basic times. Nevertheless, just as one expects skilled workers to have proper command of their trade, so any practising work study analyst must have an accurate capability for assessing the rate at which an operative is working.

Factors affecting the rating

(1) Effectiveness. This implies application of correct and effective methods, the good signs being correct choice of tools, shortest path of movement, adherence to the best method, avoidance of unnecessary activities, tidiness and systematic arrangement of tools and materials.
(2) Skill. Sureness of touch or sequence, intelligent application of movements and events, effective use of both hands and so on.
(3) Speed. This implies diligence, steadiness and continuity, the good signs being rhythm, speed of movement, steady effort, making the job look easy.

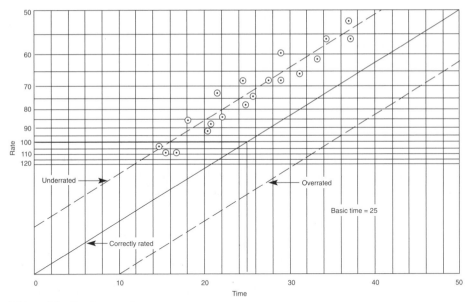

Figure 4.2 Rating graph.

Table 4.1 Various rates of working.

Rate	Description	Comparable walking rate	
		Miles/h	km/h
0	No activity	0	0
50	Very slow, unskilled, unmotivated	2	3.2
75	Not fast, average skill, disinterested	3	4.8
100	Brisk, qualified skill, motivated	4	6.4
125	Very quick, high skill, highly motivated	5	8.0
150	Exceptionally fast, intense effort and concentration	6	9.6

Source: Adapted from Alan Heap (1987).

Factors that can influence observed time but not necessarily the rating include: quality of tools used; type and quality of materials worked on; working conditions; learning period required before the task becomes familiar; interruption of supply of materials; quality of working drawings; supervision; and quality specification. These factors are difficult to assess and are best included by taking a large number of studies to give a representative sample.

The observer should also guard against malpractices whereby, for example, workers being timed to set standards for a bonus incentive scheme may try to give the impression of working at standard rating while hoping that disguised inefficiencies will go unnoticed by the study officer. While observers must be aware of such practices, they must also try to assess the true effort required for the task. For example, the same rating could be assessed for light and heavy tasks, which would normally be carried out at different speeds even by a qualified and motivated worker.

BASIC TIME

Basic time is the time required for a qualified worker to carry out a certain task with the standard/average/normal rate of working. In practice the worker could not be expected to complete the work within this time without adequate rest or relaxation. This is obtained by the following formula:

$$\text{Basic time} = \text{Observed time} \times \frac{\text{Observed rating}}{\text{Standard rating}}$$

If, for example, a qualified worker working at a steady rate of 100 performs a task in 15 minutes without rest or relaxation, the basic time for that task will be $15 \times 100/100 = 15$ minutes. If the time taken for the same task by another operator is, say, 12 minutes and the rate given is 125, the basic time will again be $12 \times 125/100 = 15$ minutes. Similarly, if the time taken is 20 minutes and the rate given is 75 then again the basic time will again be $20 \times 75/100 = 15$ minutes. This indicates that the basic time, as it should be, is the same irrespective of the rate of working or the operative if the observer has given a correct rating. This is fundamental to accurate time studies.

RELAXATION ALLOWANCES

During a time study, it is usual to exclude any elements of relaxation, idle or waiting times so that the basic time is not affected by the degree of relaxation enjoyed by any individual worker. However, an allowance must be made for relaxation as no one can be expected to work without recovering from fatigue, a visit to the toilet, a smoke, a chat with a fellow worker and so forth.

These relaxation allowances fall into two categories, 'fixed allowances' and 'variable allowances', and are normally made by adding a percentage to the basic time. Fixed allowances are meant for the operative's 'personal needs' and 'basic fatigue' and are considered a minimum requirement. These include an occasional stretch, a visit to the toilet, having a drink of water and so forth and can be assessed with a reasonable degree of accuracy. They are, however, not adequate to compensate for varying effort required for construction operations and to protect the long- and short-term health of a worker. For example, a worker breaking up a concrete slab with a jack hammer in dusty conditions needs more relaxation than a machine driver sitting at the controls in the relative comfort of the cab. This is overcome by supplementing with 'variable allowances', which consist of 'additional fatigue allowances' and 'environmental allowances'. These are very difficult to assess but many companies and industries make their own recommendations.

Typical ranges of values that can be considered for construction operations are shown in Figure 4.3 (Harris and McCaffer 1995), alternatively, the reader may refer to the Local Authorities Management Services and Computer Committee (LAMSAC) recommendations for further typical values applicable to the UK industry (LAMSAC 1971). Readers may also refer to Price (1990a, b) for a more accurate but complex method of evaluating relaxation allowances for construction workers, which include a 'basic allowance' and a 'health and safety allowance', the former being the minimum allowance and the latter incorporating mental cost, environmental cost, metabolic cost and local muscle fatigue.

CONTINGENCY ALLOWANCE

In addition to relaxation allowances a further amount is added to the basic time to cover contingencies, which are difficult to assess but which almost certainly occur. Typical contingencies are: adjustment and maintenance of tools; waiting time caused by subcontractors; machine breakdowns; material shortages; unexpected site conditions such as poor ground, high winds and bad weather; learning time; one-off tasks; design changes; getting instruction and so on. An allowance of up to 5% is usually sufficient for this purpose under properly organised site conditions, but the

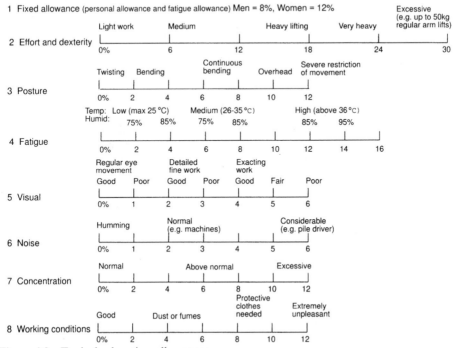

Figure 4.3 Typical relaxation allowances.

level can sometimes reach 100% or more depending on the job conditions.

STANDARD TIME

Standard time is the 'proper' time required for a qualified worker working at standard rating to complete a task. If this is achieved then the worker is considered to have achieved 'standard performance', which is defined in BS 3138 as 'the rate of output which qualified workers will naturally achieve without over-exertion as an average over a working day or shift provided they are motivated to apply themselves to their work'. To establish standard time it is therefore necessary to include relaxation and a contingency allowance. Thus:

$$\text{Standard time} = \text{Basic time} + \text{Relaxation allowances} + \text{Contingency allowance}$$

A worker can achieve standard performance in different ways, for example, by working at a slower rate and having less relaxation, or at a faster rate and having more relaxation. In practice, however, the relaxation breaks will be scattered throughout the time taken to complete a job or element of work. Because the factors affecting relaxation vary considerably from site to site due to the varying nature of construction work, the difference between standard time and basic time for a job can be quite large. As a consequence, most data banks of output times are kept as basic times with the user applying appropriate allowances as necessary.

THE REQUIRED NUMBER OF OBSERVATIONS

The basic time for an element of work or an operation, which is the basis for calculating standard times, can vary from cycle to cycle for two reasons. First, in reality it is unlikely that an observer will have perfect judgement to assess accurately the worker's rating and take full account of the effort required every time. If this can be done, the basic time for a task would be the same irrespective of the worker being observed for any multiple of observed times and ratings, as seen earlier. Second, the observed time itself can change not only due to rate of work but also to a large number of other variables which are difficult to include in rating. Thus, it is necessary to observe several cycles and select the mean basic time.

The correct sample size is difficult to determine accurately but the simplest method is to plot the cumulative average basic time, preferably for a short cycle element, against the number of observations, as demonstrated in Figure 4.4. When the line begins to stabilise, sufficient observations have probably been taken. There can be situations where a sufficient number of observations cannot be taken from one site or workplace since construction operations are insufficiently repetitive for enough observations to be made. However, with well-trained staff the intangibles caused by changes in the workplace can be taken into consideration, to permit the inclusion of data from similar elements observed at different sites.

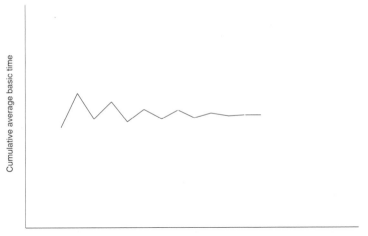

Figure 4.4 Cumulative mean basic time.

4.3.2 Time study procedure

Figure 4.1 shows the outline procedure adopted for any work measurement exercise with the first three stages, Select, Record and Examine, being common to any work measurement technique. The reason for selecting a particular operation would be to achieve any one or more of the uses previously identified, but unless the study is carried out as part of a method study, the work selected should use a suitable method and be carried out in a planned environment. This aspect is looked into at the 'record' and 'examine' stages, and method improvement may be carried out, perhaps through method study, before proceeding.

Once the operation to be studied is selected the best work measurement technique can be decided upon. For existing repetitive or cyclic operations time study is clearly an appropriate method. During the record stage the analyst should study the operation without timing, watching a few cycles until he or she understands it thoroughly and obtaining explanations from the supervisor or workmen as necessary.

The operation should then be broken down into elements to facilitate subsequent synthesis, as described later in the chapter. For example, a tower crane can be used for lifting form work and reinforcement, pouring concrete and so forth. Therefore, records of lifting, slewing and moving times at different heights would be valuable in assembling activity times for, say, placing concrete in a high-rise building. In this way direct observation can, in principle, be avoided when the data bank has developed to include most construction tasks and elements. The number of elements will, however, depend on the objective but should be carefully selected so that the break points that separate two elements are clearly identifiable during field observation.

Once these stages have been done, time study involves three broad stages: (i) planning for field data collection, (ii) on-site data collection, (iii) data analysis and compilation.

PLANNING FOR FIELD DATA COLLECTION

This stage involves decisions on the time study method, equipment to be used and preparation of data collection forms. The timing method will be either fly-back or cumulative depending on the operation to be measured. The former may be suitable to measure one operative but when there are more than one with work elements starting and finishing at different times, cumulative timing will be the only alternative. The equipment to be used mainly consists of a suitable stop-watch considering the timing method, convenience and the facilities available as previously described, a study board, and pencils, supplemented by a hand calculator, tape measure, micrometer and so on, depending upon the type of work.

Preplanned time study observation forms can be of any form, again depending on the type of work to be observed, but the conventional format is suitable for most construction operations (see Figure 4.6). Operations of a purely cyclical nature can be more efficiently recorded using break points rather than elements (see Figure 3.19).

ON-SITE DATA COLLECTION

In order to take good time studies, the observer must not only concentrate on clear and accurate timing and recording operations but must also maintain a friendly relationship with the operatives being studied. Before the study begins, it is therefore necessary to approach the workers to be observed and their foreman and explain the purpose of the exercise, with discussions where necessary with the parties and the operatives to understand any difficulties or features of the job. In most cases workers are likely to cooperate, particularly if the final result is to be increased earnings or less fatiguing work. When time study is new to the workforce it is a good policy to discuss it with the union representatives on-site and to answer all questions quite frankly. On no account should the observer resort to secret timing because it invariably leads to labour unrest.

When these problems are sorted out, on-site observation can commence but before starting timing it is essential to gather as much detail about the work as possible. This information will include the layout of the workplace, a cross-section of the work, weather and site conditions, date, time, identification of workers under study, and notes about site access, proximity of material supplies, tools and equipment used and so forth. These can be recorded in a study top sheet as shown in Figure 4.5 and can be used irrespective of the work measurement technique.

Once all of these details are complete, actual timing can commence with the observer positioned at a suitable place so that everything that is taking place can be seen throughout the study period. The actual observed time for each element should then be recorded with the stop-watch and the observer must additionally make a

TIME STUDY TOP SHEET		Sheet No:.....
Contract: *ABC carpark*	Location: *Wolverhampton*	Study Ref: *AJ/PO/250*
Operation: *Concreting of first floor slab*	Site conditions: *Average*	Weather: *Cool and bright, 15 °C*
Gang: *A - Crane driver* *B - Loader to skip* *C,D,E,F - Concrete labourers*	Plant and equipment: *Crawler crane with 0.5m³ skip and 1 inch poker vibrator*	Materials used: *Ready mixed concrete*

Brief description of job and method:

Ready-mixed concrete is supplied to site by trucks; B discharges concrete to skip when arrived; A lifts, slews, positions concrete into slab; C,D,E & F pour, spread, vibrate, tamp and trowel

List of elements and break points:

Fetch & prepare tools	Vibrate	Trowel	Skip arrives at truck	Skip arrives at pour area
Clean	Spread		Skip leaves truck	Skip leaves pour area
Discharge concrete	Level & tamp			

Layout of workplace and cross-section of job:

Plan view of slab — 40 m × 50 m

(cross-section both ways) 150 mm, 750 mm, 10 m

Time started : *8:35 am*

Time finished : *10:32 am*

Elapsed time : *117 min*

Total observed time : *702 man minutes*

Total observed time : *530 man minutes*
(excluding idle time)

STANDARD TIME AND STANDARD OUTPUT:

484 Standard minutes to pour 7.5m³ covering 50m² of floor slab

(see summary sheet for details)

Prepared by: *AJ*

Figure 4.5 Time study top sheet showing outline and results.

TIME STUDY SHEET

Study Ref: *AJ/PO/250*
Sheet No:

ELEMENTS	R	CT	OT (min)	BT (min)	ELEMENTS	R	CT	OT (min)	BT (min)
Start time			0.0		B fills skip	100		0.5	0.5
CDEF fetch floats, shovels, vibrator and climb to slab	100		2.0	8.0	A waits	IT		(0.5)	
A positions crane	100		2.0	2.0	CF wait	IT		(1.0)	
B guides A	100		2.0	2.0	DE level and tamp	90		1.0	0.9
		2.0					11.0		
CDEF/ a.b.	100		3.0	12.0	A lifts, slews & positions	90		2.5	2.2
A/ a.b.	100		3.0	3.0	B waits	IT		(2.5)	
B/ a.b.	100		3.0	3.0	CF wait	IT		(5.0)	
		5.0			DE level and tamp	90		5.0	4.5
B fills 0.5m³ skip	100		0.4	0.4			13.5		
A waits	IT		(0.4)		DE discharge concrete	90		1.4	1.3
CDEF clean out base	80		1.6	1.3	C vibrates	100		0.7	0.7
		5.4			F spreads with shovel	100		0.7	0.7
CDEF getting instructions from foreman	100		6.4	6.4	A waits	IT		(0.7)	
A lifts, slews & positions	100		1.6	1.6	B waits	IT		(0.7)	
B waits	IT		(1.6)				14.2		
		7.0			A returns to B	90		2.0	1.8
A lifts, slews & positions	100		1.0	1.0	B waits	IT		(2.0)	
B waits	IT		(1.0)		C vibrates	100		2.0	2.0
C starts vibrator	100		1.0	1.0	DF spread with shovel	100		4.0	4.0
DE wait	IT		(2.0)		E waits	IT		(2.0)	
		8.0					16.2		
DE discharge concrete	90		1.0	0.9	B fills skip	100		0.4	0.4
C vibrates	100		0.5	0.5	A waits	IT		(0.4)	
F spreads with shovel	100		0.5	0.5	C vibrates	100		0.4	0.4
A waits	IT		(0.5)		DE level and tamp	90		0.8	0.7
B waits	IT		(0.5)		E floats	100		0.4	0.4
		8.5					16.6		
A returns to B	90		2.0	1.8					
B waits	IT		(2.0)						
C vibrates	100		2.0	2.0					
DE level and tamp	90		4.0	3.6					
F spreads with shovel	80		2.0	1.6					
		10.5							
C/F					C/F				

R - Rate; CT - Clock time; OT - Observed time; BT - Basic time

Figure 4.6 Time study observation sheet.

judgement on the effective rate of working of the subject under observation, for the reasons described previously.

Figure 4.6 shows recording of these times (using a continuous decimal stop-watch) and rate for two cycles of a concreting operation. The elemental times will vary depending on the circumstances, between, say, 0.5 and 5 minutes and it is a good principle to take a reading at every 2–3 minutes for longer cycle elements such as floating of a floor surface, which can last for perhaps half an hour with no significant breaks in the worker's rhythm. This will also help to record any rate changes in between (see Figure 4.6). Accurate timing of repetitive cycle elements can be obtained by clear identification of break points, perhaps with the assistance of sharp movements or noise, for example, the noise of a skip striking the ground, or pulling the mixer lever.

Whenever an ineffective time is encountered during observation, it must be properly timed and recorded, with a clear description and including IT (ineffective time) in the rating column. These ineffective times may include rest or relaxation, wasting time for unnecessary refinement, correcting mistakes, carrying out unrelated work or idle or waiting time caused by interference such as waiting for materials, fellow workers, plant breakdowns and so on, and must be ringed so that they can be taken out of subsequent calculations (see Figure 4.6).

Before finishing on-site observations the total work content completed during the study period should be recorded. For example, in a concreting operation this may be the total number of skips handled, the total volume of concrete poured and the total area covered. In a bricklaying operation it may be the total area covered or the number of bricks laid. With this, on-site observation is over; the actual calculation of basic times and standard times is usually carried out in the office.

Indeed, complete generalisation of construction operations is often difficult. For example, the time for placing concrete by a crane will vary with several factors such as the size and type of skip, the size of the opening in the shuttering, the quantity of concrete poured and so forth. The effect of these variables can be readily incorporated by plotting the basic times obtained against changes in a variable or combination of variables, as will be seen later in the chapter.

ESTABLISHMENT OF BASIC TIME AND STANDARD TIME

The elemental times can now be worked out using clock time readings at the break points and are then entered under observed time (OT) and subsequently converted to basic times, as described previously (see Figure 4.6).

Work elements recorded on the time study form in addition to those identified before the study, such as fetching various tools, preparing form work and so on, are important but of limited value in that form and should be grouped together to be of practical use considering the fact that they bear a direct relationship to some physical aspect of the job done. For example, the time spent on positioning various tools, positioning scaffold boards, cleaning out the slab before concreting and so on can all be regrouped under 'fetch tools and prepare'.

These basic times are now transferred to the abstract sheet shown in Figure 4.7,

TIME STUDY ABSTRACT SHEET

Study No:
Study Ref:
Date:
Time unit:

ELEMENTS	BASIC TIMES															Total BT	Frequency Per	Qty.	Unit BT
Fetch tools and prepare	8.0	2.0	2.0	12.0	3.0	3.0	6.4	3.5	5.5							45.4	Job	1	45.4
Pour concrete to slab	0.9	1.3	1.1	1.0	0.9	1.1	1.0	0.8	0.9	1.1	1.2	1.0	0.9	0.9	0.9	15.0	Skip	15	15.0
Spread with shovel	2.1	4.7	3.6	3.5	3.4	3.2	3.7	3.5	3.4	3.3	3.3	3.4	3.5	3.6	3.7	51.9	m³	7.5	6.9
Vibrate with poker	2.5	3.1	2.4	2.3	2.5	2.6	2.7	2.5	2.4	2.3	2.1	2.5	2.1	2.0	2.5	36.5	m³	7.5	4.9
Level and tamp	9.0	8.5	9.0	8.6	8.7	9.0	8.6	8.8	8.9	9.0	8.6	8.5	9.0	8.4	8.7	131.3	m²	50	2.6
Float and trowel	2.0	1.8	2.5	1.9	2.0	1.8	2.0	2.1	1.8	2.0	1.9	1.9	1.9	2.0	1.8	29.4	m²	50	0.6
Fill skip	0.4	0.5	0.4	0.5	0.4	0.4	0.4	0.5	0.5	0.4	0.5	0.6	0.5	0.5	0.6	7.1	Skip	15	0.6
Crane lifts, slews, positions	2.6	2.2	2.5	2.2	2.6	2.3	2.3	2.4	2.0	2.5	2.5	2.3	2.5	2.4	2.3	35.6	Skip	15	2.4
Crane returns to position	1.8	1.8	1.7	1.8	1.9	2.0	1.8	1.8	1.7	1.8	1.9	2.0	1.8	1.9	1.9	27.6	Skip	15	1.8

Figure 4.7 Time study abstract sheet.

which contains subsequent records of elements for 15 cycles. The calculations are self-explanatory and the last column provides an average basic time for each element to be used for subsequent synthesis, as described later in the chapter. The elements and the total basic times are then transferred to a summary sheet and relaxation and contingency allowances are added as described previously (Figure 4.8).

The basis for calculating relaxation allowances is the systematic analysis of those factors involved in an element that would necessitate compensating relaxation if the operative were to maintain a consistent rate of working over a long period. The resultant times are the standard times for different elements of the job and are then related to the job quantities to give unit standard times. These can be used for any of the applications described previously or to develop time standards for other operations using other work measurement techniques, as described later in the chapter. It should be noted that the example demonstrated in Figures 4.5–4.8 is meant to illustrate the time study procedure but in a complete study there may be other elements such as 'clean out workplace', 'wash and clean tools' and so forth that must be incorporated since they are part of the operation.

4.3.3   Limitations of time studies and trends

Despite the importance of work measurement data obtained from stop-watch studies there are several inherent constraints that prevent it being regularly applied in construction operations. The notable ones are:

(1) Reliable data can only be collected from experienced work study practitioners who are very scarce in the construction industry.
(2) The number of workers studied by one observer is limited (maximum of about five by an experienced work study practitioner), which requires employment of several observers, making manual study prohibitively expensive.
(3) When activity break points are not clearly identifiable, there can be differences of opinion as to when one phase is completed and another started. Such errors can be significant, particularly if several observers are involved and data are compared and combined.
(4) The information obtained by time studies is limited to the times recorded and facts that can be interpreted from the observer's notes, which may not cover sufficient details such as interdependencies among components, exact reasons for taking longer or shorter elemental times. These will increase the variability and reduce accuracy.
(5) The data cannot be assembled quickly, especially in civil engineering, where the variables on-site complicate the interpretation of information as the relaxation and contingency allowances needed often considerably exceed the required basic time.

TIME STUDY SUMMARY SHEET											Study No:

Study Ref:

Operation: / Date:

Concreting of 150 mm first floor slab with ready-mixed concrete using crawler crane and 0.5 m³ skip.

Time unit:

ELEMENTS	Total BT	Relaxation (%) 1	2	3	4	5	Con (%)	Total (%)	Total SMs	Qty.	Unit std. Times
Fetch tools and prepare	45.4	10	2	-	-	2	5	5	24	56.3	Job	56.3/job
Pour concrete to slab	15.0	10	2	-	-	2	5	5	24	18.6	15 skips	1.3/skip
Spread with shovel	51.9	10	5	2	-	2	5	5	27	65.9	7.5m³	8.8/m³
Vibrate with poker	36.5	10	2	0	4	2	5	5	28	46.7	7.5	6.3/m³
Level and tamp	131.3	10	4	3	-	4	5	5	31	172.0	50m²	3.5/m²
Float and trowel	29.4	10	2	4	-	4	5	5	30	38.2	50m²	0.8/m²
Fill skip	7.1	10	2	-	-	2	4	5	23	8.7	15 skips	0.6/skip
Crane lifts, slews, positions	35.6	10	-	-	-	4	4	5	23	43.8	15 skips	2.9/skip
Crane returns to position	27.6	10	-	-	-	4	4	5	23	34.0	15 skips	2.3/skip
TOTAL	379.6									484.0		

PERFORMANCE:

Performance including idle time = 484 × 100/702 = 68.9 P

Performance excluding idle time = 484 × 100/530 = 91.3 P

Figure 4.8 Time study summary sheet.

Thus, except in special situations, manual time studies are seldomly carried out in the UK construction industry and have been superseded by computerised data collection and analysis, as discussed later in the chapter.

4.4 WORK MEASUREMENT BY ACTIVITY SAMPLING

Activity sampling, also referred to as work sampling, particularly in the USA, is a family of sampling techniques depending on the degree of sophistication applied. At one extreme, it can be used for quick appraisal of site efficiency and at the other extreme (called 'rated activity sampling') for work measurement. Activity sampling is gaining more and more acceptance in the industry as a reliable productivity measurement technique. Because of its wide range of applications, this technique is discussed in detail in Chapter 5.

4.5 SYNTHETICS AND SYNTHETICAL ESTIMATING

The standard times produced using time studies can only be used for other similar jobs. Many tasks in construction work, however, are not truly repetitive. For example, concreting requirements in different projects may use different skip sizes at different heights on different structural elements. To establish estimating data a different time study would be needed in each case, making such studies prohibitively expensive and impractical. Furthermore, proper use of standard times can only be obtained if they are available during the planning and estimating stages. To overcome this disadvantage the technique of *synthesis* or *synthetical estimating* was developed (Figure 4.9). The underlying principle of synthesis is to build up time standards for an operation to be carried out from previously conducted time studies, not necessarily from those of identical nature.

4.5.1 Developing synthetics for synthetical estimating

Predetermined standard times for different work elements – for example, standard times developed for vibrate, level and tamp and so on in the previous time study example – are called *synthetics*. Reliable synthetics for typical situations can only be

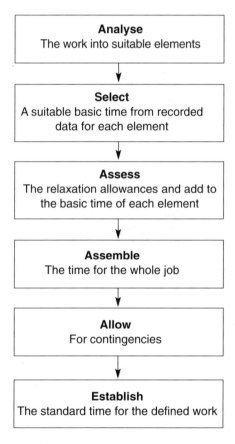

Figure 4.9 Synthetical estimating process.

established by combining several time studies carried out on different sites, under different conditions and on different operatives. However, before combining data from several studies, individual basic times should be examined carefully to check for unreasonable variations and the corresponding time studies re-examined to determine the reasons. In some cases, it may be possible to adjust the times for typical conditions or to devise a simple mathematical formula to explain the variation. Except in simple situations, this is generally carried out by a statistical analysis first, to identify significant variables that affect basic times, and then to express basic times as functions of these significant variables. This can be demonstrated using an example taken from Price (1991).

EXAMPLE

Table 4.2 shows basic element times (synthetics) for various activities of a concreting gang developed from a study carried out during concreting of two roof slabs using a crane and skip. Clearly, the basic time required for work element 'pour concrete' will be affected by the total volume of concrete to be placed and that for 'trowel concrete' will be affected by the total area to be trowelled. Thus, in order to develop synthetics to establish basic times for other operations these basic times have to be related to a set of logical variables as shown in the table. For example, based on data in Table 4.2, the basic time for 'pour concrete' can be expressed as 0.792 times the volume and that for 'trowel concrete' can be expressed as 1.55 times the area. Combining all of them, the basic time for a concreting operation can be expressed mathematically as:

Table 4.2 Basic element times for concrete gang.

Activity	Variable	Basic time (min)	General (G)	BT + G (min)	Units	$\dfrac{BT + G}{Units}$	
Prepare tools	Occasions	40	–	–	1	40 min	
Clear tools	Occasions	20	–	–	1	20 min	
Transfer tools	Occasions	15	–	–	3	5 min	
Pour concrete	Volume	25	1.1	26.6	33.6 m^3	0.792	4.38 min/m^2
Vibrate concrete	Volume	115	5.0	120.5	33.6 m^3	3.586	
Shovel concrete	Area	123	5.3	128.3	98.9 m^2	1.300	
Tamp concrete	Area	69	3.0	72.0	98.8 m^2	0.728	4.61 min/m^2
Trowel concrete	Area	147	6.4	153.4	98.8 m^2	1.550	
Cover concrete	Area	98	4.2	102.2	98.9 m^2	1.034	

Source: Price (1991).

$$\text{Basic time (first pour)} = 60 + 4.38 \text{ volume} + 4.61 \text{ area}$$
$$\text{Basic time (subsequent pours)} = 5 + 4.38 \text{ volume} + 4.61 \text{ area}$$

These equations include time spent on trowelling and covering, which may not always be required. Thus, they can be modified by deducting the corresponding element times as follows:

$$\text{Trowel but not cover, Basic time} = 60 + 4.38 \text{ volume} + 3.57 \text{ area}$$
$$\text{Cover but not trowel, Basic time} = 60 + 4.38 \text{ volume} + 3.06 \text{ area}$$
$$\text{Neither trowel nor cover, Basic time} = 60 + 4.38 \text{ volume} + 2.02 \text{ area}$$

To obtain basic times for varying slab depths, area can be replaced by volume (V) and depth (D), as follows:

$$\text{Basic time} = 60 \times 4.38V + 4.61V/D$$

It is represented graphically in Figure 4.10.

However, these equations and graphs cannot be fully relied upon to obtain basic times for typical concreting operations since they are based on only one study.

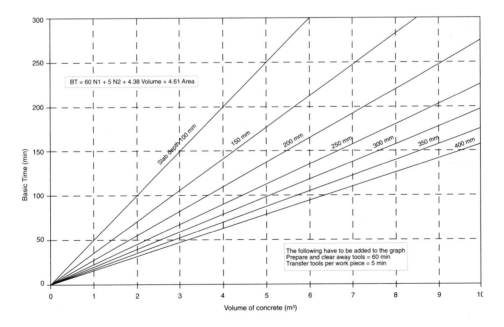

Figure 4.10 Basic times for concrete gangs against volume of concrete for various slab depths. *Source*: Price and Harris (1985).

This could be overcome by collecting more data, for example over 70 concrete pours in this example, covering different placement methods and types of pour and carrying out combined statistical analysis to develop generalised synthetics. These generalised or typical synthetics are shown in Table 4.3 and can be used to establish reliable basic times for any concreting operation. For further details, see Price and Harris (1991).

Synthetics such as those developed above provide basic data required by management for estimating, planning and control and should therefore be stored in a properly organised synthetics library. A synthetics library is never complete as additional data may be supplied constantly through time studies carried out on new operations or as a result of method improvements. The work elements that do not have a constant basic time under all conditions should be stored in the form of a graph, a set of graphs or tables, as shown in the concreting example. Situations where these variations can be eliminated by, say, standardising the method or size of unit and so on should be clearly indicated in the synthetics. Basic times are generally stored instead of standard times since the relaxation and contingency allowances adopted for individual studies may very often be related to particular site conditions, which may not be typical.

The system of filing synthetics in a library should be logical and designed to keep the number of records to a minimum to help efficient retrieval. Synthetics can be identified using an appropriate coding system and stored as computer records in a

Table 4.3 Generalised concrete model.

Operation	Equation*	Correlation coefficient	Variable
Prepare tools	$= 11.7 + 0.501\ V$	$R = 0.50;\ 0.27 < R, < 0.67$	All pours
Pour	$= 5.45 + 1.76\ V$	$R = 0.84;\ 0.72 < R < 0.91$	Slabs
Pour	$= 16.1 + 1.18\ V$	$R = 0.60;\ 0.43 < R < 0.93$	Beams and walls
Pour	$= 4.79 + 9.65\ V$	$R = 0.61;\ 0.12 < R < 0.86$	Columns
Vibrate	$= 3.46\ V$	$R = 0.91;\ 0.83 < R < 0.95$	Slabs
Vibrate	$= 5.69\ V$	$R = 0.92;\ 0.76 < R < 0.98$	Beams and walls
Vibrate	$= 22.8\ V$	$R = 0.90;\ 0.72 < R < 0.97$	Columns
Shovel	$= 8.07 + 0.737\ A$	$R = 0.89;\ 0.83 < R < 0.93$	All pours
Tamp	$= 10.7 + 1.12\ A$	$R = 0.93;\ 0.89 < R < 0.95$	All pours
Trowel	$= 27.6 + 2.79\ A$	$R = 0.90;\ 0.70 < R < 0.97$	Double trowel
Trowel	$= 1.51\ A$	$R = 0.97;\ 0.86 < R < 0.98$	Single trowel
Cover	$= 8.62 + 0.861\ V + 0.202\ A$	$R = 0.74;\ 0.43 < R < 0.89$	All pours
Clear	$= 6.83 + 0.31\ V$	$R = 0.60;\ 0.38 < R < 0.86$	Others
Clear	$= 16.2 + 0.859\ V$	$R = 0.80;\ 0.34 < R < 0.95$	Pump
General	$= 0.13\ C$	$R = 0.89;\ 0.77 < R < 0.95$	Skip
General	$= 0.0775\ C$	$R = 0.79;\ 0.64 < R < 0.88$	Direct and pump

* V=volume; A=area; C=sum of activities excluding 'general'; R=correlation coefficient; $A < R < B$, where A and B are 95% confidence limits for R.
Source: Price (1991).

suitable database format. They can then be transferred to estimating and planning software for their efficient application in productivity improvement.

4.5.2 Synthetical estimating

The first step in establishing standard time for a new operation using synthetics is to determine the method by which the operation is to be carried out and to make a list of work elements involved in the operation. Appropriate time standards can then be obtained from various elements in the synthetics library. Indeed, the smaller the size of the elements, both in the breakdown of the new operation and in the synthetics library, the easier it becomes to build up the time for the whole series of the task in the new job.

Given a proper synthetics library, the technique can be used to build up time standards for almost any operation by taking synthetics from completely different operations. In situations where only basic times are obtained from the synthetics library for the reasons mentioned previously appropriate allowances must be added to suit the working conditions of the new operations. The technique can be incorporated into unit rate or operational rate estimating methods currently used by estimators in construction companies, and no doubt as data banks are developed and improved by individual concerns, the use of standard data will increase the accuracy of estimating and hence improve productivity.

EXAMPLE

A floor slab with a depth of 250 mm and area of 500 m^2 is to be concreted using a crane and skip. The slab is ready to be concreted and the operation requires single trowelling of the surface after concreting. Weather conditions at the site are cool and dry and working conditions are average. What will be the standard time required for a concreting gang to complete the operation?

SOLUTION

The total volume of concrete to be placed $= 500 \times 0.25 = 125$ m^3.
Build-up of time standards can be carried out in tabular form as shown in Table 4.4. As can be seen, appropriate synthetics have been extracted from the synthetics library (in this case Table 4.3) and values for area and volume have been substituted to arrive at basic element times. Appropriate relaxation and contingency allowances have been added to develop standard times for different elements.

From Table 4.4, the total standard time required to complete the operation = 3582 minutes or 59.7 labour hours. If the concreting gang consists of six workers, the standard duration required would be 59.7/6 = 10 hours. Crane time and mixing time (if site-mixed concrete is used) are to be added to this figure to obtain standard time for the full operation.

Table 4.4 Build-up of time standards from synthetics.

Element	Synthetic (Table 4.3)	Basic time	Relaxation allowances (%)						Contingency (%)	Total allowances (%)	Total standard minutes
			1	2	3	4	5	6			
Prepare tools	11.7+0.501 V	74.4	10	2	–	–	2	5	5	24	92.3
Pour	5.45+1.67 V	214.2	10	2	–	–	2	5	5	24	265.6
Vibrate	3.46 V	432.5	10	2	–	4	2	5	5	28	553.6
Shovel	8.07+0.737 A	376.6	10	5	2	–	2	5	5	29	485.9
Tamp	10.7+1.12 A	570.7	10	4	3	–	4	5	5	31	747.7
Trowel	1.51 A	755.0	10	2	4	–	4	5	5	30	981.5
Clear	6.83+0.31 V	45.6	10	2	–	–	2	5	5	24	56.6
General	0.13 C	321.0	10	2	–	–	2	5	5	24	398.1
Total											3581.3

4.6 ANALYTICAL ESTIMATING

One of the problems of synthesis is the difficulty in obtaining synthetics for all the elements of a new operation, particularly when the synthetics library is incomplete. This makes it necessary to assess or estimate elemental times for missing synthetics, and the development of standard times in this way is called *analytical estimating*. Often, experience, proper judgement, similar historical data, performance handbooks and estimating manuals can be used to help in this process. For example (given the type of equipment, type of soil, conditions of loading and dumping sites, characteristics of haul road and distance), it is possible to establish output values or cycle times for an earthmoving operation by analytical estimating using equipment performance handbooks (see Caterpillar 1996).

4.7 COMPARATIVE ESTIMATING

Comparative estimating is a technique used to obtain standard times for new operations by comparing with other similar, yet not identical, tasks and is particularly useful in situations where synthesis or analytical estimating cannot be applied. The technique requires nothing more than common sense and proper judgement, and involves taking a series of studies of operations of a similar nature (benchmarks) and assessing the time required for an unstudied operation by comparing with the benchmark jobs. This is very useful in estimating time requirements for a large number of one-off jobs that occur in every site, which does not warrant a study but is not quite the same as anything already timed. The method is very popular due to its relative simplicity.

4.8 WORK MEASUREMENT USING FEEDBACK

One of the cruder ways of obtaining output values or time standards is to adopt actual output recorded and fed back from ongoing or historical projects. This system is frequently used by contractors, particularly when it forms part of a progress and cost control system. Clearly, the output data obtained from feedback is not as accurate as that obtained by scientific work measurement, for three main reasons: (i) there is no formal rating of workers' performance; (ii) various inefficiencies, interruptions and delays specific to particular sites have not been excluded, making them non-typical; and (iii) the recorded output values, resources used and timing can have significant variations from reality since they are generally completed at the end of the working day and very often by unqualified personnel. Thus, work measurement by feedback should not be relied upon for construction operations unless strict controls are made to obtain the real output values. However, these data are often used for estimating, planning and controlling, with obvious shortcomings that are inherent in present-day construction.

4.9 PRODUCTION PLANNING USING SITE FACTORS

Planning times for construction operations may be established in two ways. The first and the conventional method is simply to calculate duration using the required standard time, the gang size and the number of working hours in a day. This method assumes that the allocated relaxation and contingency allowances are sufficient to allow delay times inherent in actual construction and that pace of work is accounted for by the workers' rate. Research has, however, repeatedly found that the work rate is more or less similar in every site when the workers are producing but output can vary significantly due to other management and motivational factors. This has led to the evolvement of a second method of establishing planning times by site factors (Broomfield *et al.* 1984).

The *site factor* method considers the causes of output variation as: (i) work rate; (ii) waiting time including relaxation; (iii) external breaks, including late starts and early quits; and (iv) official break times. Four site factors are included to explain variation due to these four causes and are related to working day, as shown in Figure 4.11. As shown, an allowance is added initially to operational basic element times comprising the operation to account for any interferences and contingencies by the factor F_i, called the interference factor. This is the time when the operative is prevented from working because of the nature of the task, and is generally of a low order when dealing with site operations as there is invariably some other work (which is part of that operation) to carry on with. This becomes significant when machines are involved and operators or machines may be compelled to idle because of the working cycle (restricted operations).

The value used for factor F_i is subjective and should be assumed depending on the operation. The resultant time is called the total basic time (see Figure 4.11). All

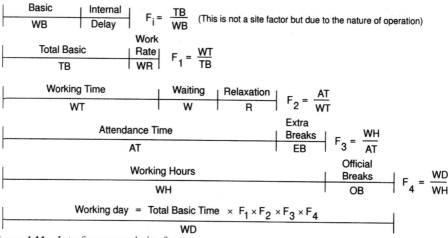

Figure 4.11   Interference and site factors.

of the other causes of low output are largely motivational or organisational problems, over which all managers should claim to have some control. They are expressed as site factors and are generally predetermined from activity sampling or time study carried out on typical construction operations under the same motivational levels and management control. Site studies have shown that overall site factors ($F_1 \times F_2 \times F_3 \times F_4$) can vary between 1.11 and 2.5 (that is, efficiency between 90% and 40%) (Price and Harris 1985).

Thus, build up of planning times using site factors involves two stages:

(1)   Determining basic operation time by combining the basic element times, work contingency allowances and internal delay allowances where appropriate.
(2)   Applying predetermined site factors F_1, F_2, F_3 and F_4 to obtain planning times.

EXAMPLE

Construction of walls in a small house requires laying of 20 000 bricks by a gang consisting of two bricklayers and a labourer. Previous time studies have revealed that the basic time for bricklaying by a three-member gang is 600 minutes per 1000 bricks under unrestricted operating conditions and that the average values for site factors F_1 (work rate), F_2 (idle time), F_3 (extra breaks) and F_4 (official breaks) are 1.03, 1.14, 1.0 and 1.07, respectively. What will be the planning time for the entire operation?

SOLUTION

Operational basic time (OBT) for 20 000 bricks	$= \frac{600 \times 20\,000}{1000 \times 60} = 200 \, \text{hr}$
Total basic time (TBT)	$= \text{OBT} \times F_i$
TBT under unrestricted conditions ($F_i = 1$)	$= 200 \times 1 = 200 \, \text{hr}$
Planning time $= \text{TBT} \times F_1 \times F_2 \times F_3 \times F_4$	$= 200 \times 1.03 \times 1.14 \times 1.0 \times 1.07$
	$= 252 \, \text{hr}$

If the gang works eight hours per day, the required duration $= \frac{252}{8} = 31.5$ days.

4.10   WORK MEASUREMENT IN PRACTICE AND FUTURE TRENDS

The literature indicates that the extent of application of work measurement techniques and the benefits obtained by such application vary widely in different parts of the world. The British industry seems to be limited in its application, and those who regularly practise work measurement are local authorities and a handful of individual organisations, with large variation in data collection techniques when compared to other European countries (Broomfied *et al.* 1984).

Germany, Sweden, the Netherlands and Finland seem to be active in application of work measurement in the construction industry. Time studies are frequently used in Germany whereas activity sampling and its modified forms are more prevalent in the Netherlands and Sweden. One of the main features of applications of work measurement data in other European countries compared to Britain is that time standards are developed by various bodies representing contractors and the data are shared by the membership. This arrangement shares the cost of work measurement among organisations and provides increased efficiency through reliable estimating, improved planning and work preparations, sets times and supplies a forum for exchange of ideas, thus promoting standardisation of methods and improved communication between parties.

As far as the future trends of work measurement techniques are concerned, time studies are too expensive and provide a degree of accuracy that is not often required in construction operations, hence activity sampling is gaining more and more acceptance. Manual data collection is being replaced by modern portable computers powered by rechargeable batteries, equipped with appropriate software, sufficient RAM, disk storage and LCD displays, making data collection more convenient and efficient (see Emsley and Harris 1986; see also Chapter 8). Also, the increasing sophistication of word processors, spreadsheets, and statistical and database packages is facilitating easier analysis and storage of information. These methods in essence help synthetical estimating and analytical estimating, and make data sharing between estimating, planning and other project management software a straightforward task. In situations where work study is considered as a regular activity of the organisation, field data collection methods have been superseded by time-lapse photography and video recording techniques to reduce the cost of data collection and to permit bringing the construction operations to a quiet office environment for analysis, as described in Chapter 5.

4.11 SUMMARY

Possession of accurate knowledge of realistic times taken to carry out construction operations is essential for successful achievement of project objectives. Such data can be efficiently applied in planning, estimating, controlling, method studies and performance comparison. Establishment of these times using time study, activity sampling, synthesis, analytical estimating, comparative estimating and feedback was explained with practical examples where necessary. The concept of site factors in establishing planning times was described. Finally, the situation in the industry with regard to application of work measurement techniques and future trends was discussed.

REFERENCES AND BIBLIOGRAPHY

British Standards Institution (1979). *Glossary of Terms Used in Work Study and Organisation and Methods* (BS 3138). London: BSI

Broomfied J.R., Price A.D.F. and Harris F.C. (1984). Production analysis applied to work improvement. *Technical Note 415, Proceedings of the Institution of Civil Engineers,* vol. 44, September, 379–386

Calvert R.E. (1981). *Introduction to Building Management* 4th edn. London Butterworth

Caterpillar (1996). *Performance Handbook*

Emsley M.W. and Harris F.C. (1986). Work study is important to construction – computers can make work study effective. *Building Technology and Management,* **11**, April, 10–15

Foster D. (1989). *Construction Site Studies – Production, Administration and Personnel.* London: Longman

Geary R. (1970). *Work Study Applied to Building.* The Builder

Harris F.C. and McCaffer R. (1995). *Modern Construction Management* 4th edn. Oxford: Blackwell Science

Heap A. (1987). *Site Productivity in the Construction Industry.* Geneva: ILO, 48

International Labour Organisation (1986). *Introduction to Work Study.* Geneva: ILO

Karger D. and Hancock W. (1982). *Advanced Work Measurement.* New York: Industrial Process

LAMSAC (1971). Manual work within Local Authorities, relaxation allowances. *Report of O&M and Work Study Panel*

Niebel B.W. (1982). *Motion and Time Study* 7th edn. Homewood, IL: Irwin

Oglesby C.H., Parker H.W. and Howell G.A. (1989). *Productivity Improvement in Construction.* New York: McGraw-Hill

Pilcher R. (1992). *Principles of Construction Management* 3rd edn. New York: McGraw-Hill

Polk E.J. (1984). *Method Analysis and Work Measurement.* New York: McGraw-Hill

Price A.D.F. (1990a). Calculating relaxation allowances for construction operatives Part I – Metabolic cost, *Applied Ergonomics*, **21**(4), 311–317

Price A.D.F. (1990b). Calculating relaxation allowances for construction operatives Part II – Local muscle fatigue, *Applied Ergonomics*, **21**(4), 318–324

Price A.D.F. (1991). Measurement of construction productivity: concrete gangs. *Technical Information Service, No. 128, CIOB*

Price A.D.F. and Harris F.C. (1985). Method of measuring production times for construction work. *Technical Information Service, No. 49, CIOB*

Winstanly W.P. (1973). Use of work study in Europe and its effect on productivity. *Occasional Paper No. 4*, The Institute of Building

5

PRODUCTION ANALYSIS USING TESTED SCIENTIFIC MODELS AND METHODS

5.1 INTRODUCTION

Construction managers should be equipped with production analysis and productivity measurement tools to monitor production efficiency throughout projects to steer construction towards maximum profit. The method study procedures discussed in Chapter 3 help to identify inefficiencies, form more effective production teams, develop optimum methods and improve site layouts and working conditions. Furthermore, the work measurement techniques described in Chapter 4 aid the measurement of productivity levels and the establishment of planning data to be used in a multitude of applications related to production control.

This chapter describes several other models and techniques that can be used to record production data, diagnose poor productivity, analyse production and measure productivity levels. It starts with a detailed discussion of activity sampling, covering its principles, statistical aspects of sampling, various activity sampling techniques and future trends. Subsequently, productivity improvement through repetition (learning curves) and production analysis using video and time-lapse photography are presented. Finally, the techniques of supervisor delay surveys, worker questionnaire and worker questionnaire sampling are discussed as diagnostic and problem solving tools for inefficiencies originating in management shortcomings.

5.2 ACTIVITY SAMPLING

One of the prime concerns of site management is to make sure that the site resources, which are in part predetermined by planning, are used most effectively during construction by constant monitoring of site productivity levels. Unlike in manufacturing industry, however, it is difficult to record the level of productivity of construction operations involving groups of workers, machines or processes because of the unstable nature of construction operations. Output values may vary over a wide margin due to such factors as bad weather, machine breakdown, poor communication, lack of supervision and so forth. Although time study methods, and cost and progress control measures can be applied in determining productivity levels or efficiency, the time between observation and subsequent reporting is usually too long to pick up inefficient sections of work quickly enough for corrective actions to be taken. Moreover, cost control systems which compare actual costs with project estimates cannot be relied upon completely because estimates are generally approximate and do not pinpoint the root cause of any low productivity levels since there may be a combination of reasons, such as degree of supervision, labour output, plant performance, site conditions, weather and so forth.

Activity sampling, also called *work sampling* or *snap-shot studies*, is a technique through which information can be obtained not only quickly and economically but also to predetermined levels of accuracy. It provides the project manager with a fairly sensitive management tool to assess the degree of activity on various sections of the construction site and to obtain benefits similar to those of time study without many of its disadvantages.

5.2.1 The principle of activity sampling

Activity sampling has always been naturally applied by human beings when forming opinions or making assessments but unless account is taken of its inherent limitations, a danger exists that the wrong inferences will be drawn. This is clearly illustrated by the following letter sent to a local newspaper by a passer-by after seeing and being disappointed with a group of construction workers (Harris and McCaffer 1995):

> Sir, I would like to make known to you a record I recently made of an exhibition of slow motion around a hole, while I have passed by on the last six occasions on my way to office each morning.
>
> First occasion   Eight men talking near the hole.
> Second occasion   The hole was deserted.
> Third occasion   Four men watching, one man priming some kind of pump, and one man holding a pneumatic drill (not working).
> Fourth occasion   Four men motionless, and sitting in various attitudes around the hole.
> Fifth occasion   Six men watching, one man working.
> Sixth occasion   Seven men watching, one man at work (one of the seven was in the hole).

After this experience, I gave up in despair and made no further records. Although I must add that the hole did get very large and deep. It has subsequently been filled in again!

Clearly, the passer-by has made a sample study but has always made observations on his way to work early in the morning before the workers had actually settled in to the day's work. If the number of observations is increased and observations are taken at random intervals throughout a working day, then according to simple statistics valid results would be obtained.

Thus, activity sampling can be defined as 'a technique in which a large number of instantaneous observations are made over a period of time of a group of machines, processes or workers. Each observation records what is happening at that instant and the percentage of observations recorded for a particular activity or delay is a measure of the percentage of time during which that activity or delay occurs'.

There is no one way to apply activity sampling to construction operations. Depending on its degree of sophistication, different objectives can be achieved, which are identified by different names as follows:

(1) Field count: for quick appraisal of site activity.
(2) General activity sampling: more detailed analysis of site efficiency and resource usage.
(3) Rated activity sampling: for work measurement.

The activity sampling concept is based on the fact that a small number of chance occurrences tend to form the same distribution pattern as the whole operation. Thus, it is a mathematical technique closely associated with statistics and the theory of probability. This aspect is explained in the following section before various activity sampling techniques are described.

5.2.2　Activity sampling theory and statistical principles

Clearly, activity sampling, being based on a sample of observations, must adhere to certain statistical principles and rules to obtain a proper representation of the whole operation. Any sampling carried out conforming to these principles and rules – or in other words, large enough to be statistically valid – can be used to predict the characteristics of an operation or project being studied with a desirable degree of accuracy. Indeed, the larger the sample, the higher the accuracy of the predictions and also the higher the time and cost involved. The desire for accuracy must therefore be balanced against the time and cost of such studies.

The principle can be illustrated using a simple example. Consider a batch of 1000 floor tiles delivered to site and required to be checked for damage. If the first one is found to be damaged it is clearly unwise to assume that the whole batch is damaged or vice versa. On the other hand, the total number of damaged tiles will not be known for certain until each one has been inspected. However, as more and more tiles are inspected it would be more certain that the total number of damaged tiles would follow the trend of the sample. If this is to be valid the samples taken must have consistent characteristics so that: (i) the condition of each tile is independent of that of any other, (ii) each tile has an equal chance of being selected and (iii) the characteristics of each tile remain constant. Examples of taking samples that do not agree with these rules are where the tiles are taken only from the top or all from one box.

The degree of certainty between the results obtained from sampling and those if all of the items were examined can be expressed using the following three concepts: (i) confidence limit, (ii) limit of error and (iii) category proportion (or proportion of the sample having the characteristic being observed).

Confidence limit provides the dependability of the result. For example, a confidence limit of 95% means that purely as a matter of chance, the answer can be relied upon 95% of the time. Clearly, the higher the confidence limit the larger the number of observations that must be made. If 100% confidence limit is required every item must be inspected. Confidence limit is often decided based on the purpose of the sample, and there is a general consensus that the 95% confidence limit is accurate enough for construction work.

The *limit of error* provides the accuracy of the estimated value given as a percentage either side of the result obtained by sampling within which the true value can be expected to fall, given the prescribed confidence limit. For example, if the limit of error is ±5% and the confidence level is 95%, the actual number of damaged tiles will fall within ±5% of the estimate obtained by sampling, and this result can be depended upon 95 times out of 100. A limit of error of ±5% is generally recognised as sufficient for construction operations.

Category proportion is the proportion of the sample that is expected to have a given characteristic. For example, if 10 tiles were found to be damaged out of a sample of 100, the category proportion of damaged tiles would be 10%. Taking another example, if a tower crane on a site is only working 40% of the time the category proportion of non-working time would be 60%. The category proportion affects the sample size required to meet the prescribed confidence limit and limit of error and it can be proved mathematically that they are related as given in the following formula (Harris and McCaffer 1995; Pilcher 1992):

$$N = \frac{Z^2 P(1 - P)}{L^2} \tag{5.1}$$

where N is the total sample size, Z is the value obtained from statistical tables depending on the confidence interval, P is the category proportion and L is the limit of accuracy required.

Table 5.1 provides sample sizes (number of observations) to be made for different values of category proportion and limits of error for 90% and 95% confidence levels. For example, if 10% damaged tiles will be allowed with the confidence limit of 95% and a limit of error of ±5%, the sample size would be 138 tiles. Alternatively, the sample size can be calculated directly using the above formula with a simplified constant ($Z = 2$) for 95% confidence level, which gives a

Table 5.1 Sample sizes required for 95% and 90% confidence levels.

Category proportion (%)	95% confidence level Limits of error (%)				90% confidence level Limits of error (%)			
	1	**2.5**	**5**	**10**	**1**	**2.5**	**5**	**10**
50:50	9604	1537	384	96	6765	1082	271	68
40:60	9220	1475	369	92	6495	1039	260	65
30:70	8067	1291	323	81	5683	909	227	57
20:80	6147	983	246	61	4330	693	173	43
10:90	3457	553	138	35	2435	390	97	24

slightly conservative value for the number of observations for a given accuracy and is often used for activity sampling studies with P usually obtained from a pilot study. The simplified formula is:

$$N = \frac{4\,P(1 - P)}{L^2} \tag{5.2}$$

EXAMPLE

A pilot study indicates that about 40% of the available working time on a section of construction work is spent on unproductive work. How many observations are required to be sure that the proportion is within $\pm 5\%$ accuracy given 95% confidence level?

SOLUTION

$$N = \frac{4 \times 0.4(1 - 0.4)}{0.05^2} = 384 \text{ observations}$$

If the workforce observed is large then the required number of observations can be achieved with a few visits but for a small workforce many visits would be required.

5.2.3 Field count

A *field count*, also known as *field rating* or *activity count*, is the simplest of activity sampling techniques and is often used to obtain a quick appraisal of degree of activity (efficiency level) of a gang, a section of construction work with several gangs or the whole site. The principle of field count is to classify activity of workers at the moment of observation into two groups, namely, *working* or *idle* (*productive* or *unproductive*).

The basic rules for carrying out a field count study are:

(1) Data are recorded using two mechanical counters (tally counters), one held in each hand, recording all of the operatives doing productive work in one counter

and those idle in the other, in the section of the construction site under review.

(2) The total number of operatives recorded should be checked against those who should be in the gang. To be a valid field count at least 75% of the operatives should be recorded, although some authors use a limit of 90% (Foster 1989).

(3) Whether *working* or *idle* must be categorised at the instant the worker is observed (snap observation), and the observations should not be rationalised, for example, the activity an operative has just completed or is about to start.

(4) Activities classified as working should include participating in active physical work, carrying material, operating a piece of equipment or receiving instructions, and those classified as idle should include waiting for another to finish work, relaxation, talking, walking empty handed and so on.

(5) The data should be recorded at random intervals touring the site during normal working hours. For more realistic results observations should be taken when operatives settle into their particular tasks or have established their rhythm of work, by avoiding observations, say, during the first half hour after commencement of work or after an official break or the last half hour before close of day or before an official break. However, this does not preclude taking special-purpose counts throughout the day, including at the beginning and end, to investigate how quickly workers settle down or slack off just before any quitting time.

Once the observations have been taken in this way, the data can be used to calculate the percentage of time when the workers are active. This is termed *activity rating*. Thus:

$$\text{Activity rating} = \frac{\text{Number of occasions observed active} \times 100\%}{\text{Total number of occasions recorded}} \qquad (5.3)$$

As a rule of thumb, it can be said that a total of 100 observations may be sufficient to identify situations having very low productivity levels, but at least 384 observations are required to obtain statistically valid results, as seen earlier (see Table 5.1). Indeed, a field count study can be made with any number of operatives. When a large section of work is observed a few tours will provide the required number; if a single gang is observed many tours may be required for results to be statistically reliable.

On construction sites, the activity rating generally falls between 60% and 80% depending on the type of work and working conditions. If the recorded activity rating is lower than this, there is something wrong in the operations and further investigation is needed. Thus, on a large site having a multitude of operations, this technique is very useful to identify weak spots where more supervision or more detailed study may be needed, either by concentrating on individual gangs, trades or a section of a site.

EXAMPLE

The site engineer on a building site felt that the overall efficiency of the workers was poor and decided to investigate the efficiency level using a field count study. The field

Clock time	Number observed working	Number observed idle	Total number assigned	Percentage observed	Percentage active (activity rating)	Remarks
			FIELD COUNT STUDY SHEET			
8:30	50	32	90	91	61	
8:50	48	35	90	92	58	
9:20	52	30	90	91	63	
10:05	45	28	90	81	62	
10:30	53	25	90	86	68	
Total	248	150	-	-	62	

Figure 5.1 Field count recording and analysis sheet.

count recordings he made using the tally counters by random tours around the site are shown in Figure 5.1. What is the overall activity rating of his site?

SOLUTION

As shown in Figure 5.1, both recording of observations and analysis can be carried out on the same sheet. Calculations show that the total percentage of workers observed during each tour (expressed as a percentage of total number of workers assigned) is always greater than 75% and hence the observations provide valid field counts. The percentage active column provides the activity rating of each round of observations but these values should not be relied upon individually as they are based on a small number of observations in this case. However, the total number of observations (398) is sufficient to provide a statistically valid activity rating, which is found to be 62% – or, in other words, workers are working only 62% of the time. The accuracy of this estimate can now be obtained using Equation (5.2):

$$L = \sqrt{\frac{4 \times 0.62(1 - 0.62)}{398}} = \pm 4.8\%$$

Thus, it can be said that the actual activity rating of the site falls within 62±4.8% with 95% confidence level.

Indeed, this kind of study can be extended to obtain a wide variety of information required for management decision making. For example, instead of only working and idle, the activities could have been divided into *working productive*, *working contributory* and *idle* according to the classification given in Chapter 2, or if it is necessary to identify idle time due to management inefficiencies, the activities can be classified as *working, idling with work* or *idling without work*. Clearly, such studies need three tally counters, preferably mounted on a board (if manual recording is envisaged). The results of such a study carried out on an actual site suspected to be poorly managed are shown in Figures 5.2–5.4 (Jayawardane 1995).

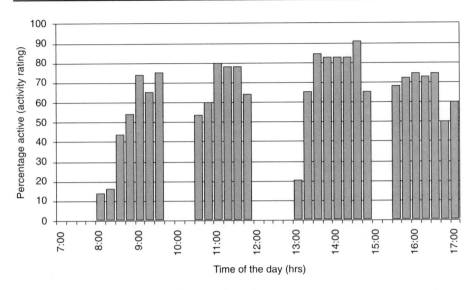

Figure 5.2 Histogram representing activity rating.

Figure 5.2 shows the variation of activity rating throughout a typical working day established with observations taken covering several days of operation. Figure 5.3 shows the percentage of worker idle time as a result of work not being assigned to the workers and Figure 5.4 indicates the percentage of waiting and relaxation time when work is available to continue. These results are very useful for site management for timely corrective action, for example, to provide increased supervision during vulnerable hours and prompt allocation of work to workers.

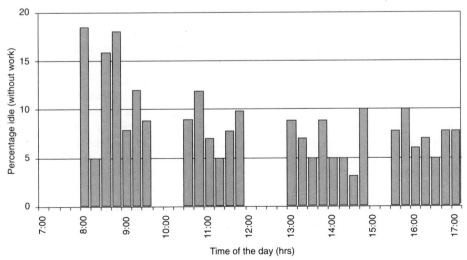

Figure 5.3 Histogram representing percentage of workers idle without work.

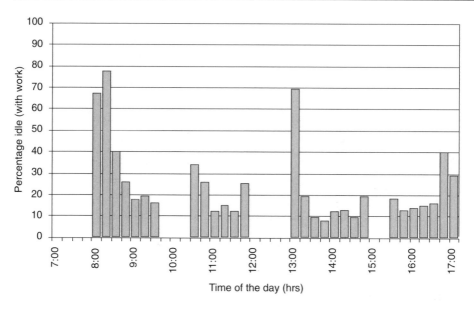

Figure 5.4 Histogram representing percentage of workers idle with work.

5.2.4 General activity sampling

General activity sampling, often referred to as activity sampling for short, is a step further in sophistication beyond the two-division field count previously discussed and is applied when a detailed breakdown of proportions of time spent on various work elements or ineffective time is required. For example, the technique can be applied to bricklaying operations to establish the proportions of workers' time spent on fetching bricks, laying bricks, cutting bricks, checking plumb, setting the line, carrying mortar, carrying bricks, idle and so on. These studies are carried out in a planned and systematic manner and can be used to highlight inefficiencies of construction activities by classifying their effectiveness to establish labour utilisation and compare the effectiveness of different methods of working.

If proportions of *productive*, *contributory* and *unproductive* times are to be identified, this method is preferred compared to an extended field count since it may perhaps be difficult to categorise activities into either productive or contributory quickly when tally counters are used. When activity sampling is used only to identify the proportions of times into these three categories, the technique is often referred to as *productivity rating* (Oglesby *et al.* 1989; Baxendale 1992; Pilcher 1992).

The technique is particularly useful in the analysis of non-repetitive or irregularly occurring activities in which complete methods and frequency descriptions are not easy to quantify. It also provides a preliminary study to evaluate the need for further study. If idle time can be broken down under various causes, such as material shortages, plant breakdown, insufficient information, extensive gang interference and so on, the exact cause of the problem can be determined.

ACTIVITY SAMPLING PROCEDURE

Activity sampling can be carried out in six basic stages.

(1) Establish the objectives of the study
(2) Carry out a preliminary survey
(3) Prepare suitable observation sheets
(4) Carry out a pilot study and establish the number of observations
(5) Record the required number of observations
(6) Calculate the results.

The procedure can be better explained with an example.

EXAMPLE

The site engineer of a major building project having large volumes of *in situ* concrete in frames noted that the productivity level of the form work gang was low and instructed the supervising officer to carry out an activity sampling study to establish the gang efficiency by determining the proportions of time the workers spent on various activities.

SOLUTION

Step 1: Establish the objectives   At this stage the purpose of the study will be clearly established, for example, whether the study is for a quick appraisal of efficiency by considering working and idle time as in field count, or a detailed appraisal by dividing into further work and idle elements, or is carried out as a work measurement exercise (described later). The required level of accuracy and the confidence level will also be decided at this stage.

For the form work example, the objective is to establish the proportion of time spent on each activity involved in erecting form work, assuming that these proportions are required with an accuracy of ±5% at 95% confidence level.

Step 2: Carry out a preliminary survey   This is to get a feeling for the problem, and the information collected will help to decide on the extent of work to be studied, the number of workers involved and the activities they carry out. Let us assume that five workers are involved in the form work gang and their activities include dismantling, cleaning, carrying, erecting and idle.

Step 3: Prepare a suitable observation form   This generally depends on the number of workers to be studied. A suitable format is shown in Figure 5.5. It is also helpful to assign suitable codes for different activity elements in a major study, to economise paperwork. The codes can be recorded on the top of the sheet for easy reference (see Figure 5.5).

Element	Code
Dismantling	1
Cleaning	2
Carrying	3
Erecting	4
Idle	5

Step 4: Carry out a pilot study and establish the number of observations The main purpose of a pilot study is to make sure that the identified activity elements are sufficient to record all the activities involved in the operation being studied, and modify if necessary, and also to calculate the required number of observations to obtain an acceptable accuracy. As seen earlier, the minimum number of observations required to have $\pm 5\%$ accuracy at 95% confidence level is 384 (see Table 5.1) or a

ACTIVITY SAMPLING OBSERVATION SHEET						
Contract: Job description: *Fixing form work to first floor* Location:			Time started: Time finished:		Sheet No: *1 of 4* Date: Observer:	
Activity Codes: *Dismantling - 1 Carrying - 3 Idle - 5* *Cleaning - 2 Erecting - 4*				Notes: *Weather bright and cool*		
Round number	Time	Workers/Machines					Remarks
		Smith	*Jones*	*Francis*	*Albert*	*Peter*	
1	*8:30*	*5*	*1*	*1*	*3*	*4*	
2	*8:35*	*2*	*4*	*1*	*1*	*2*	
3	*8:40*	*2*	*5*	*4*	*3*	*2*	
4	*8:45*	*3*	*3*	*4*	*4*	*4*	
5	*8:50*	*3*	*3*	*5*	*4*	*4*	
6	*8:55*	*1*	*1*	*4*	*4*	*1*	
7	*9:00*	*4*	*5*	*2*	*2*	*5*	
8	*9:05*	*4*	*4*	*3*	*5*	*3*	
9	*9:10*	*5*	*4*	*4*	*4*	*4*	
10	*9:15*	*4*	*3*	*5*	*4*	*4*	*Pilot study over*
11	*9:20*	*1*	*1*	*3*	*4*	*5*	
12	*9:25*	*4*	*5*	*2*	*2*	*4*	
13	*9:30*	*5*	*4*	*1*	*4*	*3*	
14	*9:35*	*4*	*5*	*2*	*1*	*2*	
15	*9:40*	*3*	*3*	*4*	*5*	*5*	
16	*9:45*	*4*	*4*	*4*	*4*	*3*	
17	*9:50*	*5*	*1*	*4*	*4*	*5*	
18	*9:55*	*4*	*3*	*2*	*5*	*1*	
19	*10:00*	*2*	*5*	*5*	*4*	*4*	
20	*10:05*	*2*	*3*	*3*	*5*	*4*	

Figure 5.5 Activity sampling observation sheet.

slightly conservative value of 400 if Equation (5.2) is applied with the category proportion of 0.5. However, if the equation is applied with the observed category proportion after a pilot study the most economic number of observations can be obtained.

Since the number of observations required is normally quite considerable it is often helpful to prepare a planned timetable of observation times. In most production work observation times are normally chosen randomly (by random number tables or computer generated random numbers) since the work patterns tend to be regular – hence the alternative term *random observation method* for this kind of activity sampling study. However, in construction work, activities by their very nature take a random time to complete, thus the observations can be taken at regular intervals. The term random observation method, therefore, is not normally used in construction studies. An observation interval of 2–10 minutes is normally used depending on the duration of activity elements and the number in the gang to be studied. Caution is, however, required in some types of building work, particularly that of a cyclical nature, to ensure that the cycle time and the observation interval or an integer multiple do not coincide, to avoid the same element being recorded all the time. The most desirable situation occurs when the sampling interval is less than any single element time. For the form work example, let us assume a five-minute observation interval.

Before commencement of actual observation, it is necessary to make sure that everyone concerned is fully informed. As discussed in time study, failure to do so may cause unrest, which can quickly escalate and feed smouldering grievances. Choose a suitable position from which to take the observations and record each activity that is in operation at the instant it is observed under the worker involved. After about 50 observations the pilot study can be closed and the required number of observations can be calculated. Based on the first 50 observations in the form work example (first 10 rounds; see Figure 5.5), the total number of counts under each activity element and the corresponding percentages are as follows.

Element	Element count	Proportion (%)
Dismantling	7	14
Cleaning	6	12
Carrying	9	18
Erecting	20	40
Idle	8	16
	50	100%

The required number of observations can now be obtained using Equation (5.2) with the largest category proportion, in this case 40%. Thus, the number of observations for ±5% accuracy at 95% confidence level is:

$$N = \frac{4 \times 0.4(1 - 0.4)}{0.05^2} = 384 \text{ observations}$$

Step 5: Record the required number of observations   Fifty observations have already been taken and to obtain the balance of 334 observations a further 67 rounds (334/5) are required. Figure 5.5 shows only the first 20 rounds of observations.

Step 6: Calculate the results   Once the required number of observations have been taken, they can be summarised as in Table 5.2. Clearly, all of the operations are within the ±5% accuracy. If the erecting percentage were 40% and exactly 384 observations were taken then the accuracy of the erecting percentage would be exactly ±5%. On the other hand, after the study if the erecting percentage were found to be, say, 44%, then:

$$N = \frac{4 \times 0.44(1 - 0.44)}{0.05^2} = 395 \text{ observations}$$

That is, a further two rounds of observations would be required to obtain ±5% accuracy. Thus, the formula can be applied any time during the study to check the number of further observations required. Furthermore, as the percentage of accuracy desired is reduced, the number of observations needed falls off rapidly.

If the results show a disproportionate amount of time being spent on certain activities – for instance, carrying and idle in the example – corrective action can then be considered, which may include increased supervision and improved layout. These studies are generally carried out on specific areas of operation, such as on gangs rather than the whole site, and are best when the number of operatives/machines observed is less than, say, ten.

Indeed, these productivity studies are relatively simple and can be carried out by junior site management. The results should be used for effective work organisation and not for questioning the operatives or as a basis for disciplining them, which if implemented will defeat their purpose and create antagonism.

The resultant activity element frequencies can be categorised into *essential*, *contributory* and *ineffective*, as in Chapter 2, and compared with established ratios

Table 5.2   Activity sampling summary sheet.

Operation	Frequency	Percentage of total, P	Accuracy, L^*	Minimum (%)	Maximum (%)
Dismantling	58	15.0	±3.64	11.4	18.6
Cleaning	48	12.5	±3.37	9.1	15.9
Carrying	67	17.4	±3.86	13.5	21.3
Erecting	150	39.0	±4.97	34.0	44.0
Idle	62	16.1	±3.75	12.3	19.9
Total	385	100.0	–	–	–

$* L = \sqrt{\frac{Z^2 P(1-P)}{N}}.$

(norms) maintained in the organisation for different trades. For example, in the form work study only erecting can be considered as productive; dismantling, cleaning and carrying are contributory and idle is clearly unproductive. The productive, contributory and unproductive ratio is therefore 39:44.9:16.1. The labour utilisation factors can now be calculated both by excluding and partially including contributory activities, as suggested by Pilcher (1992). Thus:

$$\text{Labour utilisation excluding contributary activities} = \frac{\text{Effective work observations}}{\text{Total observations}}$$

$$= \frac{150 \times 100\%}{385} = 39.0\%$$

$$\text{Partially including contributary activities} = \frac{\text{Effective observations} + \frac{1}{4}\text{Contributary})}{\text{Total observations}}$$

$$= \frac{150 \times \frac{1}{4}(173) \times 100\%}{385} = 50.2\%$$

5.2.5 Rated activity sampling

Rated activity sampling is a further step of sophistication beyond general activity sampling and can, if applied carefully, be used as a work measurement technique to determine production output data for use in estimating, planning and control. It is especially suitable for gang work where there are too many members for easy observation by normal time study. The basic procedure adopted for rated activity sampling is the same as that described for general activity sampling, but when snapshot observations are taken on operatives or machines the performance level is assessed at each observation on the standard rating scale (described in section 4.3 under 'Time study') and recorded in addition to the activity being carried out. Thus, unlike field count or general activity sampling, which does not require special training or expertise, rated activity sampling should be carried out by an experienced observer. Since the primary objective of such studies is to establish standard times or output data, they are carried out on individual operations with a relatively smaller time interval, usually 1–2 minutes, and on organised sites. Furthermore, as with conventional time studies, all of the other information required for establishing standard output data, such as details of working conditions, layouts and output during observation period, should also be recorded. The technique can be better explained using an example taken from Jayawardane et al. (1995a).

EXAMPLE

The rated activity sampling technique was to be used to establish standard times for a bricklaying operation. The study was planned and executed as described previously and observations were recorded throughout a typical working day. Figure 5.6 shows the first 19 rounds of observations taken on a bricklaying gang consisting of two bricklayers and one labourer. As can be seen, activities have been recorded using code numbers assigned to various activities and a rate has been

RATED ACTIVITY SAMPLING OBSERVATION SHEET									
Contract: *Boot houses* Job description: *Half thick pointed brickwork/ GF* Location: *Leicester*				Time started: *8:30am* Time finished: *3:53pm*			Sheet No:*1* Date: *../ ../97* Observer: AKWJ		
Notes: *Facing brickwork of half thick is constructed in ground floor using perforated common bricks. Construction is carried out from outer side. Working height varies from 0.6m to 1.4m. See a separate sheet for workplace layout (not provided) Weather bright and cool.*									
		Workers/Machines							
		BL 1		*BL 2*		*L 1*			
Round number	Time	*Aty.*	*Rate*	*Aty.*	*Rate*	*Aty.*	*Rate*	*Aty.*	*Rate*	Remarks
1	*8:30*	*2*	*100*	*2*	*100*	*13*	*100*			
2	*8:31*	*5*	*100*	*5*	*100*	*13*	*100*			
3	*8:32*	*1*	*100*	*5*	*100*	*13*	*80*			
4	*8:33*	*2*	*100*	*4*	*100*	*15*	*80*			
5	*8:34*	*4*	*100*	*5*	*100*	*18*	*90*			
6	*8:35*	*23*	*-*	*7*	*80*	*18*	*90*			
7	*8:36*	*2*	*100*	*1*	*100*	*13*	*100*			
8	*8:37*	*6*	*100*	*5*	*100*	*13*	*100*			
9	*8:38*	*5*	*100*	*6*	*90*	*13*	*100*			
10	*8:39*	*15**	*90*	*15**	*90*	*22*	*-*			** fixing meter boxes into the wall*
11	*8:40*	*15**	*90*	*15**	*90*	*31*	*-*			
12	*8:41*	*15**	*90*	*15**	*90*	*18*	*90*			
13	*8:42*	*9*	*90*	*20*	*-*	*18*	*90*			
14	*8:43*	*4*	*100*	*2*	*100*	*18*	*100*			
15	*8:44*	*9*	*100*	*3*	*100*	*18*	*90*			
16	*8:45*	*15*	*100*	*10*	*100*	*23*	*90*			
17	*8:46*	*1*	*90*	*28*	*-*	*19*	*80*			
18	*8:47*	*8*	*90*	*8*	*90*	*22*	*-*			***for future use*
19	*8:48*	*2*	*100*	*2*	*100*	*14***	*90*			*(Not to the workplace)*
										Contd..

Figure 5.6 Rated activity sampling observation sheet.

Table 5.3 Element codes and descriptions.

Code	Description
1	Fetch mortar
2	Spread mortar
3	Pick up brick
4	Butter brick
5	Lay brick
6	Tap brick
7	Fill joints
8	Finish/point joints
9	Check/plumb/level
10	Cut brick
11	Measure
12	Set line
13	Distribute mortar
14	Distribute bricks
15	Ancillary work
16	Other work
17	Unload bricks
18	Mixer operation
19	Cleaning workplace
20	Help mate
21	Help labourer
22	Relaxation
23	Waiting
24	Recovery
25	Extra breaks
26	Instruction/inspection
27	Walk empty handed
28	Talk
29	Redo work
30	Search
31	Away
32	Read drawing

attached to each observation that can be rated. The codes used are shown in Table 5.3, where the bricklaying operation has been broken down into 32 elements. This detailed breakdown has been adopted to facilitate subsequent synthesis, described in Chapter 4.

The data collected are summarised in Table 5.4, where the number of occasions of each activity element observed under different operatives, the corresponding percentages and the average rates are shown. For example, the activity 'fetch mortar' (code 1) was observed nine times under bricklayer 1 and this value expressed as a percentage of the total number of observations is 1.4. His average rate of carrying out this activity is 99. The number of times observed, in this case nine, is equivalent to nine minutes because the observations were taken at one-minute intervals. Thus, the basic time spent by bricklayer 1 in fetching mortar can be established using the equation given in the subsection 'Basic time' in section 4.3, and is found to be 8.9 minutes.

Table 5.4 Summary of data analysis with respect to activities.

Code	Bricklayer 1				Bricklayer 2				Labourer				Total			
	No.	%	Rate	BT	No.	%	Rate	BT	No.	%	Rate	BT	No.	%	Rate	BT
1	9	1.4	99	8.9	18	2.8	99	17.8	0	–	–	–	27	4.2	99	26.7
2	23	3.6	99	22.8	21	3.3	101	21.2	0	–	–	–	44	6.9	100	44.0
3	11	1.7	100	11.0	15	2.3	99	14.8	0	–	–	–	26	4.0	99	25.8
4	7	1.1	101	7.1	4	0.6	95	3.8	0	–	–	–	11	1.7	99	10.9
5	41	6.4	100	41.0	25	3.9	99	24.8	0	–	–	–	66	10.3	100	65.8
6	3	0.5	93	2.8	4	0.6	103	4.1	0	–	–	–	7	1.1	99	6.9
7	0	–	–	–	0	–	–	–	0	–	–	–	0	–	–	–
8	27	4.2	99	26.8	22	3.4	99	21.8	8	1.2	90	7.2	57	8.9	98	55.8
9	7	1.1	99	6.9	5	0.8	98	4.9	0	–	–	–	12	1.9	98	11.8
10	5	0.8	98	4.9	1	0.2	100	1.0	0	–	–	–	6	0.9	98	5.9
11	1	0.2	100	1.0	0	–	–	–	0	–	–	–	1	0.2	100	1.0
12	4	0.6	90	3.6	3	0.5	87	2.6	0	–	–	–	7	1.1	89	6.2
13	0	–	–	–	0	–	–	–	25	3.9	90	22.6	25	3.9	90	22.6
14	0	–	–	–	0	–	–	–	87	13.6	93	80.9	87	13.6	93	80.9
15	30	4.7	96	28.8	30	4.7	96	28.8	16	2.5	93	14.8	76	11.8	95	72.4
16	16	2.5	99	15.9	15	2.3	97	14.6	1	0.2	80	0.8	32	5.0	98	31.3
17	0	–	–	–	0	–	–	–	1	0.2	100	1.0	1	0.2	100	1.0
18	0	–	–	–	0	–	–	–	15	2.3	94	14.1	15	2.3	94	14.1
19	0	–	–	–	2	0.3	90	1.8	12	1.9	86	10.3	14	2.2	86	12.1
20	0	–	–	–	1	0.2	–	1.0	0	–	–	–	1	0.2	–	1.0
21	3	0.5	–	3.0	3	0.5	–	3.0	0	–	–	–	6	0.9	–	6.0
22	6	0.9	–	6.0	7	1.1	–	7.0	16	2.5	–	16.0	29	4.5	–	29.0
23	1	0.2	–	1.0	1	0.2	–	1.0	0	–	–	–	2	0.3	–	2.0
24	3	0.5	–	0.3	3	0.5	–	3.0	1	0.2	–	1.0	7	1.1	–	7.0
25	0	–	–	–	1	0.2	–	1.0	0	–	–	–	1	0.2	–	1.0
26	4	0.6	–	4.0	7	1.1	–	7.0	1	0.2	–	1.0	12	1.9	–	12.0
27	1	0.2	–	1.0	5	0.8	–	5.0	5	0.8	–	5.0	11	1.7	–	11.0
28	2	0.3	–	2.0	8	1.2	–	8.0	7	1.1	–	7.0	17	2.6	–	17.0
29	1	0.2	–	1.0	0	–	–	–	0	–	–	–	1	0.2	–	1.0
30	3	0.5	–	3.0	2	0.3	–	2.0	4	0.6	–	4.0	9	1.4	–	9.0
31	5	0.8	–	5.0	9	1.4	–	9.0	15	2.3	–	15.0	29	4.5	–	29.0
32	1	0.2	–	1.0	2	0.3	–	2.0	0	–	–	–	3	0.5	–	3.0
Total	214	33.3	99	211.5	214	33.3	98	211.0	214	33.3	92	200.7	642	100	96	623.2

Source: Jaywardane *et al.* (1995a).

Table 5.5 shows the activity sampling abstract sheet. Only the first 19 activities have been considered to establish basic and standard times because the activities beyond 19 are unproductive and need not be present in an efficient bricklaying operation. Appropriate relaxation and contingency allowances can now be added as shown and standard times can be established. The number of bricks laid by the gang during the observed period was 919 and the standard times obtained have been proportionately increased to establish the time required to lay 1000 bricks, as shown in the last column. Standard time for each element can then be used to develop

Table 5.5 Activity sampling abstract sheet.

Code and activity	Overall time (min)	Basic time (min)	Total allowances (%)	Standard time (min)	Quantity	Standard time per 1000 bricks
1 Fetch mortar	27	26.7	16	31.0	919	33.7
2 Spread mortar	44	44.0	16	51.0	919	55.5
3 Pick up brick	26	25.8	16	29.9	919	32.5
4 Butter brick	11	10.9	16	12.6	919	13.7
5 Lay brick	66	65.8	16	76.3	919	83.0
6 Tap brick	7	6.9	12	7.7	919	8.4
7 Fill joints	0	0	14	–	919	–
8 Finish/point joints	57	55.8	14	63.6	919	69.2
9 Check/plumb/level	12	11.8	10	13.0	919	14.1
10 Cut brick	6	5.9	16	6.8	919	7.4
11 Measure	1	1.0	10	1.1	919	1.2
12 Set line	7	6.2	10	6.8	919	7.4
13 Distribute mortar	25	22.6	16	26.2	919	28.5
14 Distribute bricks	87	80.9	16	93.8	919	102.1
15 Ancillary work	76	72.4	16	84.6	919	92.1
16 Other work	32	31.3	16	36.3	919	39.5
17 Unload bricks	1	1.0	14	1.3	919	1.4
18 Mixer operation	15	14.1	16	16.4	919	17.8
19 Cleaning workplace	14	12.1	16	14.0	919	15.2

Source: Jayawardane *et al.* (1995a).

output data for other operations using the principle of synthesis described previously.

Activity sampling data can easily be used by management to obtain a variety of information for decision making; for example, to find out whether work is equitably distributed among gang members (balanced gangs) and to pinpoint workers not meeting acceptable performance levels. For example, considering again that only the activities up to number 19 are essential in bricklaying, it can be established, based on the data in Table 5.4, that the total number of counts taken on bricklayers 1 and 2 and the labourer are 184, 165 and 157, respectively. This implies that bricklayer 1 is working more effectively than bricklayer 2 and, the total number of observations taken on each worker being 214, the activity ratings for bricklayers 1 and 2 and the labourer are 85.9%, 77.1% and 73.4%, respectively. This shows that work is reasonably well distributed among the workers. Put another way, the ratio of bricklayers' activities and labourers' activities should approximate to, or preferably be equal to, the bricklayer/labourer ratio for a balanced gang. Thus:

$$\text{Bricklayer/labourer ratio} = \frac{184 + 165}{157} = 2.22$$

This implies that, according to the nature of the activities on-site, one labourer can effectively serve 2.22 bricklayers. Clearly, proportions of bricklayers being impractical, two bricklayers assigned is the most satisfactory solution.

The investigation of equitable work distribution, gang balance or pinpointing workers not meeting acceptable performance levels could have been established more accurately using basic times for each element under different workers (see Table 5.4), rather than activity counts. This is because basic times represent the workers' actual effort by adjusting for slow and fast workers with appropriate rating. However, in general, ratios established by activity counts are sufficiently accurate for this purpose. For more details about the above discussion and how several studies are combined to develop reliable standard times, see Jayawardane *et al.* (1995a, b).

5.2.6 Activity sampling in practice and trends

As far as the application of activity sampling is concerned, it is probably the most widely used production analysis tool in the construction industry because of its relative simplicity. Rated activity sampling is also becoming more and more popular as a reliable work measurement technique and is widely used in Europe because traditional time studies are expensive and provide an accuracy greater than that required for construction work.

As in time study, much of the data gathering and analysis is now performed on hand-held computers and/or microcomputers using commercially available or self-developed software; for example, see Emsley and Harris (1986) and Chapter 8. Application of activity sampling is vast and models have been developed to predict future values of unit rate productivity and learning rates using work sampling data (Handa and Abdalla 1989). The validity of the technique for reliable production analysis has also been proved (Liou and Borcherding 1986).

5.3 PRODUCTIVITY IMPROVEMENT THROUGH REPETITION (LEARNING CURVES)

A *learning curve* (or *experience curve*) is a graphical representation of the relationship between unit cost or unit production time and the number of consecutive units produced.

Anyone who has performed the same task over and over again in succession appreciates that it takes less time to perform the task each time it is repeated. Many construction activities exhibit this phenomenon, known as the learning or experience effect. Learning curves can be applied to individuals, gangs or organisations. *Individual* or *gang learning* is the improvement that results when people repeat a process and gain skill or efficiency from their own experience; that is, *practice*. This is attributable to several factors, such as: (i) increased knowledge about the task being performed both by the management and workers, (ii) greater familiarity with the job, (iii) better coordination, (iv) improved job organisation, (v) more effective use of tools, methods and processes and so on. *Organisational learning* results from practice as well as from changes in strategy, administration, procedures, equipment and so on. In general, complex and labour-intensive repetitive tasks provide the best opportunities for productivity improvement through individual learning. If properly applied, incorporation of the learning development phenomenon when planning repetitive construction activities provides a more reliable production forecast over the duration of the project, resulting in more accurate scheduling and budgeting, and, consequently, better competitive bidding.

5.3.1 Learning curve theory

Learning curve theory is based on three assumptions: (i) the time required to complete a given task or unit production will be less each time the task is undertaken; (ii) the unit time will decrease at a decreasing rate; and (iii) the reduction in time will follow a predictable pattern. The time required to perform successive iterations of the same process generally takes the form shown in Figure 5.7. The lower curve shows the unit time and the upper curve represents the cumulative average time as the total number of units increases. Both of these methods of data presentation are generally applied with learning curves. As shown, the cumulative average time does not decrease as fast as the unit time because the time is being averaged.

To obtain the maximum benefit from learning development, research on learning curve theory has focused on developing mathematical models that describe the time per cycle (or cost per cycle) as a function of the cycle number by fitting models to historical data. Such models provide mathematical means for predicting or measuring improvements in productivity in repetitive work.

5.3.2 Learning curve models

A number of learning curve models have been introduced since the original work of Wright (1936) based on best geometric functions that fit collected data. Three widely known models are shown in Figure 5.8 and are briefly described in the following subsections.

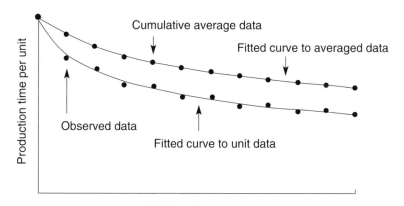

Figure 5.7 Impact of learning on repetitive processes.

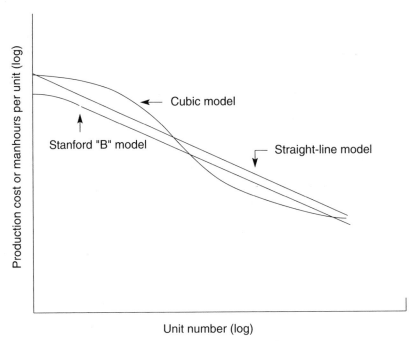

Figure 5.8 Typical learning models plotted on log–log scale.

STRAIGHT-LINE MODEL

The straight-line model, also called the Boeing model (Wright 1936) assumes that every time the number of cycles doubles, the time per cycle decreases by a constant percentage. This relationship can be expressed mathematically as:

$$Y_X = aX^n \tag{5.4}$$

where X is the unit number, Y_X is the number of direct labour hours (or cost) required for unit X, a is the number of direct labour hours (or cost) for the first unit, n is the slope of the logarithmic curve, $\log_{10} L/\log_{10} 2$, and L is the learning rate expressed as a percentage.

   When Equation (5.4) is plotted arithmetically, the curve is hyperbolic, but when it is plotted on a log–log scale the model yields a straight line, hence the name (Figure 5.8). The learning rate is the most significant parameter of the straight-line model, which decreases as the reduction in time due to learning increases (see Figure 5.9). When there is no reduction in time for subsequent cycles the learning rate is 100%. A learning rate of 90% indicates that the second cycle requires only 90% of the time of the first cycle, the fourth cycle requires only 90% of the time of the second cycle, the eighth cycle requires only 90% of the time of the fourth cycle, and so on. Thus, as the value of the learning rate decreases, a larger learning improvement effect can be anticipated. By convention, the percentage learning rate is used to identify any straight-line model. The straight-line model is the most

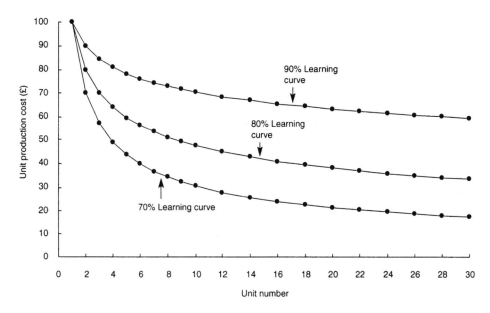

Figure 5.9 Arithmetic plot of 70%, 80% and 90% learning curves.

commonly used model for construction activities (Gates and Scarpa 1972, 1978; Diekmann *et al.* 1982; Oglesby *et al.* 1989).

STANFORD 'B' MODEL

This model, an improvement on the straight-line model, assumes that improvement in labour performance due to previous learning will be smaller at the beginning of the project but will eventually increase to approximately the same pattern as the straight-line model (see Figure 5.8). The model can be expressed mathematically as:

$$Y_X = a(X + b)^n \qquad (5.5)$$

where Y_X, a, X and n have the same meanings as earlier and b is a factor describing the level of experience acquired before commencement of work.

CUBIC MODEL

This is also referred to as the S model due to its shape. It incorporates multiple learning rates (or changing slopes; see Figure 5.8) and is given by:

$$\log Y_X = a + n_1 \log X + c(\log X)^2 + d(\log X)^3 \qquad (5.6)$$

where Y_X, a, and X have the same meanings as earlier, n_1 is the slope of the initial logarithmic phase, $\log_{10} L_1 / \log_{10} 2$, L_1 is the initial learning rate expressed as a percentage, and c and d are constant coefficients that are estimated using the basic equation of the model and another data point along the curve.

For further details about these models and several other models, see Spencer (1986), Thomas *et al.* (1986), Hijazi *et al.* (1992), Carlson (1973), Tanner (1985), Spears (1985), Everett and Farghal (1994), Lutz *et al.* (1994) and Karger and Hancock (1982).

Indeed, mathematical models such as these are only approximations of the real-life situation and too much emphasis on such models will obscure the true situation. Learning curves cannot be generalised to suit all forms of activities, and the type of model and, in particular, the model parameters are uniquely applicable to the specific situation in which they are fitted and tested. Thus, caution is required in selecting a particular model to predict future performance. In situations where a reasonably accurate mathematical model cannot be fitted a trend line fitted to actual data should be used to provide future performance.

5.3.3 Factors affecting the learning rate

All of the learning curve models are functions of the learning rate which is either assumed to be constant – for example, the straight-line model – or a variable – for example, the cubic model. The maximum benefit of learning development can only be obtained by a proper understanding of the factors affecting the learning rate and by taking actions so as to obtain the minimum learning rate and maximum learning development. The factors that generally affect learning are shown in Figure 5.10.

Among the factors listed, the characteristics of the task have the greatest impact on learning rate (Tanner 1985), followed by management characteristics. Indeed, proper management with effective planning, suitable incentive programmes, safety precautions and making available the required materials and tools, provides a conducive climate for rapid learning. Recent research in the construction industry has shown that the introduction of measured incentives has a significant positive effect on the rate of learning, while changing gang members during the process has a significantly negative effect (Duff *et al.* 1987). All of the other factors listed in Figure 5.10 have some effect on learning, and management should foster the positive factors so that the maximum benefits of learning development can be harnessed.

5.3.4 Learning curve application in practice

Recent research indicates that the most suitable mathematical model to describe the learning development obtained during repetitive construction for completed projects is the cubic learning curve (Thomas *et al* 1986; Everett and Farghal 1994). These best-fit curves cannot be used for the remaining cycles of the same project since the curve is plotted after completion of all cycles and hence can be of use for similar projects carried out in the future. In situations where the learning curve tool is used to predict the future performance of the same process, it has been proved that the straight-line model provides the best prediction (Everett and Farghal 1994), and the model is developed based on the unit data rather than the cumulative average data

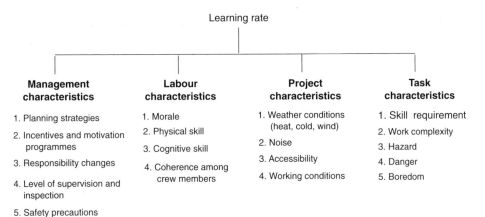

Figure 5.10 Major factors determining learning rate.

(Everett and Farghal 1997a, b). Recent research has also provided further tools for predicting future performance more accurately with varying methods of fitting curves, data representation and simulating learning development by modelling learning rates in simulation environments. See Farghal and Everett (1997), Everett and Farghal (1997a, b), Hijazi *et al.*(1992) and Lutz *et al.* (1994) for further details.

5.3.5 Guidelines for maximising learning development

The following list provides some guidelines for management to obtain maximum benefit from learning development when assigning work to personnel, both professional and craftsmen:

(1) Proper selection of workers by thorough evaluation of skill requirements.
(2) Provision of effective training to speed up the learning development.
(3) Motivation, as productivity gains based on learning cannot be achieved without a proper reward. Profit sharing and group incentives can significantly improve the rate of learning.
(4) Allow for work specialisation but be careful that boredom does not interfere.
(5) Allocate one or very few jobs at a time, because learning is faster on jobs completed one at a time.
(6) Provide the necessary tools and equipment to assist the performance.
(7) Provide quick and easy access to help.
(8) Allow workers to help redesign their tasks.
(9) Existence of proper standards because without a comparison base performance cannot be measured.
(10) Simplification of tasks because the simpler the task, the easier it is to learn.
(11) Avoid discontinuity because interruptions require relearning.
(12) Avoid employee turnover because new employees require learning, thereby changing the unit time and the learning rate.

(13) Proper repetition; that is, maintaining the same work content as far as possible.

EXAMPLE

A contractor has been constructing 25 single-storey houses in a residential estate under a continuity contract. So far, 20 houses have been completed and the client has decided to continue the project to build a further 75 houses, for which the contractor is keen to bid and win the contract. The total cost incurred by the contractor for each of the 20 houses completed is shown in Table 5.6. What is the learning rate achieved by the contractor? Assuming that the contractor is confident in maintaining the same learning rate throughout the project and that the mark-up is 20%, what will be the contractor's most competitive bid value for the new contract consisting of 75 houses?

SOLUTION

The house number and the corresponding cost when plotted on a log–log scale indicated a linear trend. A regression line fitted to the data resulted in a goodness of fit coefficient (R^2) of 0.995, confirming that the straight-line model accurately predicts the learning development trend (Figure 5.11). The resultant equation is:

Table 5.6   Unit costs of the first 20 houses.

House number	Cost (£)
1	50 000
2	45 000
3	38 800
4	36 400
5	34 250
6	33 000
7	31 500
8	30 600
9	29 950
10	29 500
11	28 530
12	27 800
13	27 475
14	27 500
15	26 500
16	26 000
17	25 780
18	25 600
19	25 000
20	24 850

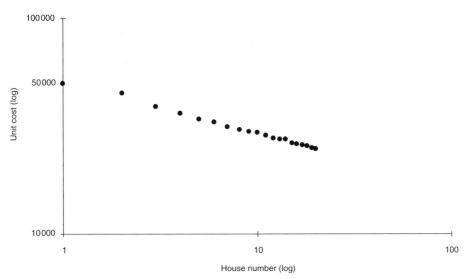

Figure 5.11 Scatter plot of house number and unit cost (log–log scale).

$$\log Y_X = 4.706 - 0.240 \log X \text{ or } Y_X = 50874\, X^{-0.240}$$

The slope of the learning curve $n = \log_{10} L / \log_{10} 2$ is therefore equal to -0.240. Solving the equation, $L = 0.8466$. The learning rate is therefore 84.66%.

The above equation can now be used to obtain the cost of construction for different houses by substituting the house number for X. For example, the cost of house number $26 = 50874 \times 26^{-0.24} = £23\,276$. The summation of total cost for houses 26–100 can be obtained by adding all the values, and was found to be £1 440 405. With a 20% mark-up the recommended contractor's bid value should be £1 728 486. If, for example, the contractor did not consider the learning development but decided to use the cost of the last built house (house 20) to estimate the bid value for the 75 houses in the new contract, with 20% mark-up, it would be 24 850×75×1.2 = £2 236 500. This indicates a top-up value of £508 014. If this were included the contractor might lose the contract.

5.4 PRODUCTION ANALYSIS USING VIDEO AND TIME-LAPSE PHOTOGRAPHY

The conventional data gathering methods for time and method studies discussed earlier involve data recording as the work proceeds and require employment of several observers, particularly when large teams are to be observed, making such data collection expensive and time consuming. Furthermore, the reliability of such data depends on the capability of the observer, and information collected in this way is limited to what the observer has already recorded using sketches, words and numbers.

Photographic techniques using camera and video provide an alternative way of recording information without these disadvantages. Furthermore, films and videos can be easily understood by anybody. They provide detailed and accurate information on all team members, equipment and their interactions, and make a permanent record of field operations for later analysis away from the hustle and bustle of the work site. Indeed, information revealed by such records cannot be denied by anybody and can be used in a multitude of other applications such as proof of certain phenomena, as an aid to justify claims, for education and training purposes and so forth, in addition to providing information required for time and method study. Data recording is carried out either by time-lapse photography or video recording, as described in the following subsections.

5.4.1 Time-lapse photography

Time-lapse photography involves taking still pictures at preselected intervals with a specially designed movie camera. Unless finer details such as hand movements are to be recorded, an interval of 3–4 seconds is often sufficient to study common construction operations as against 18 or 24 frames per second in normal real-time filming. Thus, a time-lapse system can record work-face activities in a very compact form, making filming far more economical. When played at normal speed several hours of operations can be viewed in minutes without diminishing understanding of the operation that has been recorded. A frame interval of even 20 seconds is not uncommon in recording construction operations and is suitable if the objective of the study is to obtain a broader view and a permanent record.

The equipment required for recording and viewing consists of a time-lapse camera and accessories such as a tripod, a projector and a screen. The equipment, which was formerly quite heavy, bulky and powered by mains electricity, is now portable, lightweight and battery powered. Other desirable features include the possibility of unattended operation for longer periods for economical recording; zoom lens to cover wide angles and long range to obtain only the desired features; automatic exposure to regulate light conditions for best pictures in an unattended camera; ability to imprint date and time on each frame to calculate elapsed time; and a battery condition indicator. The projection equipment should be capable of running frame by frame, and several times faster than normal speed either forward or backward to provide maximum flexibility in reviewing.

5.4.2 Video recording

Video recording techniques have several advantages over time-lapse systems for recording work-face activities and have become the current choice. Some of the advantages include: (i) no film processing like in time-lapse and hence instant replay; (ii) capability of recording audio signals in addition to pictures; (iii) equipment less expensive and more reliable, and becoming even less expensive; and (iv) purchasing and repair facilities readily available.

Video recording can be carried out in three ways. The first and most common method is to use a portable camera, a special cassette recorder/player, and a television type screen with facilities to view tapes by individual frames either backward or forward at user selected speeds up to about ten times faster than the normal speed of recording. The second method is a video time-lapse system where the camera records on the tape continuously and a special but expensive editor selects and records individual frames from the tape at selected intervals, thereby producing the equivalent of time-lapse and providing a compact record. The third way is to set the camera to record pictures at selected intervals as with time-lapse but this produces a far less clear picture and the user has little choice of speed during replay.

Similar to time-lapse photography, some of the characteristics to be considered in selecting equipment are: portability; the degree of resolution; automatic focus and exposure control; the magnitude of the zoom ratio; the ability of character generation; editing facilities; existence of frame and time counters; colour and sound facilities; the length of battery life; the quality of freeze-frame pictures; and the ability to play back both forward and backward at varying speeds up to about ten times normal speed with good picture resolution. If continuous filming is carried out, which is the current economical choice, selected segments of different tapes can be combined using a normal editor to organise data for efficient analysis and viewing.

5.4.3   On-site data collection using time-lapse or video

Preplanning for time-lapse or video recording is crucial for successful study. As with all field data collection, the purpose of the exercise must be communicated clearly to all the parties involved and questions should be answered frankly. The camera position will depend on the arrangement of the workplace, and what is to be recorded and the degree of detail required. General guidelines are that it should be located at a higher elevation and at a reasonable distance away from the work face to ensure that equipment and personnel will not obstruct the view and to avoid possible distraction caused by the presence of the camera and the taping operation. For time-lapse studies, the work-face activities can then be recorded at a suitable rate as discussed earlier, that is with 3–4 second intervals between frames for common production analysis, 1–2 seconds for details covering hand movements and 10–20 seconds to obtain a broader record. Video recording is generally continuous, using cassettes with a maximum recording time of four hours.

Before actual recording, the project details and other information such as date, weather, sketch of camera placement and so forth are customarily recorded at the beginning of the film or tape to aid understanding during viewing. In time-lapse this is usually done by photographing text written on paper or a board but in video it may be entered using the character generation facility. Any additional notes that need to be attached to frames during recording can also be carried out in the same way. It is also usual to film the overall site aspect to provide a proper orientation to the viewer before the camera is set up to record a specific area. If the filming is monitored by an operator, the camera view can be altered to capture other pertinent information affecting the operation being studied or another view can be recorded using a second camera, particularly in video recording since the two can easily be combined for analysis.

When covering large teams with different trades, an arrangement should be made to distinguish between them. The best way to do this is to provide them with hard hats of different colours or to paint their hats using easily removable paints. Once the necessary recording has been carried out the films or tapes can then be used for several applications as discussed below. Clearly, time-lapse films must be processed before viewing, but unless editing and combining several tapes are required for efficient compilation video tapes can be played back instantly.

5.4.4 Viewing and analysis of time-lapse and video

The main advantage of time-lapse photography is the recording of all facets of an operation in a compact form, which allows viewing at a faster rate. For example, if an operation is recorded at a rate of one frame every 4 seconds and played at a rate of four frames per second the operation can be viewed 16 times faster than the normal speed of work. The jerky effect produced, like old silent movies, does not cause a problem for interpretation. Indeed, the speed can be controlled at any time to suit the viewer's objectives. Similarly, video playing can be at either normal speed or several times faster, again depending on the purpose.

It is often beneficial to show the recordings to the workforce first, because this will provide opportunities for effective brainstorming, with faults and suggested improvements coming spontaneously from the workers themselves. The same thing can be carried out with other groups – managers, engineers, supervisors, foremen or all as a group – as a medium for method improvements and to improve on-the-job communications. With a preliminary analysis and tentative recommendations prepared by the analyst before such brainstorming sessions, management time can be best utilised in selecting alternatives and evaluating new ideas. Inviting viewers unfamiliar with the operation is often useful because they can view with an open mind, without prejudice. These informal viewings often reveal obvious shortcomings to help improve methods and communication among parties, and provide the added advantages of building up team spirit, positive attitudes and a high level of commitment, thus indirectly contributing to improved productivity.

However, fine-tuning of operations with a detailed understanding of interferences, waste time, excessive movements, duplicated efforts and inefficient methods can only be obtained after reviewing the recording several times (usually three to five times) at varying speeds to suit the analyst. A sensible approach is to review the recording from one standpoint at a time; for example, (i) flow of workers and materials, (ii) equipment utilisation and balance, (iii) safety and working conditions, (iv) study activities of each piece of equipment, worker or group of workers and so on. Using the frame numbers or elapsed time the information can then be transferred to detailed method study tools, such as flow diagrams, flow process charts and multiple activity charts, for detailed analysis. All of these and other uses, described below, are possible with the flexibility of being able to stop, rewind and rerun at various speeds, enabling assessment of all facets of operation from different perspectives.

In addition to the production analysis and method studies discussed above, time-lapse and video recordings can be used for several other applications:

(1) Using the frame number, or in modern equipment the digitised time on the picture, data required for time studies can be recorded by observing break points in the operation, eliminating the disadvantages of conventional data collection.
(2) Similarly, data required for activity sampling studies can be picked up to investigate and quantify the degree of activity. Here, again, the film or tape can be rerun to capture missing information, change the observation interval or concentrate on a different set of operatives and so on.
(3) The information recorded provides a permanent record of past activities and can be used for training of both workers and management. Indeed, a well-prepared video with combined vision and sound features is a superior communication and teaching aid for people at all levels.
(4) These records are also invaluable for proving the conditions of actual situations, for example for dispute resolution and justification of claims.

5.4.5 Future trends

Time-lapse photography is rapidly being replaced by video forms of recording because of their comparative advantages, as discussed earlier. With the ability to pick up audio signals in video recordings and the development of sophisticated software, much of the tedium of transferring data for time or method study can be eliminated by coding a video tape sound track. For example, once the video tape and computer are synchronised, the computer, using audio sensors, can directly identify the break points on a cyclic operation based on a distinct audio signal such as the frequency of the engine sound or the striking of a skip on the floor recorded on the video sound track. This enables automatic recording of cycle element times in the computer data files when the video is played. With the continuous improvement of computer hardware and software, it may soon be possible to record from a distance, capture the whole picture and recreate it in digitised form that enables the computer program to recognise a specific resource or piece of equipment for further analysis.

Some of these advanced features are already successfully applied in productivity improvement. For example, a computer-based Cyclone-Timelapse analysis system has been developed and successfully applied in the industry for the study, analysis, simulation and design of construction operations (Antill and Woodhead 1990, page 325). It processes films (time-lapse or video) of construction operations and prepares a variety of work-as-executed management reports of field activity. Required data are stripped from the film using a special computer-driven projector and critical events are registered. During the running of the film a Cyclone model of the work in progress captures the technological structure of field operations. A comprehensive software package enables the user to select and carry out multi-level planning and management studies of the process by generating a variety of reports, such as portrayal and summary of resource utilisation, investigation of gang sizing details or multiple activity charts of new or existing operations and establishment of data-based estimating approaches to construction operations.

5.5 SUPERVISOR DELAY SURVEYS

Asking the workers themselves is often regarded as the best means of acquiring information about production problems. The use of *supervisor delay surveys* (SDS), also called *foreman delay surveys*, is one such method whereby production problems are exposed by supervisors through the identification of causes and quantification of delays in the daily routine of their workforce. Since the problems are identified by the supervisors themselves, SDS is aimed at determining the effect of factors outside the supervisor's control, such as badly scheduled material deliveries, lack of information or equipment and so forth. The technique provides reasonably accurate information, avoids adversarial relationships with the workforce and can be administered through the existing resources and channels of communications at little extra cost. Furthermore, it encourages improved communication between trades and management through active supervisor participation in problem identification and solution, fostering positive morale. Although the SDS does not reveal the efficiency of the method or the gang, it provides a good indication of where to direct detailed investigations in addition to revealing management shortcomings.

5.5.1 Conducting supervisor delay surveys

The required information is provided by the supervisor completing a SDS report at the end of the working day. A typical SDS report form is shown in Figure 5.12; it can be modified to suit any specific situation or type of work but note that greater detail should be avoided to minimise estimating errors. Depending on the circumstances, SDS can be conducted at a wide range of frequencies and durations, such as daily survey and weekly reporting throughout the project, a two-week survey on a quarterly basis, daily survey for one week on a monthly basis and so forth. The latter is considered to be adequate for most construction operations.

As with all data collection surveys, details should be communicated clearly to all supervisors at a meeting attended by all supervisors and higher management before implementing the survey. The instructions should: (i) clearly indicate that the programme is intended to highlight the problems outside the supervisors' control and is not an evaluation of their own performance; (ii) assure the support of higher management, job security and non-punishment for honest reporting, preferably by higher management itself; and (iii) show how to record the details of the delays, quoting examples. The message can be clearly communicated with the help of a data collection form (see Figure 5.12) and an explanatory handout, as shown in Figure 5.13 (Tucker *et al.* 1982). The supervisors should also be informed about how the forms are to be distributed, and when they should be completed and collected. The most convenient arrangement is to utilise the same channels used for time cards and

SUPERVISOR DELAY SURVEY FORM			
Date: Name of supervisor:		Trade:	
Work area:		Number in gang:	
Problems causing delay	Number of hours lost	Number of men involved	Total manhours lost
1a Waiting for materials (on-site)			
1b Waiting for materials (outside delivery)			
2 Waiting for tools and equipment			
3 Lack of access			
4 Plant breakdowns			
5a Changes/redoing work (design errors)			
5b Changes/redoing work (site errors)			
6 Move to other work area			
7 Waiting for information			
8 Lack of continuity			
9 Overcrowded work areas			
10 Inclement weather			
11 Other			
Comments:			

Figure 5.12 Supervisor delay survey form.

information should be filed immediately after the day's work, before the day's events have been forgotten.

5.5.2 Presentation of delay summaries and their use in productivity improvement

Having collected SDS data for a sufficient period of time to obtain a representative picture of production delays – for example, five consecutive days per month – the data can be summarised either manually or using a computer for each significant cause and each trade, as shown in Figure 5.14. To highlight the magnitude of delays visually under various causes for the entire site or for individual trades, the results can be presented in a pie chart as shown in Figure 5.15.

INSTRUCTIONS FOR SUPERVISOR DELAY SURVEYS

A. Introduction

1. What is a supervisor delay report? It is a tool for the management to help the supervisor do his job. It is a simple daily account of problems that create delays in the work which the supervisor may not be able to directly control.

2. What does the supervisor delay report do? It makes sure the site manager has a chance to see what problems are causing delays for the gangs so that he can take corrective action to fix the problem depending on its severity.

B. Using the supervisor delay reports

1. You will be required to report only about five days per month, as directed by your supervisor.

2. The attached delay report form provides a checklist to record man hours lost to common problems. Space is provided to write other problems. When a report is required, you should put down the total man hours lost each day for each problem. Space is also provided for any other comments.

3. During the day, try to notice every time anyone in your gang has a serious delay (more than 15 minutes) and at the end of the day record the total lost time for each problem on the report form.

4. Supervisor delay surveys will work only if you take a few minutes at the end of the day to think about your delays and to record them. Otherwise, they will be just another piece of paperwork.

5. The summary of your reports will show which problems are the biggest across the site. The management can evaluate the cost of these problems and justify spending effort and money to do something about them.

C. Examples of problems to report

1. Your gang needs a poker vibrator. Because of delay in getting it five men in your gang wait half an hour each. Record two and a half hours lost for 'Waiting for tools and equipment'.

2. Your entire eight-man gang spends the entire eight-hour day reworking pipe spools because of off-site fabrication error. You record 64 man hours lost for 'Changes/redoing work'. While doing this work, six men are delayed half an hour each because the chainfall breaks. You record three hours lost to 'Plant breakdowns'.

D. Goals of supervisor delay reports

1. Short term – fixing of day-to-day problems by the site management, when the cost of fixing is less than the cost of delay.

2. Long term – (a) improvement of procedures based on supervisor's comments and (b) improved engineering packages as engineering personnel become more aware of their impact on construction costs.

E. Why should I fill it out?

1. Now is your chance to talk to top management, directly.

2. Problems that are really bad can be fixed right away if possible.

3. Top management cannot do anything without the support of the supervisor, so communicate your thoughts, ideas, even wishes back to them.

4. You have nothing to lose, but a few minutes of your time.

Figure 5.13 Explanatory handout for supervisor delay surveys. (Adapted from Tucker *et al.* 1982.)

SUPERVISOR DELAY SURVEY SUMMARY FORM									
Project:					Date:				
Supervisor area:									
Problems causing delay	Carpentry	Equipment	Masonry	Mechanics	Painting	Steelwork		TOTAL	PERCENTAGE
Waiting for materials (on-site)									
Waiting for materials (outside delivery)									
Waiting for tools and equipment									
Lack of access									
Plant breakdowns									
Changes/redoing work (design errors)									
Changes/redoing work (site errors)									
Move to other work area									
Waiting for information									
Lack of continuity									
Overcrowded work areas									
Inclement weather									
Other									
TOTAL									
PERCENTAGE									

Figure 5.14 Supervisor delay survey summary form.

Once the summary results are available they should be discussed with the supervisors participating in the survey to identify the root causes and to explore solutions. These discussions also yield other benefits. For example, it satisfies the supervisors' curiosity to see the outcome of their participation, provides an opportunity for them to participate in active discussions with higher management in suggesting solutions, and motivates them to increase their commitment to future surveys, especially if higher management indicates that actions are being taken to

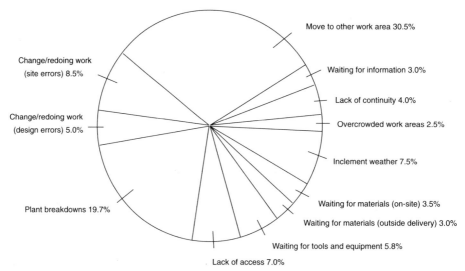

Figure 5.15 Pie diagram of supervisor delay survey results.

solve at least some relatively simple problems highlighted by the SDS technique. Very often, by effective preplanning and diligent application of the method study procedures discussed earlier, further improvements can be effected.

Subsequent use of SDS would indicate whether the corrective actions were proving effective by the reducing percentage of delays. A monthly cycle is recommended because it keeps supervisors familiar with the procedures, allows time for positive management action and prevents the programme from becoming too routine. An example indicating overall improvement at site level is shown in Figure 5.16. Similar graphs can be plotted to investigate improvements at individual trade level. In addition to being a cost effective technique which is particularly useful for evaluating administratively-related problems, SDS has the following advantages:

(1) Delays to particular groups of workers are highlighted immediately through generation of a credible problem list.
(2) Information is provided on particular aspects such as materials, subcontractor interference, information, plant and equipment and so on.
(3) Information is current and the whole project can be readily monitored.
(4) Can be used as a fast, easy to administer and relatively inexpensive troubleshooting device for projects experiencing serious productivity problems.
(5) Can be used as an ongoing productivity improvement programme, providing continuous feedback of production problems to site management for their action and maintaining a direct communication link between supervisors and higher-level site management.
(6) Most useful on projects with a large workforce where logistics and communications are most complex.

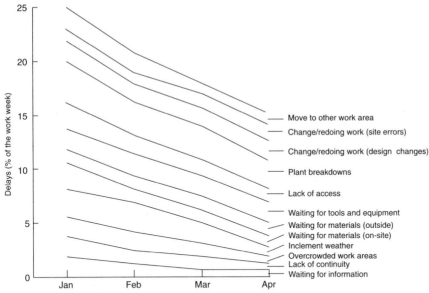

Figure 5.16 Results of regular supervisor delay surveys.

5.6 OTHER PRODUCTION ANALYSIS TECHNIQUES

Two more recently developed production analysis techniques are *worker questionnaire* (WQ) and *worker questionnaire sampling* (WQS), also called craftsman questionnaire sampling. There is not much evidence of their wide application in the construction industry; nevertheless, they provide similar benefits to SDS and are suitable when a detailed account of delays and unproductive times originating from management shortcomings is required.

5.6.1 Worker questionnaire

The technique involves information gathering through a self-administered questionnaire among construction workers and supervisors, with the main objective of investigating the problems that adversely affect workers' productivity and motivation. The questionnaire usually requires workers to estimate loss of time due to various causes, rank the severity of the problems and even to provide potential solutions to productivity problems caused by management shortcomings and support-related problems. Clearly, such questionnaires should be carefully designed to suit the specific situations by considering such factors as the purpose, length and type of project, possible causes of low productivity, the time required to complete questionnaires, and the attitudes and abilities of respondents. Typically, main areas of the questionnaire might include:

- Introduction, with the purpose clearly indicated and confidentiality guaranteed
- Trade, present location of work and type of work
- General level of satisfaction with working conditions and supervision
- Provision of health and welfare facilities
- Availability, suitability and quality of materials
- Availability and condition of tools
- Availability, reliability and condition of plant and equipment
- Availability, suitability and condition of scaffold
- Gang interference and overcrowding with other trades
- Instruction and inspection delays
- Rework.

Under each of the above causes, the questionnaire might include questions to discover: (i) whether workers have to wait or move to another area because of delays; (ii) how many hours per week are lost due to such delays; and (iii) exact details of the problem and possible suggestions in the workers' opinion to improve the situation. However, there are no hard and fast rules in designing or administering the questionnaires. What is required is a clear understanding of the purpose supported by common sense. Depending on the circumstances, the questionnaires can be simple, requiring 10–15 minutes to answer, or more detailed, where 30–45 minutes may be required. Questionnaires may be administered to groups of, say, 10–50 people at a time. As with all the other surveys, careful planning, organising and implementation are required, with necessary introductory sessions to convey the purpose, assure confidentiality of information and clarify doubts, as with SDS. On large and long-duration projects, the questionnaire can be administered more formally, say, once every six months or when there are special circumstances. Less formal approaches can be adopted for small, short-duration projects. The information gathered can be most effectively analysed and the results presented quickly using microcomputer systems; for example, see Stall (1983). Additional information may also be gathered through worker or supervisor group interviews. Important findings should be shared with the workers.

The advantages of the WQ technique include:

(1) The provision of timely information about production problems due to management shortcomings enabling managers to take prompt corrective action.
(2) A direct worker–management link that brings job satisfaction and motivation of workers.
(3) A means for monitoring the effect of any productivity improvement programme.
(4) More accurate and revealing information about production problems since information is collected directly from the workers and not through the normal channels of communications, where information can be lost or manipulated for the benefit of either the sender or the receiver.

The disadvantages include:

(1) Unlike SDS, delay time estimates in the WQ are usually requested as number of hours lost per week and hence are subject to under or over-estimating, casting doubt on the validity of the estimates. See Chang and Borcherding (1985) for details.
(2) A significant amount of worker time is spent in completing the questionnaire, thus losing productive time.
(3) Similar to SDS, it does not provide information about the efficiency of construction methods or the competence of the workforce.

5.6.2 Worker questionnaire sampling

Worker questionnaire sampling (WQS) aims to achieve the same purpose as WQ but with reduced effort by restricting the survey to a sample of workers selected on the basis of activity sampling theory. The procedure is very similar to activity sampling; the WQS administrator tours the site and randomly selects workers and supervisors by sight. The selected workers are then asked whether they were engaged in *productive* or *unproductive* work (with a clear description of productive and unproductive work) at the time when they were chosen. If they were engaged in unproductive work, they are asked to indicate the detailed causes by completing a simple questionnaire. The idea is to capture the detailed causes of unproductive work, which cannot usually be ascertained by activity sampling. The procedure is repeated by making random tours of the site exactly like activity sampling until a sufficient sample size is obtained. Results can be compiled similarly to activity sampling studies. The technique has several advantages compared to WQ: it requires less time and effort, provides more reliable information since information is collected while activities are still fresh in workers' minds, and it can be applied regularly as a diagnostic tool. On the other hand, it provides less detail than WQ.

Indeed, the reliability of information provided by craftsworkers in both the WQ and WQS techniques will depend strongly on their attitudes towards management and their motivational levels. Although the validity of these techniques has been proven by applying them to a few sites (Chang and Borcherding 1984, 1985), they are only recommended in favourable job climates.

5.7 SUMMARY

Construction managers should be equipped with production analysis and productivity measurement tools to monitor production efficiency throughout projects. In addition to the techniques described in Chapters 3 and 4, several other models and methods – activity sampling, learning curves, video and time-lapse photography, supervisor delay surveys, worker questionnaire and worker questionnaire sampling – were presented in this chapter as further tools to record production data, diagnose poor productivity, analyse production and measure productivity levels. These techniques were illustrated with examples where necessary.

REFERENCES AND BIBLIOGRAPHY

Antill J.M. and Woodhead R.W. (1990). *Critical Path Methods in Construction Practice* 4th edn. Chichester: John Wiley & Sons

Baxendale A.T. (1992). Measuring site productivity by work sampling. In *The Practice of Site Management* Vol. 4 (Harlow P.A., ed.), pp. 157–165. London: CIOB

Calvert R.E. (1981). *Introduction to Building Management* 4th edn. London: Butterworth

Carlson J.G.H. (1973). Cubic learning curves: precision tool for labour estimating. *Manufacturing Engineering and Management*, **71**(5), 22–25

Chang L.M. and Borcherding J. (1984). Craftsman questionnaire sampling for construction productivity. *Transactions of the AACE*, pp. H.2.1–H.2.4

Chang L.M. and Borcherding J. (1985). Evaluation of craftsman questionnaire. *Journal of Construction Engineering and Management ASCE*, **111**(4), 426–437

Diekmann J.R., Horn D.L. and O'Connor M.H. (1982). Utilisation of learning curves in damage for delay claims. *Project Management Quarterly*, 67-81

Duff A.R., Pilcher R. and Leach W.A. (1987). Factors affecting productivity improvement through repetition. In *Proc. 5th Int. Sym. Managing Construction Worldwide* Vol 2: *Productivity and Human Factors in Construction* (Lansley P.R. and Harlow P.A., eds.), CIB W65, September 1987, pp. 634–645. London: E&FN Spon

Edlin N.N. and Egger S. (1990). Productivity improvement tools: camcorders. *Journal of Construction Engineering and Management ASCE*, **116**(1), 100–111

Emsley M.W. and Harris F.C. (1986). Work study is important to construction – computers can make work study effective. *Building Technology and Management*, April, 10–15

Everett J.G. and Farghal, S.H. (1994). Learning curve predictors for construction field operations. *Journal of Construction Engineering and Management ASCE*, **120**(3), 603–619

Everett J.G. and Farghal, S.H. (1997a). Data representation for predicting performance with learning curves. *Journal of Construction Engineering and Management ASCE*, **123**(1), 46–52

Farghal S.H. and Everett J.G. (1997b). Learning curves: accuracy in predicting future performance. *Journal of Construction Engineering and Management ASCE*, **123**(1), 41–45

Foster D. (1989). *Construction Site Studies – Production, Administration and Personnel*. London: Longman

Gates M. and Scarpa A. (1972). Learning and experience curves. *Journal of the Construction Division ASCE*, **98**(CO1), 79–101

Gates M. and Scarpa A. (1978). Optimum number of crews. *Journal of the Construction Division ASCE*, **104**(CO2), 123–132

Handa V.K. and Abdalla O. (1989). Forecasting productivity by work sampling. *Construction Management and Economics*, **7**, 19–28

Harris F. and McCaffer R. (1995). *Modern Construction Management* 4th edn. Oxford: Blackwell Science

Hijazi A.M., AbouRizk S.M. and Halpin D.W. (1992). Modelling and simulating learning development in construction. *Journal of Construction Engineering and Management ASCE*, **118**(4), 685–700

Jayawardane A.K.W. (1995). Wastage on building sites in Sri Lanka. *Asia Pacific Building and Construction Management Journal*, **1**(1), 51–70

Jayawardane A.K.W., Price A.D.F. and Harris F.C. (1995a). Measurement of brickwork and blockwork productivity: part A. *Building Research and Information*, **23**(2), 81–86

Jayawardane A.K.W., Price A.D.F. and Harris F.C. (1995b). Measurement of brickwork and blockwork productivity: part B. *Building Research and Information*, **23**(3), 147–155

Karger D. and Hancock W. (1982). *Advanced Work Measurement*. New York: Industrial Process

Liou F.S. and Borcherding J.D. (1986). Work sampling can predict unit rate productivity. *Journal of Construction Engineering and Management ASCE*, **112**(1), 90–103

Lutz J.D., Halpin D.W. and Wilson J.R. (1994). Simulation of learning development in repetitive construction. *Journal of Construction Engineering and Management ASCE*, **120**(4), 753–773

Oglesby C.H., Parker H.W. and Howell G.A. (1989). *Productivity Improvement in Construction*. New York: McGraw-Hill

Pilcher R. (1992). *Principles of Construction Management* 3rd edn. New York: McGraw-Hill

Rogge D.F. and Tucker R.L. (1982). Foreman-delay surveys: work sampling and output. *Journal of the Construction Division ASCE*, **108**(CO4), 592–604

Spears W. (1985). Measurement of learning and transfer through curve fitting. *Human Factors*, **27**(3), 251–266

Spencer W. (1986). Comparing learning curves. *Production Engineering*, May, 56–58

Stall M.D. (1983). Analysing and improving productivity with computerised questionnaires and delay surveys. *Project Management Quarterly*, **XIV**(4), 69–79

Tanner J. (1985). The learning curve. *Production Engineering*, May, 72–78

Thomas H.R. (1991). Labour productivity and work sampling: the bottom line. *Journal of Construction Engineering and Management ASCE*, **117**(3), 423–444

Thomas H.R. and Daily J. (1983). Crew performance measurement via activity sampling. *Journal of Construction Engineering and Management ASCE*, **109**(3), 309–320

Thomas H.R. and Holland M.P. (1980). Work sampling: a comparative analysis. *Journal of the Construction Division ASCE*, **106**(CO4), 519–534

Thomas H.R., Holland M.P. and Gustenhoven C.T. (1982). Games people play with activity sampling. *Journal of the Construction Division ASCE*, **108**(CO1), 13–22

Thomas H.R., Guevara J.M. and Gustenhoven C.T. (1984). Improving productivity estimates by work sampling. *Journal of Construction Engineering and Management ASCE*, **110**(2), 178–188

Thomas H.R., Mathews C.T. and Ward J.D. (1986). Learning curves models in construction productivity. *Journal of Construction Engineering and Management ASCE*, **112**(2), 245-258

Tucker R.L., Rogge D.F., Hayes W.R. and Hendrickson F.P. (1982). Implementation of foreman-delay surveys. *Journal of the Construction Division ASCE*, **108**(CO4), 577–591

Wijesundera D.A. and Harris F.C. (1987). Video and computer application in production analysis. In *Proc. 5th Int. Sym. Managing Construction Worldwide* Vol 2: *Productivity and Human Factors in Construction* (Lansley P. R. and Harlow P. A., eds.), CIB W65, September 1987, pp. 758–766. London: E&FN Spon

Winstanly W.P. (1973). Use of Work Study in Europe and its Effect on Productivity. *Occasional Paper No 4*, The Institute of Building

Wright T.P. (1936). Factors affecting the cost of aeroplanes. *Journal of Aeronautical Science*, February, 124–125

6

PRODUCTION PLANNING AND CONTROL

6.1 INTRODUCTION

In order for a project to succeed, well-prepared plans by all the parties involved are essential. In the first instance the client needs to have a clear understanding of the functions and design scope of the building or civil engineering works, from which an outline plan of construction can be determined. In this manner the major activities and stages will be identified early on and budget estimates of the cost of the work properly ascertained.

If this phase can be thoroughly executed in conjunction with the appointed project manager (either internal or external to the client's organisation) targets are more likely to be achieved. Thereafter, more detailed preplans and cost estimates are prepared for the client's consideration, enabling alternatives to be evaluated for suitability and function, not least budget limitations.

The types of contract and managerial arrangements covering the relationships between client, project manager, planning supervisor for safety, designer(s), contractor(s), subcontractors and suppliers can also be determined when this phase of early planning for the client has been fully worked through. Thereafter, designers and contractors can be invited to bid or negotiate for the work as appropriate, when the benefits of good drawings and preplanning will prove essential in bringing the project on time, to cost and to the quality anticipated. Once the contractor is engaged on site, usually very detailed contract plans are subsequently prepared by the contractor's management team, based upon the preplans and programmes, and thereafter monitored for progress by the client's project manager or representative.

The methods of planning used vary depending on the size, nature of project, complexity and experience of the combined team and of course the client's needs. Bar charts are generally adopted for presentation at meetings, these often being reconstructed from networks (for example critical path method (CPM) or PERT), precedence diagrams or line of balance (LOB) charts, from which resource levels and cash flows are analysed or decided, together with procurement schedules for materials suppliers and subcontractors. Indeed, by breaking the contract plan into smaller elements and with cross-referencing to the contractor's activities, estimates, monitoring of construction costs against the budget and even calculating bonus or incentive payments to individual workers is possible provided sufficient effort is given to measuring and collating work done – a task often difficult to achieve accurately and readily because of the fragmentation of work commonly in evidence on site.

This chapter describes how to carry out project planning and control in a broader sense, covering common planning methods such as CPM, precedence diagrams and LOB including worked examples. The planning process is described, drawing on the previous discussions relating to the techniques used for method improvement, work measurement and activity sampling to explain the principles and approaches to construction planning. The importance of project control and associated tools such as bar charts and S curve techniques are described. Integration of planning with estimating, budgetary control and costing is highlighted together with a summary of the application of computer systems. Finally, quality management and safety in relation to planning are highlighted, all acting as a focus to other chapters.

6.2 PLANNING METHODS

There are several planning methods to choose from and the selection of a technique for a particular application depends on the factors mentioned above. Some of the widely used techniques and the situations where they are most suitable are now discussed.

6.2.1 Networks

Network analysis has been variously described as activity on the node, critical path method or diagram, and performance evaluation and review technique (PERT), all of which essentially require the construction elements to be determined and sequenced in order and the time for construction calculated. Logic sequencing and time analysis are usually the most straightforward aspects, with the decisions on the type of elements (that is, full activities or sub-tasks) and the duration of each needing experienced practitioners to make assessments based upon the drawings, quantities of work, materials, working space available and construction practicalities. When this latter phase has been achieved the activities are normally listed with their associated durations and resources as shown in the example below:

Activity list	Resources	Duration (days)
Brickwork to walls	2 Bricklayers	7
First fix joinery and windows	1 Carpenter and 1 Labourer	3
Erect roof	3 Carpenters	4
First fix services	2 Electricians	5
Install gas services	1 Subcontractor	4
Install electricity	1 Subcontractor	2
Finishes	2 Craft and 1 Labourer	6
Prepare paths	2 Labourers	5
Prepare driveway	2 Labourers	2

DRAWING THE ACTIVITY LOGICAL SEQUENCES

The succession logic linking each activity is determined using a network technique. Sometimes the sequencing of an activity is obvious – for example roofing normally follows columns or walls – whereas other activities are more flexible, such as external works to a building, which may broadly start and finish within the project itself. Clearly, experience is necessary in judging these relationships. Nevertheless, the notation requires each activity to be defined and given numbered start and finish nodes (events), as shown in Figure 6.1. All events must be allocated unique numbers which may be in any order to suit, including the use of alphanumeric versions if preferred. The links between events are the activities.

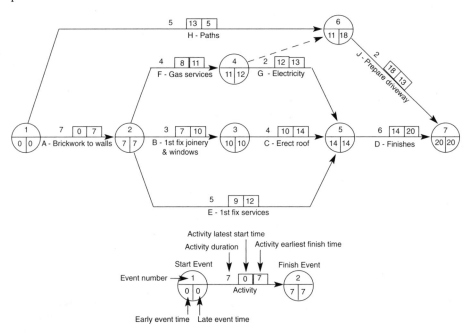

Figure 6.1 Activity plan represented in arrow network form.

Good convention places the activity description below the line to avoid clutter, while the durations (hours, days, weeks and so on) together with the resources required are normally sited above the line.

Dummy activities, usually shown by dashed lines, can be inserted to force logic. For example, activity 6–7, prepare driveway, cannot be started until the gas main, activity 2–4, has been laid. Dummy activities are also required for unique identification of activities when they are identified by event numbers. Depending on the purpose of the dummy activity, they are referred to as either 'logic' dummies or 'identity' dummies.

PRODUCING THE SCHEDULE

Once the project activities are represented in a network form as in Figure 6.1 a project schedule can be produced with activity durations and activity resources assigned, network time analysed, floats calculated and activity times established as described below.

Activity duration   Before the start and finish times of the activities can be determined, the duration of each needs to be calculated. This task is presently the least well understood. Many planners use rule of thumb estimates – for example, one bricklayer can complete 50 bricks per hour, 5 m³/hr of concrete can be placed by a crane and so on.

Unfortunately, this kind of data tends to include a generous allowance for contingencies – for example, lost time to be anticipated – which can amount to perhaps 100% of basic time for average construction work. Other more scientific approaches involve collection of work study data and forming regression type equations of the form:

$$Y_c = C_0 + C_1 X_1 + C_2 X_2 + \ldots C_n X_n \tag{6.1}$$

where Y_c, might be cubic metres of concrete placed per hour, for example. C values are various constants, while X_1 could be size of pour in cubic metres, X_2 plan area of pour in square metres, X_3 depth of pour, X_4 number of workers in the gang and so on, as described in detail in Chapter 4.

The effort needed to secure data of this quality is presently beyond the willingness of most firms to make available the resources to fund the work study task, but clearly is essential if accurate estimates and plans are demanded. Indeed, unless reliable activity durations are used in the network, the final calculated times will only be very approximate – a situation unfortunately commonly associated with the method as currently used in the industry.

Activity resources   By way of emphasis, the activity duration estimate must take account of the fundamental resources requirement for execution. For example, in Equation (6.1), X_4 would represent these aspects. In practice, however, rules of thumb are probably unavoidable in gauging the right balance, and typically the appropriate size of gang working in a confined area might have to be assessed from experience, unless data banks of accurate basic times and the influential variables were extensive enough to establish the regression relationships.

Assuming all these elements can be ascertained, carrying out the timing calculations is fairly straightforward.

Time analysis Managers generally wish to know the earliest and latest times that each activity can start, the corresponding earliest and latest finish times, and the path through the network with the shortest combined time, this being the 'critical path' that determines the completion time for the project.

The calculations shown in Figure 6.1 illustrate the earliest event times, established by travelling from node 1 along each path (a process referred to as 'forward pass'), and the latest event times, established by travelling back from node 7 (referred to as 'backward pass'). If manual analysis is carried out the convention is that the earliest event time of the first event is considered to be zero and the latest event time of the last event is considered equal to its earliest event time, in this case 20 days.

Where two or more paths combine – as, for example, events 5 and 6 – the longest path obviously determines the earliest event time. The reverse is true for latest event times; that is, the smallest value must be chosen to avoid delaying the project completion time.

Float time The forward and backward passes allow 'total', 'free' and 'interfering' float to be calculated, total float being the time an activity start can be delayed without delaying the project end date. For example, the total float of activity 1–6 is determined from the latest event time of node 6 (18 days) minus the earliest event time of node 1 (zero), minus the activity duration (5 days), to produce $18 - 0 - 5 = 13$ days float. Of course, using up all the total float on an activity will have the equivalent knock-on effect on the succeeding activities, thereby using up some of their total float also.

Consequently, planners and managers also like to see free float, which is the time an activity can be moved without affecting succeeding activities. It is determined by subtracting the earliest event time of the start node from the earliest event time of the finish node and subsequently deducting the duration of the activity between these two nodes. For activity 1–6 this produces $11 - 0 - 5 = 6$ days of free float.

The difference between the two is called interfering float, and its use will affect succeeding activities; for example, float on 6–7 will be used. Figure 6.2 illustrates the situation of float times diagrammatically.

Activity times Once the network is time analysed, activity start and finish times can be established. Each activity has an earliest start time (EST), a latest start time (LST) and corresponding earliest and latest finish times (EFT and LFT). The EST of an activity is equal to the earliest event time of the start node. EFT can then be established simply by adding the activity duration to EST. For example, the EST of activity 1–6 is zero and the EFT is $0 + 5 = 5$. LFT of an activity is equal to the latest

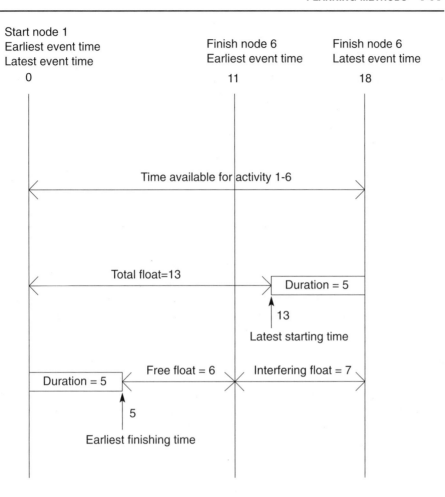

Start node 1
Earliest event time
Latest event time
0

Finish node 6
Earliest event time
11

Finish node 6
Latest event time
18

Time available for activity 1-6

Total float=13

Duration = 5

13

Latest starting time

Duration = 5

Free float = 6

Interfering float = 7

5

Earliest finishing time

Figure 6.2 Float calculation.

event time of the finish node. The LST can then be established simply by deducting the activity duration from the LFT. For example, the LFT of activity 1–6 is 18 and the LST is therefore $18-5=13$. Activity schedules consisting of these activity times and total floats are usually presented in a tabular form as in Table 6.1 or diagrammatically represented as in Figure 6.1. Of course there is no one best way to present these schedules and several presentation formats are used by different authors and by various project planning software packages.

RESOURCE ALLOCATION

Time limited If the resources for the activities can be made available to suit the earliest or latest activity times the usage diagrams or histograms for all resources are

Table 6.1 Time analysis results in tabular form.

Activity	Duration	EST	EFT	LST	LFT	Total float	Resources
1–2	7	0	7	0	7	0	2
2–3	3	7	10	7	10	0	3
2–4	4	7	11	8	12	1	1
3–5	4	10	14	10	14	0	3
2–5	5	7	12	9	14	2	2
4–5	2	11	13	12	14	1	1
1–6	5	0	5	13	18	13	2
6–7	2	11	13	18	20	7	2
5–7	6	14	20	14	20	0	3

as in Figures 6.3 and 6.4, respectively. Clearly, any manipulation of activity times between these two extremes uses up float time, but enables some smoothing of resource levels to be achieved. The process is called *time-limited resource analysis*, where it can be seen that some adjustment of the schedule can be considered without affecting the total project duration.

Resource limited In practice, resources cannot be provided instantly, nor is the 'hiring' or 'firing' of labour desirable, the preferred solution being a steady build-up of requirements to be held reasonably constant and reduced towards the end of the project. For example, if a limit of five workers were imposed then the end date of the project would have to be extended, which could be achieved by delaying activities 2–4 and 4–5 by four days and pushing the project completion time to 24 days as shown in Figure 6.5.

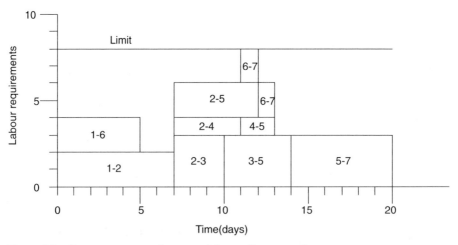

Figure 6.3 Resource aggregation at activity earliest start time.

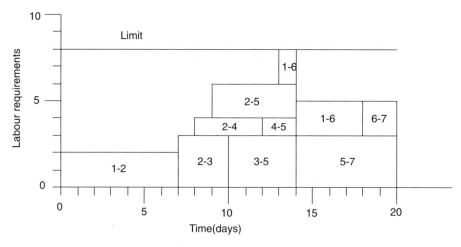

Figure 6.4 Resource aggregation at activity latest start time.

In a more complex situation with 500 activities and maybe 20 categories of resource the scheduling becomes complicated and computer assistance is almost essential. Frequently, different activities may start simultaneously, for example 2–5, 2–4, 2–3, only prevented by resource levelling limitations, where in the previous instance activities 2–4 and 4–5 were arbitrarily selected for delay. Hence, some sort of rule is needed, especially when computer software is used for the analysis, priority for activities with the least float often being adopted. Of course, different priority options will produce different schedules and need to be considered carefully before application.

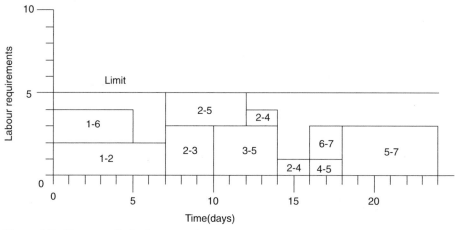

Figure 6.5 Resource limited aggregation.

BAR CHART (AND LINKED BAR-CHART)

While networking techniques are preferred in forcing the logical relationships between activities to be established, the final diagrammatic presentation is somewhat abstract and unappealing to the eye. Consequently practitioners have continued to use bar (Gantt) charts for day to day use as the final schedule.

The process simply requires the earliest or latest start of each activity as determined by network analysis together with the duration to be drawn as a bar diagram. The list of activities is usually assembled down the left-hand margin and their durations (hours, days, weeks and so on) drawn horizontally as a bar, as shown in Figure 6.6 for the previous example using earliest start dates. Sometimes the logic or dependency links (dashed lines in the diagram) are included to aid understanding. Commonly the activity resources are also included in the diagram and the corresponding histogram obtained. It can be seen that the usage pattern is identical to Figure 6.3, as expected.

Level of detail   The bar diagram is commonly chosen for scope design plans, pre-tender plans, and contractors' tender plans, where only the major activities shown in weeks or months, together with phase, end and procurement dates, are needed. During actual construction more detailed analysis is necessary, illustrating the sequence of, for example shuttering, concrete pours and so on. Durations are thus likely to be needed in days or even hours from which daily or weekly work gang schedules can be prepared and the procurement dates checked for delivery and storage.

PROGRESS CONTROL

Re-analysis of the network times during the construction phase is a fundamental task in ascertaining the projected situation for each future activity after current progress has been superimposed for completed and partly completed activities. The procedure illustrated in the bar chart (Figure 6.6) indicates how the network update reschedules the tasks in the light of progress. For example, if the programme time now was the end of week 15, the state of progress on all activities would be ascertained from the completed construction work, which is shaded on each bar. Activity 5–7 is showing a one-week delay, having not yet started, while the plan requires a start at week 14. Thus in this case, since the activity is on the critical path, the project is most likely to overrun by one week at least, unless remedial action, such as activity crashing, is undertaken.

ESTIMATING AND COST CONTROL LINKED TO PLANNING

The network plan (or linked bar chart) should serve as the vehicle to monitor control of all aspects of the project from inception to completion and handover to the client. It is thus a key element in preparing the estimate and subsequent monitoring of costs, whether for the client, designer, contractor, subcontractor or materials supplier. In particular, the costs of time-dependent items such as labour and regular

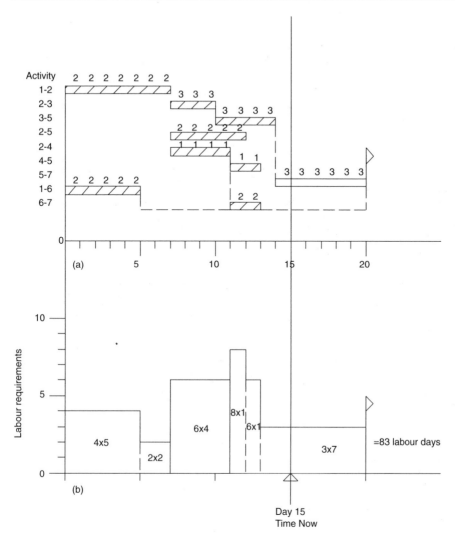

Figure 6.6 (a) Linked bar diagram and (b) resource histogram.

resources such as concrete, reinforcement and machines on-site are best estimated using the diagram. The process is relatively straightforward once the activity durations and resource requirements have been established and converted into unit costs (£/hr, £/m^3 and so on) in line with the limits used in the plan. Thus in the simple case illustrated in Figure 6.6, if the labour costs were £100 per labour day then the area under the resources histogram (labour days in this example) multiplied by the cost rate provides the estimated cost of labour resources, that is 83 labour days or £8300. Similar histograms can be prepared for the other resources, such as concrete, steel and so forth, and when aggregated, together with minor or specific items, produce the cost estimate for the project.

By carrying out a similar process but on the progress diagram, with actual resources used rather than planned resources, the cost of work to date can in principle be obtained, the difference or variance between estimate and costs being a guide to likely profit after other variances, such as overheads, change orders and claims for additional work, have been determined and included.

CUMULATIVE COST CURVE (S CURVE) PRESENTATION OF ESTIMATES AND COSTS

The unit costs derived from the labour histogram of Figure 6.6 can be represented cumulatively and plotted against time as shown in Figure 6.7 to produce an S shaped estimate. Also shown is a hypothetical cost curve derived from the progress bar diagram, where the delay in activity 5–7 for example, indicates a likely cost overrun.

A further superimposition of the phased payments by the client will enable a saw-tooth cash flow diagram to be produced, the maximum outlay being £2600 at any one time.

In reality the situation is likely to be slightly more complicated since the client normally retains approximately 5% of the contractor's figure until completion, and the contractor might also delay payments to subcontractors and front-end load early activities, thereby shifting the S curve to the right. Also, the cash-in would include the contractor's undisclosed profit, which must be deducted from this particular curve to gain a true comparison with the estimate, for cash flow purposes. Counter measures can be taken, such as increasing the resources and crashing the duration, to meet the time schedule in the case of a delay arising.

CRASHED ACTIVITIES

The network diagram assumes activity durations based on standard time estimates derived from basic time observations, and theoretically cannot be reduced. However, application of extra resources to an activity, and/or overtime working could assist in producing a quicker time, but of course at extra cost; indeed, congestion is a likely outcome, causing a nonlinear shortening to the crash time and cost as shown in Figure 6.8.

DETERMINING THE ACTIVITIES TO CRASH

For the example shown in Figure 6.1 the standard cost and estimated crash cost/ duration of each activity are shown in Table 6.2. The cost per day of crashing is shown as a linear amount for simplicity, whereas in practice the true rate is likely to be curvilinear. It can also be seen that the standard duration and crashed time for activities 1–6 and 6–7 are the same and hence there is no opportunity to crash those activities.

Examination of the crash cost daily rates indicates that some activities are cheaper per day than others, and these would normally be selected first. Also, closer inspection suggests that crashing all of the activities at the same time would be an

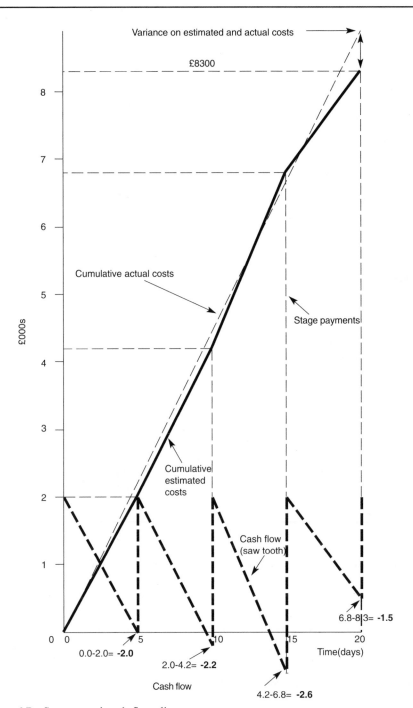

Figure 6.7 S curve and cash flow diagram.

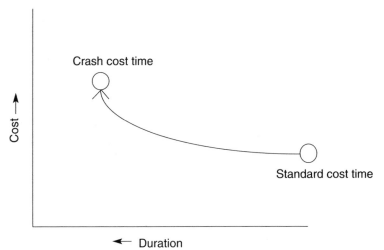

Figure 6.8 Crashed activity.

Table 6.2 Activity cost details.

Activity	Standard duration	Standard cost (£)	Crashed time	Crashed cost (£)	Crash cost per day (£)
1–2	7	1400	5	1700	150
2–3	3	900	1	1400	250
3–5	4	1200	3	1400	200
2–5	5	1000	4	1175	175
2–4	4	400	3	700	300
4–5	2	200	1	600	400
5–7	6	1800	3	2700	300
1–6	5	1000	5	1000	–
6–7	2	400	2	400	–
		£8300			

inefficient use of resources since those not on the critical path would not reduce the overall time of the project. Hence careful analysis is necessary, starting firstly by crashing activities on the critical path, and progressing to those with float that will subsequently introduce additional critical paths. The activity with the least expensive crash rate is the first action point, followed by the next expensive as follows:

Step 1

Action	Project duration	Rate	Amount	Crash cost
Crash 1–2 by 2 days	18	150	300	£8600
Crash 3–5 by 1 day	17	200	200	£8800
Crash 5-7 by 3 days	14	300	900	£9700

It is observed that although activity 2–3 has a cheaper crash rate than 5–7, the effect of crashing embraces the need to crash 2–4, 4–5 and 2–5 in that order since they will also form identical critical path durations, and thus produce combined high crash cost rates.

Step 2

Action	Project duration	Rate	Amount	Crash cost
Crash 2–3 by 1 day		250		
and 2–4 by 1 day	13	300	550	£10 250

Step 3

Action	Project duration	Rate	Amount	Crash cost
Crash 2–3 by 1 day,		250		
4–5 by 1 day and		400		
2–5 by 1 day	12	175	825	£11 075

If the total project duration is not reduced by the same number of days crashed from a critical activity, then crashing would have introduced one or more additional critical paths. In these situations, as carried out in the above example, durations should be reduced from critical activities either common to all critical paths or from several critical activities of all the critical paths to effect reduction of total project duration.

EFFECT OF INDIRECT COSTS

The maximum direct cost of the project with a critical path time of 12 days is £11 075, compared to £8300 at normal duration, also however with the potential saving in site variable overheads. For example, if these were £400 per day the total costs at the different crash durations would be as in Table 6.3. The optimum occurs at a crash cost rate of £300 per day on activity 5–7 to produce an earliest finish time of 14 days at direct cost of £9700.

Table 6.3 Effect of indirect cost on the total project cost.

Project time (days)	Direct costs (£)	Indirect costs (£)	Total cost (£)
20	8300	8000	16 300
18	8600	7200	15 800
17	8800	6800	15 600
14	9700	5600	15 300
13	10 250	5200	15 450
12	11 075	4800	15 875

6.2.2 Precedence diagram for critical path analysis

The need for dummies and event nodes in arrow networks can be distracting and is avoidable by the adoption of a precedence notation, where only activities and their logical relationships are needed. Figure 6.1 can be redrawn in this style as Figure 6.9, the forward and backward passes being determined in the same manner as for arrow networks, but with the time values representing the activities rather than the event nodes. Float is also calculated in a similar way. For example, total float for activity E is the LFT minus the EST less the duration, that is $14-7-5=2$.

ACTIVITY RELATIONSHIPS

The precedence style enables a greater choice of relationships between activities, for example:

(1) Finish–Start (for example, activity A, B in Figure 6.9)
(2) Finish–Finish (for example, activity J, D)
(3) Start–Start (for example, activity A, H)
(4) Part complete–Start
(5) Part complete–Finish
(6) Finish–Part complete

Relationships (4), (5) and (6), which are shown as ladder overlaps in Figure 6.10a, can be translated as shown precedently in Figure 6.10b. The difficulty of appreciating the complexity of the overlapped sequences has rendered both styles cumbersome and the straightforward connections (1), (2) and (3) are commonly preferred, albeit at the expense of subdividing activities to represent the stages as shown in Figure 6.11.

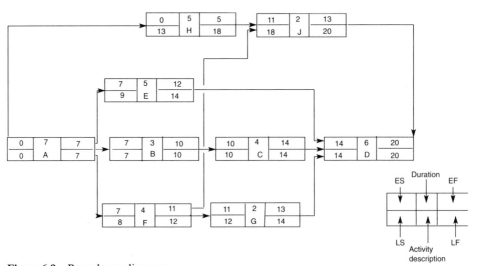

Figure 6.9 Precedence diagram.

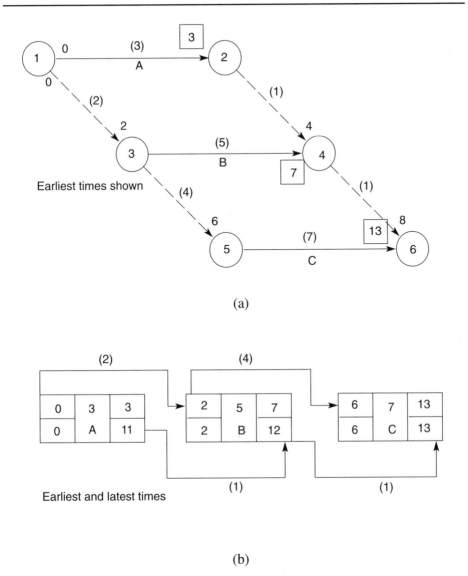

Figure 6.10 (a) Ladder and (b) precedence overlaps.

6.2.3 Line of balance

Some building situations involve much repetitive work, for example finishing trades, housing, jetty construction and road pavement layered surfaces. While networks and bar charts can be used to plan operations the logical relationships become very complex, as can be seen in Figure 6.12, and are better represented as a line of balance reflecting the rates of production to be applied to each trade, as shown in Figure 6.13.

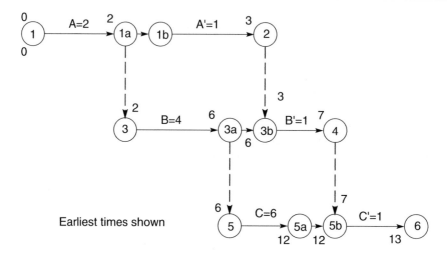

Earliest times shown

Figure 6.11 Subdivided activites.

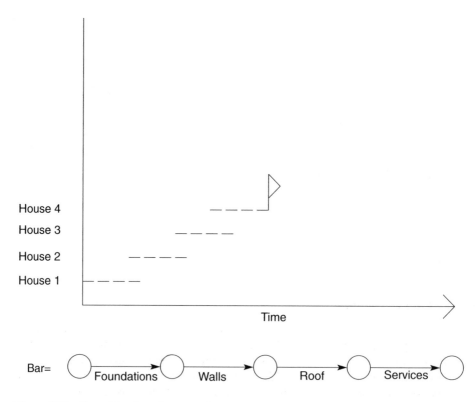

Figure 6.12 Repetitive bar plan.

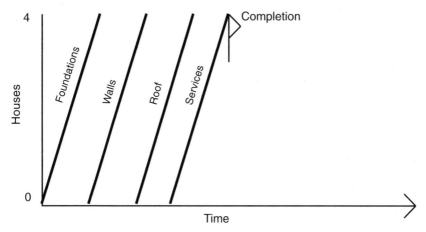

Figure 6.13 Line of blance plan.

This method allows the planner to experiment with different rates, that is gradients on the graph, to interpose buffer times between trades and even to have split gradients part way through an activity. The key element is assignment of the appropriate gang sizes to activities.

PREPARATION OF A LINE OF BALANCE: AN EXAMPLE

The construction plan for a building involves the sequence of activities shown in Table 6.4, with each activity to be completed before the logically succeeding activity can begin. The planner and estimator have assessed the standard time labour hours for each activity (column 2) from suitable data held as basic time values, together

Table 6.4 First attempt line of balance.

Activity or operation (C1)	Labour hours per house (C2)	Theoretical team size at four houses per week (C3)	Gang size per house (C4)	Actual team size (C5)	Actual rate of production (C6)	Time in days for one house (C7)	Time in days from start of first house to start of last house (C8)	Minimum buffer (C9)
Substructure	104	10.4	3	9	3.46	4.33	56.35	5
Superstructure	272	27.2	6	24	3.53	5.67	55.24	5
Glazing	50	5.0	2	4	3.20	3.13	60.93	5
Joinery	276	27.6	4	28	4.06	8.63	48.03	5
Services	134	13.4	4	12	3.58	4.19	54.47	5
Plaster	124	12.4	3	12	3.87	5.17	50.39	5
Painting	93	9.3	3	9	3.87	3.88	50.39	–

with the allocation of gangs in each building (column 4). The total number of houses to be built is 40 and the nature of the contract demands a target completion of 4 dwellings per week, allowing for five days of eight hours in each week. The planner also prudently inserts a five-day buffer between succeeding activities in each dwelling to facilitate coordination of trades and eliminate interference (column 9).

Proposed plan

(1) The logic diagram is first established (Figure 6.14).
(2) The estimated labour hours for each activity are inserted in the table together with the associated gang sizes and buffer times; that is, columns 2, 4 and 9 in Table 6.4.
(3) The theoretical team size for each activity; that is, the combined total of workers on the activity (column 3), is determined.

$$\text{Theoretical team size} = \frac{\text{Target rate of build} \times \text{Labour hours per dwelling}}{\text{Number of working hours per week}}$$

(4) The theoretical team size is adjusted up or down to produce an exact multiple of the gang size for the activity (column 5).
(5) Calculate the actual rate of production (column 6).

$$\text{Actual rate} = \frac{\text{Actual team size} \times \text{Target rate of build}}{\text{Theoretical team size}}$$

(6) The time in days for one dwelling (column 7) is determined.

$$\text{Time for one dwelling} = \frac{\text{Labour hours for one dwelling}}{\text{Number of workers in gang} \times 8 \text{ hours/day}}$$

(7) Calculate the time lag, that is the time in days from the start on the first dwelling to the start on the final dwelling (column 8)

$$\text{Time lag} = \frac{(\text{Number of dwellings} - 1) \times 5 \text{ days in the week}}{\text{Actual rate of build}}$$

Table 6.5 shows alternative possibilities in rounding up/down for the actual team sizes, the tables being plotted as graphs in Figures 6.15 and 6.16 respectively, to produce slightly different completion times caused by the changed rates of production in the teams.

Figure 6.14 Line of balance diagram activities logic.

Table 6.5 Second attempt line of balance.

Activity or operation (C1)	Labour hours per house (C2)	Theoretical team size at four houses per week (C3)	Gang size per house (C4)	Actual team size (C5)	Actual rate of prod. (C6)	Time in days for one house (C7)	Time in days from start of first house to start of last house (C8)	Minimum buffer (C9)
Substructure	104	10.4	3	12	4.62	4.33	42.25	5
Superstructure	272	27.2	6	30	4.41	5.67	44.19	5
Glazing	50	5.0	2	6	4.80	3.13	40.63	5
Joinery	276	27.6	4	28	4.06	8.63	48.03	5
Services	134	13.4	4	16	4.78	4.19	40.79	5
Plaster	124	12.4	3	12	3.87	5.17	50.39	5
Painting	93	9.3	3	9	3.87	3.88	50.39	–

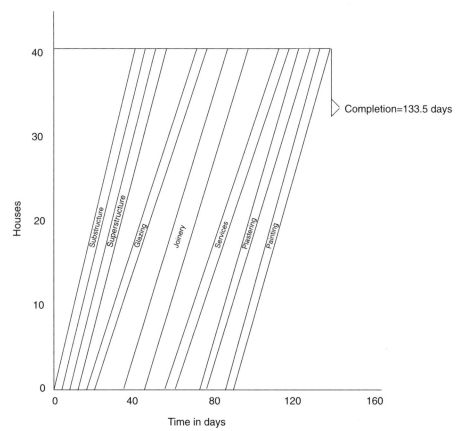

Figure 6.15 LOB example.

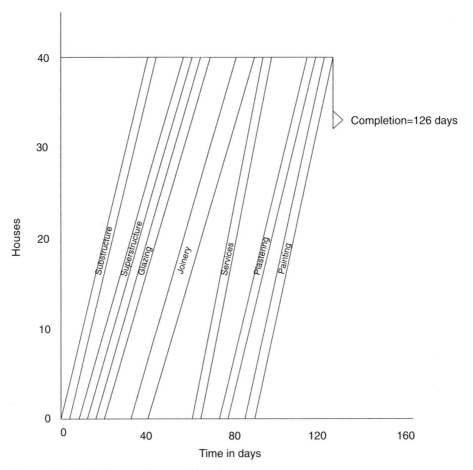

Figure 6.16 LOB improved completion time.

EFFECT OF LEARNING

The constant team rates are unlikely to be achieved in practice and an expectation of slower production during approximately the first quarter of the activity should be allowed, and possibly also towards the end of the activity as workers perceive potential loss of employment. Hard data are yet to be established for accurately estimating the reduction but curves of the shape shown in Figure 6.17 are typical.

PROGRESS MONITORING

The line of balance is ideal for pictorially representing actual progress to date by shading the proportion of each activity completed at time now. For example, Figure 6.18 shows substructure and superstructure complete at week 60 (time now for update purposes), with joinery and services on schedule, but glazing behind plan and

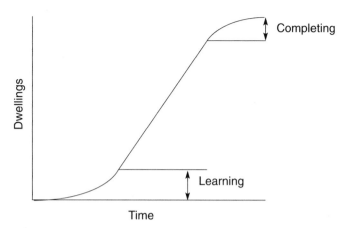

Figure 6.17 Learning and completing effects.

needing action to speed up. The calculations are similarly determined as for the original schedule but based on the time now situation for each team and activity.

Also when monitoring progress, caution should be exercised to include all of the detailed aspects of an activity when ascertaining the proportion of work completed, otherwise severe distortion will arise at the end of the project when these items eventually come to light.

SPACE–TIME DIAGRAMS

Some projects such as highways, multi-span bridges, pipelines and similar work involving distance are often best planned using a combination of bar chart and LOB principles, with distance from the start point drawn along the bottom of the diagram and time depicted vertically. Hence an unbroken horizontal line represents an activity taking place continuously at a fixed date, for example holidays. When the line has a gradient then work progresses steadily at a uniform rate along the chainage path, typically drainage, road surfacing and so on. When the line is formed as a rectangle or parallelogram the operation is taking place over a given period at each chainage point, thereby directly resembling the LOB derivation such as finishes, cut and fill and so on. Finally a vertical line, as in the bar chart, denotes a fixed position activity carried out over a given duration. A combination of all five types of representation is illustrated in Figure 6.19.

6.2.4 Estimating phase in relation to planning

Planning and estimating go hand in hand, especially pre-tender planning, and the two activities are often carried out in one department. The two widely used estimating approaches, unit rate estimating and operational estimating, require planning and estimating data to be stored in slightly different manners.

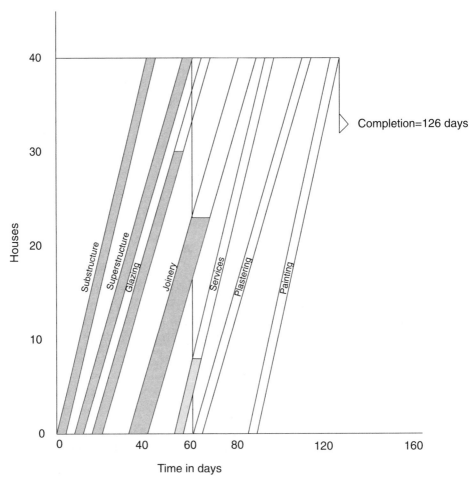

Figure 6.18 LOB showing progress update.

UNIT RATE METHOD

The essential feature for both designers and constructors involves establishing a reliable database of historical work study records comprising standard output rates for resources, for example labour hours per cubic metre of concrete placed by a 0.5 m³ skip or the equivalent regression formula as shown earlier. A comprehensive catalogue would embrace all of the resources associated with such an activity, including the associated equipment and materials – for example, aggregate amounts per cubic metre – all of which could be automatically assembled by appropriate software. An accompanying cost database would also need to be held, made up of the company prices and cost of additional items to be bought in for the activity; for example, materials and subcontractor costs.

Where the estimate is simply developed from a bill of quantities and working on a unit rate principle of estimating, spreadsheet type software linked to the database

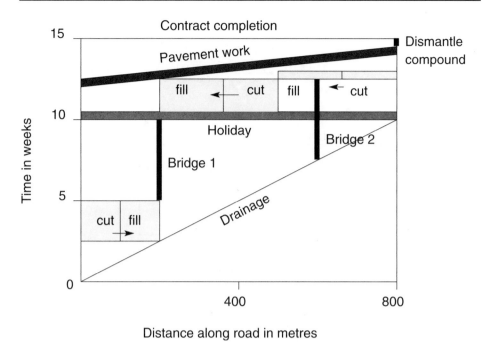

Figure 6.19   Space–time chart for road construction.

provides a relatively uncomplicated system since little more than adding the costs of the resources associated with each bill item ultimately produces the total direct cost estimate of the project to which overheads and mark-up can then be added and spread back over the items. Building type work embracing repetitive tasks – for example brickwork, plastering, tiling and so forth – are ideally suited to this form of estimating.

OPERATIONAL METHOD

The unit rate method assumes each resource item to be in continuous usage without enforced gaps in progress. Unfortunately in complex building and civil engineering in particular, resources tend to follow irregular work patterns. For example, concreting activities may be spread over a large site, requiring the gang to move frequently, thus incurring delays. In this situation the favoured method of estimating labour and equipment resources costs is to link the costs over all the associated activities, termed a 'Hammock' activity (Figure 6.20). Special computer software is then required to perform the estimating function, since the hammocks often do not correlate easily with a bill of quantities presentation of items. Indeed, since the hammocks are time related they generally require data from the planning stage; for example, earliest or latest times for the start and finish nodes of the hammock to be input into bespoke estimating packages where cost rate build-up and ultimate final project cost estimates of all the hammocks are prepared. The final re-apportioning

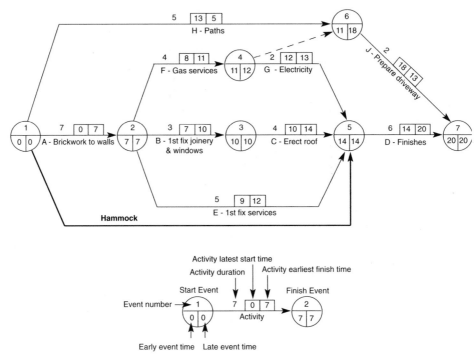

Figure 6.20 Hammock activity.

of estimated costs is commonly done by manual transfer back to the associated bill of quantities, with minor adjustments incorporated as necessary.

6.2.5 Computerised applications

Developments in computer software continue to strive for the integrated package whereby CAD design and construction plans, cost estimates, bill of quantity preparation, cost monitoring, procurement scheduling, change orders and variations, and not least invoicing and payments link together in a seamless web. Indeed, sophisticated software of this standard is already a feature of manufacturing industries, but not yet in construction, where often incompatible computer packages still have to be partially manually driven.

In principle many of these processes could be executed through a sophisticated network planning computer package. In reality, however, firms prefer to develop in-house software and associated databases to reflect the nuances of the company and coding systems for control. Hence a computerised system still tends to be made up of independent packages involving integration, for example, with the estimating process receiving information from the planning function such as work study data and details on start times of activities, resource schedules and requirement periods and so on. If every item including materials, equipment and subcontractors' quantities and costs were included fully the cost estimate would also be produced. In practice this level of detail generally proves difficult to organise at the contract stage, since stage payments normally require accurate measurements to be taken of work completed on-site costed at tender rates adjusted for agreed variation/change orders and sometimes further complicated by the bill of quantity interface package.

Importantly, a computerised construction system can serve many other useful functions besides providing estimates and calculations of activity times and resources/procurement schedules; for example, monitoring of 'time now' progress and updating of the schedule combined with S curve evaluation of work done and comparison with actual costs. The latter would have to be supplied through a computerised finance system giving details of wage payments, salaries, materials/subcontractor invoices and so on. Not least, accurate site measurement of work completed, including materials held on-site, in transit and actually built into the project, would be essential if true comparisons with the progress schedule were to be reliable. Unfortunately, because of the coarse-grained nature of most construction plans and cost coding systems, only very broad monitoring trends are achievable.

OTHER COMPUTER APPLICATIONS

Potentially, the ability to simulate different construction methods and evaluate impacts on plans, resources and costs (as will be described in Chapter 8) presents similar opportunities for construction as already enjoyed in manufacturing. Other novel possibilities might embrace bar-coding systems for stock control and materials ordering, including holding drawings registers and record keeping in general. Video conferencing and close-circuit televised managerial communication, both on sites and between sites and the outside world, could also develop in the relatively near future, as has already been demonstrated in other industries. Indeed, the rapid developments of the Internet are increasingly facilitating email communications, particularly the World Wide Web, where voice, pictures, data, tables, diagrams, different operating systems and file storage formats can be transferred. So, for example, site-based staff could log into a local Internet service provider via a modem and access information located at head office and elsewhere on the Web site.

6.3 QUALITY MANAGEMENT AND PLANNING

Traditionally, quality assurance and its counterparts, quality control and assessment, have been difficult to achieve in terms of client satisfaction, with the image of the industry perceived to be unreliable in this respect. Thus, the introduction of strategies adopted in other industries is likely to be required, with quality procedures such as ISO 9000 forming a foundation approach. Here, all phases of planning, production monitoring and ultimately control need to embrace solid quality procedures and processes together with mechanisms for performance measurement.

As far as individual projects are concerned, the major scope lies in obtaining quality performance from suppliers and subcontractors, for example through the supplier chain network concept originally developed for component contractors to the automobile manufacturers.

The principle requires suppliers to comply with procedures as set out, for example, in the ISO 9000 standard, but more importantly to follow best practices identified in successful arrangements. Obviously the lead would have to be taken by the larger clients, design practices and contractors in order to enforce set standards on suppliers and, indeed, avoid under-achievers in the procurement system. Unfortunately, the plethora and variety of clients and contractors is likely to hinder implementation of firm quality management processes, but this should nevertheless be seen as a step towards bringing about a total quality management (TQM) culture to both the tendering and supply elements in procurement. This aspect is discussed in detail in Chapter 9.

6.4 SAFETY MANAGEMENT

The introduction of the Construction Design and Management (CONDAM) regulations by the Health and Safety Executive requires clients engaged on all but very small-scale construction to take into account the importance of design for safety. Here, the influence of the independent safety planning supervisor appointed by the client and responsible for the preparation of a safety plan covering the project from inception to completion will impact on both the designer's and the contractor's planning processes, especially with respect to consideration of design in relation to construction methods. Furthermore, the contractor will also need to demonstrate compliance with the safety plan in terms of established procedures, action records and so forth, which therefore should form an integral part of the planning, progress monitoring and control tasks outlined earlier.

6.5 SUMMARY

This chapter drew on the previous discussion relating to techniques used in methods improvement, work measurement and activity sampling to explain the principles and approaches to construction planning from enquiry to completion of a project, including worked examples of CPM, precedence diagram and line of balance methods. Integration of planning with estimating, budgetary control and costing was also highlighted, together with a summary of the application of computer systems. Finally, incorporation of quality and safety during planning was briefly discussed, all acting as a focus to other chapters.

REFERENCES AND BIBLIOGRAPHY

Antill J.M. and Woodhead R.W. (1990). *Critical Path Methods in Construction Practice* 4th edn. Chichester: John Wiley & Sons
Calvert R.E., Coles D. and Bailey G. (1995). *Introduction to Building Management* 6th edn. London: Butterworth-Heinemann

ECI (1994). *Total Productivity Management – Guidelines for the Construction Phase*, Productivity Task Force, European Construction Institute

Fellows R., Langford D., Newcombe R. and Urry S. (1983). *Construction Management in Practice*. London: Longman

Harris F.C. (1994). *Modern Construction and Ground Engineering Equipment and Methods*. London: Longman

Harris F.C. and McCaffer R. (1995). *Modern Construction Management* 4th edn. Oxford: Blackwell Science

Harris R.B.(1978). *Precedence and Arrow Networking Techniques for Construction*. Chichester: John Wiley & Sons

Lockyer K.G. (1991). *Critical Path Analysis and Other Project Network Techniques*. London: Pitman

Lockyer K.G. and Gordon J.H. (1996). *Project Management and Project Network Techniques* 6th edn. London: Pitman

Mawdesley M., Askew W. and O'Reilly M. (1997). *Planning and Controlling Construction Projects*. London: Longman

McCaffer R. and Baldwin A.N. (1991). *Estimating and Tendering for Civil Engineering Works* 2nd edn. Oxford: Blackwell Science

Neal J.M. (1982). *Construction Cost Estimating and Project Control*. Englewood Cliffs, NJ: Prentice Hall

O'Brien J.J. (1993). *CPM in Construction Management* 4th edn. New York: McGraw-Hill.

Paulson B. (1994). *Computer Applications in Construction*. New York: McGraw-Hill

Peurifoy L., Ledbetter W.B. and Schnexnayder C. (1996). *Construction Planning Equipment and Methods* 5th edn. New York: McGraw-Hill

Pilcher R. (1992). *Principles of Construction Management* 3rd edn. New York: McGraw-Hill

Price A.D.F. and Harris F.C. (1985). Methods of measuring production times for construction work, *Technical Information Service Paper 49*, Chartered Institute of Building

Schuette S. and Liska R. (1994). *Construction Estimating*. New York: McGraw-Hill

Sher W. (1996). *Computer-aided Estimating: A Guide to Good Practice*. London: Longman

Thompson P.A. (1981). *Organisation of Economics of Construction*. New York: McGraw-Hill

Wearne S.H. (1989). *Control of Engineering Projects*. London: Thomas Telford

CONSTRUCTION WORKFORCE MOTIVATION

7.1 INTRODUCTION

In Chapter 2 insights into construction workers' personality and perception of production problems in the working environment were presented. A knowledge of workers' problems must be complemented with an understanding of motivation in the drive to optimise construction productivity. Motivation, aptly described as an inner generator of actions and reactions, is of interest to managers as a means to an end – the optimisation of the human resource in the production process. This chapter describes the application of conceptual theories and empirical studies for construction workforce motivation, together with an analysis of the results of a survey on the relative importance of motivation and demotivation variables. Financial incentives are also discussed with special reference to their application.

7.2 UNDERSTANDING CONSTRUCTION WORKFORCE MOTIVATION

Different authors construe construction operative motivation differently, often to their own particular bias. Some interpret it as meaning 'incentive', some 'motivation' and others as a reflection of the degree of 'satisfaction' based on the general notion that a satisfied worker will produce more. All basically refer to the same aspect – turning on the production 'generator' inside the individual. Two broad groups of studies in construction operative motivation predominate, namely *conceptual*, which examines existing theories with respect to the construction operative without scientific testing, and *empirical*, which has to do with findings from experiments and observations.

7.2.1 Conceptual studies

Unfortunately, none of the existing general management theories on motivation is construction industry based. Nevertheless, Maloney and McFillen (1983) advocated that instead of concentrating on differences between construction and other industries, similarities should be sought that permit the adoption and transfer of existing knowledge. No single specialised theory of construction operative motivation has evolved but only applications of well-established general theories.

APPLICATION OF MASLOW'S THEORY TO CONSTRUCTION WORKERS

Maslow's hierarchy of needs theory is based on a hierarchy of five principal classes of needs, namely, (i) physiological, (ii) security, (iii) love and belonging, (iv) esteem and (v) self-actualisation (Figure 7.1).

Although logical, this hierarchy has not been subjected to any serious empirical verification; it is not surprising, therefore, that most applications of the theory as a conceptual base for motivating construction operatives are rather subjective and at best descriptive.

However, Schrader (1972), Haseltine (1976) and Neal (1979) adopted the Maslow model as a base for construction operative motivation, with Schrader in particular believing that American construction workers can meet physiological needs when employed by earning sufficient income. Haseltine also claims that most 'working people' have satisfied these basic needs and believes that the next level – safety needs, including job security, and

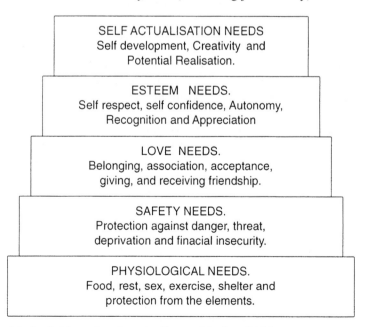

Figure 7.1   Maslow's hierarchy of needs. *Source:* Maslow (1971).

protection against danger, threat and deprivation – is also satisfied for many US workers. Schrader is of the opinion that safety needs, especially the job security aspect, do not motivate as strongly as in other industries, primarily because construction workers have become used to changing jobs from time to time.

Social interaction, claims Schrader, is a major motivator for construction operatives, emphasising that many construction workers fulfil their desire to become a member of a group by making serious efforts to work with their 'buddies' and form cliques. This view is also supported by Zelst's experiment on the effects of operative behaviour on construction productivity, where individuals were allowed to choose whom to work with, resulting in reduced turnover and improved productivity.

Schrader also believes that construction workers satisfy ego needs through competition, praise or upliftment of status, processes that are often frustrated in the USA for example, by construction union restrictive practices. The Hawthorne experiment (Homans 1963), however, indicated that ego, though often difficult to measure, *can* motivate.

Self-actualisation needs, the last in Maslow's hierarchy, were suggested by Schrader as rarely fulfilled in construction terms. For instance, workers who might have been promoted stick to their craft rather than accepting onerous responsibilities as foremen or supervisors.

Unfortunately, while these studies by and large failed to show proof of the hierarchy of needs conceptualised by Maslow, they are nevertheless commended as good 'eye openers' to construction operative motivation.

APPLICATION OF THEORIES X AND Y TO CONSTRUCTION WORKERS

MacGregor's *Theory X* is a series of propositions felt to be the conventional conception of management's task in harnessing human energy to meet organisational requirements. The propositions include:

- Management responsibility for organising the elements of productive enterprise – money, materials, equipment, people – in the interest of economic ends.
- With respect to people, the process of directing and motivating efforts, controlling their actions and modifying behaviour to fit the needs of the organisation.
- Without active intervention by management, people would be passive – even resistant to organisational needs.
- People are indolent and would work as little as possible.
- People lack ambition, dislike responsibility and prefer to be led.
- People are inherently self-centred and indifferent to organisational needs.
- All people are by nature resistant to change.
- People are gullible and not very bright – the ready dupes of the charlatan and the demagogue.

MacGregor believed that conventional organisational structures, practices and managerial policies reflect and reinforce these assumptions, a view further reinforced by Bennis, who claimed that Theory X is not only alive in industrial organisations but also in basic assumptions behind advertisements, political rallies and the management of welfare and health institutions in the USA.

Theory Y contains another set of propositions:

- Work is natural for most people; they do not avoid it.
- If individuals are committed to the organisation's objectives, they will get satisfaction from helping to achieve these goals and thus be self-motivated.
- The strength of commitment is related to the reward it brings.
- In a non-threatening atmosphere, most people will accept and even seek responsibility.
- Creative problem solving is a potential of many individuals, not just a few.

MacGregor's Theory Y implies that human growth is self-generated and furthered in an environment of trust, feedback and authentic human relationships. Theory Y excludes 'pseudo growth' forced on an individual by the supervisor through manipulation, no matter how well intentioned, or by the use of fear. A good leader should therefore understand the conditions conducive to creating a climate of growth and then do their best to promote such a climate.

Haseltine (1976) in supporting MacGregor (1960) emphasised that the traditional management techniques of providing good pay, good working conditions, excellent fringe benefits and continuous employment are not necessarily effective motivators in construction because they satisfy only the first two needs, which by themselves do not motivate.

In contrast, the concept of satisfaction before production is evident was denounced by Brayfield and Crocket (1955) as being simplistic, the relationship being complex and variable between individuals. Also, the motivational techniques enumerated by Schrader (1972) emphasised the higher needs as a basic extension of Theory Y. Furthermore, Haseltine recommended a progressive Theory Y approach to the construction setting.

APPLICATION OF HERZBERG'S THEORY TO CONSTRUCTION WORKERS

Herzberg (1968) identified the following eight different schemes and approaches by management to motivating employees in his motivation-hygiene theory:

(1) Reducing time spent at work
(2) Spiralling wages
(3) Fringe benefits
(4) Human relations training
(5) Sensitivity training
(6) Communication
(7) Job participation
(8) Employee counselling.

These were described as KITA (kick in the ass) approaches to motivation, with a strong resemblance to traditional means of getting an animal (pet) to obey commands and having short-term 'movement' effects, not 'motivation'. True motivation pulls not pushes; pushing only effects temporary 'movements' in behaviour and could be costly to maintain because the effect wears off quickly, calling for replacement.

Likening motivation to installing a generator in employees, Herzberg postulated that 'the factors involved in producing job satisfaction (and motivation) are separate and distinct from factors that lead to job dissatisfaction' and importantly are not opposites. In other words, the opposite of job dissatisfaction is not job satisfaction, and vice versa.

Herzberg identified two basic needs: (i) the basic *biological* requirement to avoid pain from the environment such as hunger, followed by (ii) *growth* relating to the unique human characteristic to progress through achievement; for example, a stimulating job content to counter the lack of good job environment.

The growth factors or motivators were:

- Achievement
- Recognition of achievement
- The work itself
- Responsibility
- Growth and advancement.

The dissatisfaction-avoidance or hygiene (KITA) factors were:

- Company policy and administration
- Supervision
- Interpersonal relationships
- Working conditions
- Salary
- Status
- Security.

Results of a survey carried out on 1675 employees concluded that 71% of the factors contributing to job satisfaction were motivators and 69% contributing to employee dissatisfaction were hygiene related.

Haseltine (1976) supports the view of Herzberg's theory as a basic extension of MacGregor's theories, implying that the traditional KITA-orientated motivational techniques are poor motivators. He also suggested that the influence of construction unions can offset most KITA motivational techniques, leaving contractors (employers) little room for manoeuvre compared to Herzberg's job enrichment technique.

The situation, however, was rather different for open shop construction workers found in the UK, the tendency here being to identify with management goals and be motivated (not only moved, as suggested by Herzberg) by KITA forces. As

Herzberg himself observed later, the enthusiasm for a job enrichment programme eventually waned (Herzberg 1977). The theory's suitability for the construction industry is therefore questionable.

EXPECTANCY THEORY AND THE CONSTRUCTION WORKER

Expectancy theory relates workers' motivation to their expectation of desired outcomes in satisfying their individual goals, including money, recognition, promotion and security.

In experiments Maloney and McFillen (1985b) applied the theory to construction operatives, suggesting different approaches instead of a wholesale introduction. With supportive evidence from the social sciences, they concluded that the concept appeared relevant when based on 'rigorous empirical research' into worker performance and motivation.

Wesley-Lees (1976) was more enthusiastic in applying the concept wholesale to construction operatives but was unable to prove or disprove suitability and concluded that the principal potential motivators to high performance concern financial incentives and job security, but they only raise productivity if operative motivation is the principal determinant of output. Unfortunately, this conclusion highlights a basic flaw in its application because, expectancy theory being holistic, it is not possible to single out financial incentives.

7.2.2 Empirical studies in construction operative motivation

There being no truly validated model for worker motivation and performance, various researchers recognised that empirical studies could provide a reasonable starting point for the development of a relevant set of theories for the construction industry. Most of the empirical studies are, however, based on existing motivation theories.

Wilson's (1979) experiment in evaluating the degree of importance that workers attach to certain motives is an example of a straightforward empirical approach to acquiring a knowledge of motivators in the construction industry. Wilson concluded that 'safety' and 'belonging' needs are the greatest motivators. These findings were subsequently tabulated against Maslow's hierarchy by Mackenzie and Harris (1974), who concluded that Maslow's theory explains motivation for a construction operative only in the early stages of the hierarchy, with the pattern becoming quite confusing later.

A similar approach applied to some Nigerian site workers revealed that the greatest motivation influences relate to physiological and safety needs, indicating that the level of economic development in a particular country may also be a strong determinant (see Table 7.1), although the hierarchy is not as dominant as suggested by Maslow (Olomolaiye and Ogunlana 1988). Indeed, Wilson (1979) and Olomolaiye and Ogunlana (1988) recommended approaching construction workers directly, without bias in favour of any theory. Both papers demonstrated that Maslow's theory can, to some extent, explain motivation in construction.

SATISFACTION AND DISSATISFACTION OF CONSTRUCTION OPERATIVES

Satisfiers do not necessarily motivate, and vice versa. In contrast, motivators actually satisfy and motivate, while demotivators largely dissatisfy and can cause deliberate withdrawal of production ability. In a comprehensive survey of 650 operatives Borcherding and Oglesby (1975) reported that productive jobs created high job satisfaction, especially when accompanied by good organisation, with the degree of satisfaction depending on the worker (Table 7.2). The recommendations for increased job satisfaction shown in Table 7.3 indicate that dissatisfaction arises when production is thwarted by poor management caused by errors in planning, scheduling or materials procurement.

Maloney and McFillen (1985a) evaluated operative satisfaction using a random population of unionised construction workers through a structured questionnaire where workers were asked about the importance attached to various job-related factors and the associated satisfaction (Table 7.4). The most important set related to the intrinsic nature of the work such as working with a craft or performing challenging tasks, with workers most satisfied when achieving high productivity and quality. Their findings are in almost perfect agreement with those of Borcherding and Oglesby, so giving a strong indication that intrinsic factors can make a significant contribution to worker satisfaction.

Table 7.1 International comparison of motivation ranking in the UK and Nigeria.

Theoretical ranking (after Maslow)	UK Operative ranking (Wilson 1979)	Nigerian operative ranking (Olomolaiye and Ogunlana 1988)
Physiological needs		
Earnings-related (fringe benefits)	3rd	1st
Safety needs		
Physical, safety, working conditions	1st	6th
Welfare conditions	2nd	–
Job security	10th	4th
Belonging needs		
Good relationship with colleagues	4th	2nd
Good orientation programme	4th	7th
Good supervision	7th	9th
Needs for esteem		
Recognition on the job	7th	5th
Need for self-actualisation		
Challenging job	9th	3rd
Participation in decision making	6th	7th

Table 7.2 Rank order of job satisfiers.

	Rank				
Satisfiers	Owners	Project manager	Superintendent	Foremen	Operatives
Job making a profit	1st	1st			
Satisfied customer	2nd	3rd			
Job completed on schedule	3rd				
Tangible physical structure	4th	6th		4th	3rd
Good workmanship	5th	2nd	2nd	3rd	1st
Owner satisfied		3rd			
Good working relationship		5th	5th	5th	
Maintain the job			1st		
Meeting challenge			2nd		
Job costs below estimate			4th		
Challenge of running the work				1st	
Maintain the job schedule				2nd	
Productive day					2nd
Social work relation					4th

Source: Borcherding and Oglesby (1975).

Table 7.3 Recommendations for increased job satisfaction.

Participants	Recommendations
Owners and project managers	Timely feedback Plan rather than restructure job content Beware of change orders Ensure good workmanship Identify with the goal of a built structure
Superintendents and foremen	Beware of the effect of challenging work in decision making Effective field planning and management support Share cost information Identify with the goal of a built structure Develop good crew relations
Operatives	Task accomplishment Identify with the goal of a built structure Maintaining good crew relations

Source: Borcherding and Oglesby (1975).

Table 7.4 Factor scale ranking of job outcomes (sample of 703 workers on different sites).

Job outcomes	Importance	Satisfaction
Intrinsic rewards	1st	4th
Opportunity	7th	7th
Interpersonal rewards	6th	3rd
Feedback	3rd	5th
Supervision	5th	6th
Performance level	2nd	1st
Extrinsic rewards	3rd	2nd

Source: Maloney and McFillen (1985b).

PARTICIPATIVE DECISION MAKING

The organisational behaviourist Vroom (1964) observed that participation helps individuals to feel that the group's decision is their own and makes them try hard to make it a success. Furthermore, the supervisor's feelings of achievement are often fulfilled when few restrictions are placed on the freedom to make decisions, while workers are more effective when charged by individual responsibility for the methods employed. Being able to accomplish tasks also results in the feeling of achievement; in construction the actual challenge of the working environment helps operative participation in the decision making process and should be allowed to flourish.

JOB CHARACTERISTICS

Application of the job characteristics model of Hackman and Oldham revealed some 'moderating variables' or 'core job characteristics' affecting worker reactions, motivation and satisfaction. Maloney and McFillen (1985b) reported:

(1) Statistically significant differences in skill variety, autonomy and feedback in construction trades.
(2) Construction workers do not see their jobs in enrichable terms.
(3) Motivating potential varies little with the degree of skill among construction operatives.
(4) Motivating potential is low in construction.
(5) There is therefore a need to restructure jobs to improve motivating potential.

7.3 MOTIVATION AND DEMOTIVATION VARIABLES

Awareness of the motivation and demotivation variables is important in effectively applying incentive schemes and is demonstrated below based on the results of an investigation into their relative importance and interrelationships.

Table 7.5 Comparative ranking of motivating variables.

Motivators	Relative index rank
Good relations with colleagues	1st
Good safety programme	7th
The work itself	4th
Overtime	15th
Fairness of pay	1st
Recognition on the job	13th
Accurate description of work	7th
Participation in decision making	10th
Good supervision	3rd
Promotion	14th
More responsibility	12th
Challenging task	11th
Job security	6th
Choosing workmates	9th
Bonus	5th

7.3.1 Motivation variables

Table 7.5 illustrates a ranking of motivating variables by UK construction workers where 'good relations with colleagues' held primary position regardless of the working environment. Earnings in particular depend on output, and output in turn (among other things) is influenced by relationships among colleagues. Thus a somewhat circular situation exists between the gang, output and earnings (Figure 7.2).

Indeed, inter-gang relationships can also affect productivity, especially if interference causes significant production problems. Harmonious and positive relationships among all workers tend to reduce gang interference, leading to improved productivity, through exchange of ideas, tools and advice. Furthermore, gang members are more likely to cooperate when tasks are challenging.

'Fairness of pay' also ranked highly, challenging Herzberg's argument that money does not satisfy and is therefore not a motivator on the grounds of a possible misconception of the role of wages in human motivation. When there is parity between pay and effort, with wages fair and equitable, a parabolic relationship as shown in Figure 7.3 may be a more accurate representation of the relationship between wages and effort.

Clearly, increases in wages as represented by points A, B and C arouse workers' effort to a 'high point', leading to conscious or unconscious withdrawal of effort until the next wage increase. Despite Herzberg's belief that this cannot continue forever, satisfaction at each wage increase pushes effort up towards an optimal level with each subcurve having an optimal wage/effort point.

Overpayment beyond the optimum level may not motivate, but underpayment leads to a conscious withdrawal of effort, so requiring monetary reward commensurate with effort in relation to achievement, satisfaction and motivation.

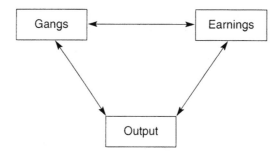

Figure 7.2 Relationship between gangs, output and earnings.

'Good supervision' encourages site safety and identifies production problems such as lack of materials, repeat work and gang interference. It is ranked highly, followed by 'the work itself' – that is being a skilled worker in a demanding and interesting trade. 'Job security' featured strongly, indicating workers' expectations of continued employment when more responsibility is entrusted and their tendency to stay longer on sites offering more self-recognition.

'Accurate work description' and 'good safety provision' were also important. Here, clear, unambiguous and easy to read drawings all pointed to a desire to avoid repeat work, particularly important in 'labour only' subcontracting.

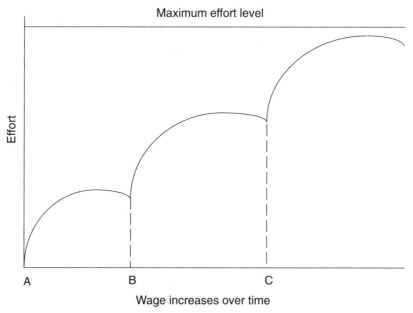

Figure 7.3 Relationship between wage increases and effort.

7.3.2 Demotivating variables

As can be seen in Table 7.6, 'disrespect' by site management ranked as the highest demotivator. It is characterised by the supervisory attitudes, for example, urging but not caring, and manifested in a lack of concern about the provision of resources, operatives' progress or levels of earnings. A supervisor who urges meeting deadlines with an uncaring or nonchalant attitude is a hypocrite.

The second ranked demotivator, 'colleagues not cooperating', especially when working with an incompetent mate, often leads to repeat work, resulting in a feeling of frustration, reduced earnings and subsequent break-up of the gang. The level of seriousness among gang members also differs with individuals; for example, a labourer may listen to the poor weather forecast for the next day and so decide to take a rest at home, while bricklayers may come to work, meet good weather but find no labourer to serve them!

'Cold weather' featured strongly, indicating much frustration for both site management and workforce during cold periods, together with 'unsafe working conditions'. 'Discontinuity of work' caused by lack of resources is yet another important demotivator.

The foregoing discussion provides some insight into worker attitudes in the working environment, and how they affect motivation to work, although the exact ranking of the relative effects of the variables discussed may vary slightly depending on circumstances.

Table 7.6 Comparative ranking of demotivating variables.

Demotivators	Relative index rank
Disrespect	1st
Little accomplishment	10th
Discontinuity of work	5th
Non-recognition	12th
Under-utilisation of skill	9th
Incompetent workmate	6th
Colleagues not cooperating	2nd
Poor inspection programme	13th
Unsafe working conditions	3rd
Urging but no one caring	11th
Hot weather	8th
Cold weather	3rd
Too much work	14th
Not enough work	6th

7.4 FINANCIAL INCENTIVES AND HOW TO MAKE THEM WORK

Section 7.2 described a selection of the modern behaviourists' work on human motivation. The classical approach championed by Adam Smith, in contrast, emphasised that money is the chief motivator (Adam, 1965):

> Workmen . . . when they are liberally paid by piece are very apt to overwork themselves and to ruin their health and constitution in a few years . . . the desire for greater gain frequently prompted them to overwork themselves and to hurt their health by excessive work.

Indeed, the construction industry in many countries, especially Britain, has over the years believed in the efficacy of financial incentive programmes (FIPs) as a robust alternative to the highly theoretical approaches to motivation as particularly practised in the USA. FIPs have been used to motivate both managerial staff and operatives in the UK construction industry for several decades; see Entwistle and Reiners (1958), Advisory service to building industry (1969) and Department of Environment (1975). It is only recently, however, that the potential of financial incentives in motivating construction workers has been recognised in the USA (Laufer and Borcherding 1981) and the indications are that there is still a lack of understanding of its applications (Liska and Snell 1992).

As in manufacturing, where financial incentives are a major motivational tool, such schemes applied to the construction industry fall broadly into two categories: those for managers and those for operatives. Irrespective of the category, the basis of financial incentives requires that a portion or all of the monetary compensation of the worker or group of workers is tied to one or several performance criteria. This is, however, not clearly evident in schemes designed for managerial staff but is the fundamental basis of those designed for operatives. As seen in Maslow's hierarchy, money may mean different things to different people depending on their physiological and psychological needs. Nevertheless, well-designed and properly introduced schemes lead to higher productivity for the employer and extra pay for the employees for their efforts. On the other hand, ill-conceived arrangements sour relationships between management and operatives and may well have the opposite effect.

7.4.1 Financial incentives for managerial staff

Financial incentives for managerial staff, from top management to field supervisors, may take the form of strictly financial incentives or semi-financial incentives. The former generally include annual salary increases or payment of a percentage of any profit earned by the company at regular intervals, usually at the end of the year, while semi-financial incentives usually include fringe benefits or perks such as free lunches, clothing allowances, medical benefits, free travel abroad for the family while on business, free advice for personal affairs, professional fees, noncontributory pension and insurance schemes, low interest loans, free education for children and so on. Indeed, an organisation can introduce many such fringe benefits depending on the motivational aspects or needs of different levels of management staff as identified in Maslow's hierarchy. Thus, relatively lower level provisions, such as medical benefits, low interest loans and so forth, could be directed to junior staff with additional higher level satisfiers for top management. There is increasing need for such benefits for managers and executives as a way around government prices and income policies, without of course violating any rules or regulations. Such benefits not only motivate but also help to retain vital staff for the company's future success.

However, linking financial benefits to performance cannot be applied directly to managerial staff because it is difficult to accurately assess individual performance. Nevertheless, in certain situations parts of profits earned by a particular project or particular assignment (if it can be accounted separately) should be paid to the staff involved, depending on their degree of involvement. This will prevent the feeling that some members earn bonuses for the others who do not contribute or contribute to a lesser extent than they are paid.

7.4.2 Financial incentives for operatives

Financial incentives for operatives can take several forms, basically divided into the following three categories:

(1) Incentives not tied to performance such as holiday pay, sick pay, cost plus rates, long service allowances, pension fund, death benefits, employer's liability insurance and so on.
(2) Incentives partially tied to performance such as profit sharing.
(3) Incentives directly tied to individual or group performance such as geared incentive schemes.

The first category is generally applicable to unionised labour or workers directly and permanently employed by the organisation, and either stems from negotiations between employers and unions or is covered by such documents as the National Working Rule Agreement in the UK. These measures are generally aimed at keeping the workforce satisfied and retained in the organisation rather than at motivating for higher productivity. The second category is mainly used for managerial staff and rarely applied to operatives. When adopted, payments are made either at the end of the project or more frequently at the end of the year, and are generally only paid to permanently employed workers. The third category, in which earnings are tied to day-to-day performance, represents the truly financial incentive scheme as regarded by both operatives and management. If properly applied, it is much more effective in yielding higher productivity. The following discussion is therefore limited to this category.

The basic approach compares individual or group performance in terms of units produced per day or at the end of the assigned job with a target fixed by management promising extra payment to operatives exceeding the target. It is generally accepted, especially in the UK, that operatives are entitled to one-third extra pay if the target is achieved; that is, 100% performance. Additional bonus is paid for any extra hours saved depending on the gearing ratio. Many schemes have been devised, particularly for the manufacturing sector, but common gearing ratios applied in construction are:

(1) 100% scheme (direct scheme): bonus paid for all the hours saved at the usual hourly rate.
(2) 75% scheme: bonus paid for 75% of hours saved at the hourly rate.
(3) 50% scheme: bonus paid for 50% of hours saved at the hourly rate.
(4) 25% scheme: bonus paid for 25% of hours saved at the hourly rate.

In the direct scheme, bonus earnings start at relatively high performance but the earning rate is high, whereas in the 25% gearing scheme bonus earnings start at relatively low performance but the earning rate is low. Depending on the circumstances, such as workforce skills and working conditions, a suitable gearing ratio can be selected. See Harris and McCaffer (1995), Foster (1989) and Oxley and Poskitt (1986) for details of gearing schemes and how they are formulated. Some guidelines on how to maximise the benefits of any financial incentive scheme are given below.

(1) Committed top management – in implementing and monitoring a financial incentive programme through initial support by providing adequate resources, developing policies and procedures with active employee participation and maintaining this commitment throughout the project. It is often said that incentives are not a substitute for poor management and unless an organised approach is pursued programmes are bound to fail.
(2) Reliable production standards – unrealistic targets set on an unsound basis have often been the cause of disputes between workforce and management. There are several methods available to set targets, such as work measurement, based on the estimate, based on data from past projects, experience, bargaining and so on. Systematic work measurement is the most reliable, as discussed in Chapter 4 (see also Section 9.7) Such targets must also be checked regularly against field performance and updated whenever necessary.
(3) Suitable gearing ratio – as the bonus starting point and the rate of earning depend on the gearing ratio, a suitable ratio must be determined to avoid worker frustration. For example, in the early stages of new operations, when learning is taking place, a low gearing ratio such as 25% or 50% may be suitable but when workers become familiar or gain skill a higher gearing ratio, such as the direct scheme, should be selected, preferably in consultation with the worker representatives to avoid any subsequent disputes.
(4) Multi-criteria targets – performance measured only on quantity leads to poor quality as operations are unnecessarily quickened, resulting in rework and damage

to the firm's reputation. Assessment of performance should therefore be tied to all the relevant criteria, namely, quantity, budget (standard or target), quality and wastage, which requires proper supervision and quality inspection in addition to quantity measurement.

(5) Effective cost-control programme – incentives being based on budgeted resources (targets) and the actual resources used, an effective cost control programme with a suitable cost-coding system is a prerequisite to any successful incentive programme. This enables accurate recording of all details and is especially important for large, complex projects having multi-level information sources. Well-trained progress and cost information staff are essential and should be held responsible for accurate supply of cost information.

(6) The unit of measure – team working predominates in construction, hence individual incentive evaluation is rarely possible. Measuring and rewarding small units such as gangs enriches individual knowledge of results and is a key component of job-related motivation. It also reduces administrative efforts but may create a feeling among the workers that they earn bonuses for others. The team size should therefore be carefully selected to obtain the maximum benefit possible.

(7) Flexibility – a 'must' in any incentive programme to accommodate an organisation's needs and changes over time; for example, new technology, new work types, different work locations, changing workforce attitudes and management strategies. Rigid programmes tend to stagnate and fail in the long run.

(8) Organisational set-up and needs – effective incentive schemes are generally not interchangeable and cannot be borrowed from another organisation. They should be designed specifically for the organisation considering its own set-up – for example, the quality and cost-control systems adopted, type of work carried out, employment conditions and so forth.

(9) Ease of administration – complicated schemes tend to reduce worker trust and confidence, increase overheads and bureaucracy and have proven to be unsuccessful. A good point to start is with an effective cost-control system, which is not only a prerequisite to an effective incentive scheme but also, more importantly, provides a tool for managers to keep track of project spending. Both systems can be integrated and administered with little difficulty using a computer system.

(10) Worker trust and confidence – successful incentive programmes must win the workers' trust and confidence. This can be encouraged through worker participation during development, implementation and maintaining of the programme, so improving communication with management to help foster a sense of belonging and pride. Furthermore, integrity and consistency must be maintained, targets should not be changed without proper reasoning and dialogue, and promised incentives must be distributed, any failure possibly having detrimental effects on productivity. Performance must also be based on objective measures such as quantity as far as possible rather than subjective measures like supervisor's rating.

(11) Short intervals between payments – research in motivation and human psychology has consistently indicated that the shorter the gap between achievement and reward, the higher the effect on inducing workers to higher productivity. Consequently, incentive payment should ideally be made as soon as possible after

evaluating performance. A weekly interval is the best but the period should not be more than a month in any case, and the cost-control systems should be able to track weekly performance to accommodate such payments.

(12) Payments for delays beyond workers' control – delays due to factors such as late instructions, material shortages, subcontractor delays, inclement weather and so on often cause implementation difficulties. Several approaches are used in these situations, depending on the understanding between the parties, the commonest being paying an 'average bonus' based on past performance, paying a fixed standard bonus or paying for the time at normal hourly rates. Frequent occurrence will be resisted, however, and management must ensure that such delays are kept to a minimum. Indeed, this not only provides smooth incentive programme but also drives productivity, as will be seen in Section 9.7.

(13) Equitable payments for similar effort – needed to avoid worker frustration if other trades are earning more, perhaps arising from unrealistic targets, inappropriate gearing ratios, reward not properly established or target impossible to set, as in maintenance work. Reference to past records, consultation with workers or unbiased management intervention can help to solve such problems.

Finally, while financial incentives can help to raise productivity and lower costs, the concept needs to be considered holistically and not simply as a list of the above factors. Furthermore, the support of other measures, such as planning, organisation and control, formulated with a specific objective tied to a specific criteria, such as to reduce the frequency of accidents, rate of turnover, overtime or quality, is essential.

7.5 SUMMARY

Conceptual studies covering theories of motivation and empirical studies applied to construction operative motivation were discussed and their effectiveness in motivating construction workers evaluated. Motivating and demotivating variables, their interrelationships and significance in workforce motivation were illustrated based on the results of a case study. Finally, financial incentives were discussed with special reference to their application for maximum productivity.

REFERENCES AND BIBLIOGRAPHY

Adam J.S. (1965). Injustice in social exchange. *Advances in Experimental Social Psychology*, **2**, 267-299

Advisory Service for the Building Industry. (1969). *The Principles of Incentives for the Construction Industry*. London: ASBI

Birchall D.W. (1977). Employee motivation in the construction industry, *Site Management Information Service CIOB*, no. 72, 1977/77

Blain B.C.R. (1986). *Bonus: A Study of Incentive Schemes Operating in the Construction Industry*. London: International Thompson

Borcherding J.D. (1977). Participative decision making in construction. *Journal of the Construction Division ASCE*, **103**(CO4), 567-575

Borcherding J.D. and Garner D.F. (1981). Work force motivation and productivity on large jobs. *Journal of the Construction Division ASCE*, **107**(CO3), 443–453

Borcherding J.D. and Oglesby C.H. (1974). Construction productivity and job satisfaction, *Journal of the Construction Division ASCE*, **100**(CO3), 413–431

Borcherding J.D. and Oglesby C.H. (1975). Job dissatisfaction in construction work. *Journal of the Construction Division ASCE*, **101**(C02), 415–434

Brayfield A.H. and Crockett W.H. (1955). Employee attitudes and employee performance. *Psychological Bulletin*, **52**(5), 415-422

Department of the Environment (1975). *Incentive Schemes for Small Builders*. London: HMSO

Entwistle A. and Reiners W.J. (1958). Incentives in the building industry, national building studies, *Special Report No. 27*, London: HMSO

Foster D. (1989). Construction Site Studies – Production, Administration and Personnel. London: Longman

Harris F.C. and McCaffer R. (1995). *Modern Construction Management*. Oxford: Blackwell Science

Haseltine C.S. (1976) Motivation of construction workers. *Journal of the Construction Division ASCE*, **102**(CO3), 497–509

Herzberg F. (1968). One more time – how do you motivate employees? *Harvard Business Review*, **46**(1), 53–62

Herzberg F. (1977). One more time – how do you motivate employees? – A retrospective commentary. *Harvard Business Review*, Sept/Oct, **55**, 523-534

Homans G.C. (1963). *Group Factors in Worker Productivities, Fatigue of Workers; its Relation to Industrial Production* 1st edn. New York: Reinhold

Laufer A. (1985). On-site performance improvement programme. *Journal of Construction Engineering and Management ASCE*, **111**(1), 82–97

Laufer A. and Borcherding J.D. (1981). Financial incentives to raise productivity, *Journal of the Construction Division ASCE*, **107**(CO4), 745-756

Laufer A. and Jenkins G.D. (1982). Motivating construction workers. *Journal of the Construction Division ASCE*, **108**(CO4), 531–545

Liska R.W. and Snell B. (1992). Financial incentive programmes for average size construction firms. *Journal of Construction Engineering and Management ASCE*, **118**(4), 667–676

MacGregor D.M. (1960). *The Human Side of Enterprise*. New York: McGraw-Hill

Mackenzie K.I. and Harris F. (1974). Money the only motivator. *Building Technology and Management*, May, 25-29

Maloney W.F. (1981). Motivation in construction – a review. *Journal of the Construction Division ASCE*, **107**(CO4), 641–647

Maloney W.F. and McFillen J.M. (1983). Research needs in construction worker performance. *Journal of Construction Engineering and Management ASCE*, **109**(2), 245-254

Maloney W.F. and McFillen J.M. (1985a). Instance of and satisfaction with job outcomes. *Journal of Construction Engineering and Management ASCE*, **3**(1), 53-73

Maloney W.F. and McFillen J.M. (1985b).Motivational implication of construction work. *Journal of Construction Engineering and Management ASCE*, **112**(1), 137-151

Maslow, A.H. (1971) '*Maslow's hierarchy of needs*' from '*A theory of human motivation*'. *Pyschological Review*, 370-396

Neal R.H. (1979). Motivation of construction workers – theory and practice. *CIOB Site Management Information Service*, no. 78

Olomolaiye P.O. (1989). A review of construction operative motivation. *Building and Environment*, **24**(3), 279–287

Olomolaiye P. O. and Ogunlana S.O. (1988). A survey of construction operative motivation on selected sites in Nigeria. *Building and Environment*, **23**(3), 179–185

Olomolaiye P. O., Wahab K.A. and Price A.D.F. (1987). Problems influencing craftmen's productivity in Nigeria. *Building and Environment*, **22**(4), 317–323

Oxley R. and Poskitt J. (1986). *Management Techniques Applied to Construction Industry* 4th edn. Oxford: Blackwell Science

Schrader C.R. (1972). Motivation of construction craftsmen. *Journal of the Construction Division ASCE*, **98**(CO2), 257–273

Vroom V.H. (1964). *Work and Motivation*. New York: John Wiley & Sons

Warren R.H. (1989). *Motivation and Productivity in the Construction Industry*. New York: Van Nostrand Reinhold

Wesley-Lees J.N. (1976). Motivation, expectancy theory and the design of payment systems, Department of Civil Engineering, Loughborough University of Technology, UK

Wilson A.J. (1979). Need-important and need-satisfaction for construction operatives. *MSc. Project Report*, Loughborough University of Technology

8

COMPUTER APPLICATIONS IN IMPROVING PRODUCTIVITY

8.1 INTRODUCTION

Productivity improvements in construction work are driven by a number of interconnecting factors; for example, wage changes in a different sector of the economy may lead to upward drift for construction workers if their loyalty is to be retained. These higher wages in the long term can then only be sustained by improvements in productivity; that is, fewer workers achieving a given level of output. Unfortunately, productivity improvements have generally lagged behind those industries able to introduce new technology and hence building price increases have tended to be inflationary.

A major element causing lack-lustre performance has been the continued presence of lost time on construction sites, where typically only half the working day is used effectively. Much can be blamed on poor organisation, where redoing work, workers moving about and machine breakdowns commonly account for up to 75% of the lost time. Clearly, better planning, monitoring and subsequent control would be beneficial. However, until the advent of the personal computer the time needed to evaluate alternative solutions was prohibitive. Today virtually all managers and engineers should have ready access to a variety of computing facilities, both at head office and on-site, allowing timely simulations to be carried out and the most economic and feasible solutions to construction problems evaluated. Furthermore, the power of modern computers is increasingly facilitating the collection and storage of useful data on many aspects affecting construction performance, which can be usefully combined with bespoke and general software relating to production planning and resources scheduling, procurement, computer aided design (CAD), estimating, cost control, record keeping, invoicing, financial management and so on.

However, good production planning remains the key to more accurate estimating and subsequent control of budgets. This chapter therefore describes some examples of computer models, mainly based on advanced operational research (OR) and expert systems (ES) to aid and improve construction planning and managerial control. It also discusses computerised collection of work study data and application of automation technology in productivity improvement.

8.2 POTENTIAL APPLICATION OF COMPUTER-BASED MODELS IN PRODUCTION PLANNING

Commonly managers choose the appropriate construction methods for a particular task in a 'rule of thumb' fashion, based on past experience, resource availability, costs and convenience, tempered by local considerations. Where time permits perhaps one or two schemes may be costed for comparison purposes. The proliferation of PCs and associated software packages, however, is increasingly facilitating more detailed evaluation of alternatives to provide marginal improvements in construction scheduling, resource balancing and economic analysis, potentially through improved application of OR. The OR Society has explained the approach as useful in developing a scientific model of a system incorporating measurements of factors, such as chance and risk, with which to predict and compare the outcomes of alternative strategies or means of control. In the main the method is suited to modelling those complex logistical problems generally highly dependent on detailed and accurate records of performance data. Hence presently only a limited range of OR methods – as, for example, adopted by manufacturing industry – can be applied to construction situations; nevertheless, simulation, linear programs and expert systems represent promising examples as demonstrated in the following summaries of recently published work.

8.3 COMPUTER SIMULATION MODELS

Simulation involves mimicking or generation of a real situation using a model which represents the real system as nearly as possible. The technique can be applied to compare different alternatives for management decision making at relatively low cost and at a much faster rate compared to real situations. It is suitable in complex situations where other mathematical modelling cannot easily be applied. Some examples are described in the following subsections.

8.3.1 Evaluating the effects of weather on construction activities

Faced with the uncertainty of predicting weather, managers are often reluctant to agree to advanced expenditure on preparations for dealing with adverse conditions. Even though quite accurate daily forecasts are now available, costing the provisions over the length of a contract continues to be a general inclusion to overall estimating figures.

A new approach combining network analysis and Meteorological Office data provides a means of simulating the effects of uncertainty. The model evaluates the effects of wind speed, rainfall and temperature for each activity in the network, by synchronising Meteorological Office hourly weather records obtained for the location near the project with the running time of the construction work (see Figure 8.1a–j). In this manner the weather patterns over the past, say, 20 years can be used

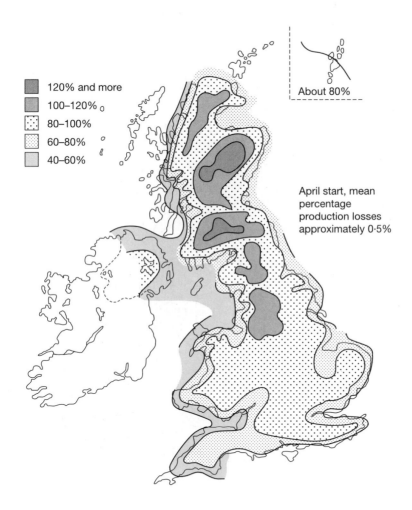

Figure 8.1a Simulated weather maps for projects of six months duration. Mean percentage production losses due to temperature on concrete-type projects started in October, concreting occupies 25% of construction period.

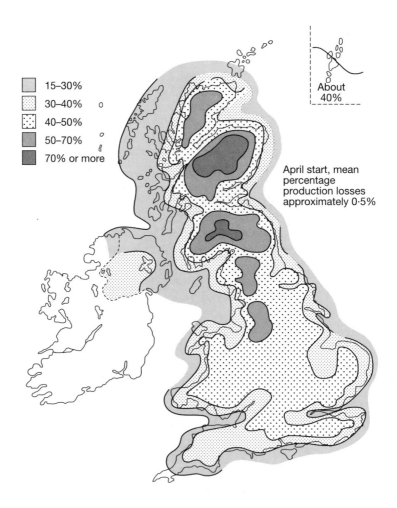

15–30%
30–40%
40–50%
50–70%
70% or more

About 40%

April start, mean percentage production losses approximately 0·5%

Figure 8.1b Temperature on concrete-type projects started in October, concreting occupies 50% of construction period.

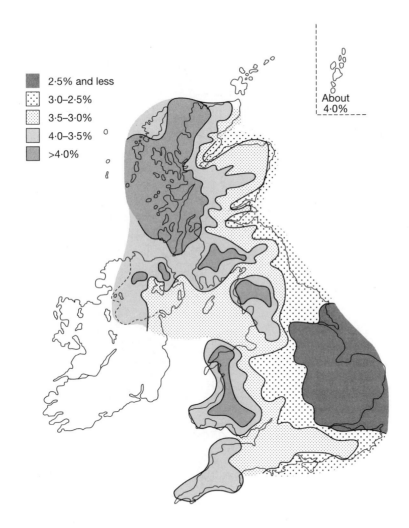

2·5% and less
3·0–2·5%
3·5–3·0%
4·0–3·5%
>4·0%

About
4·0%

Figure 8.1c   Rainfall on projects started in April.

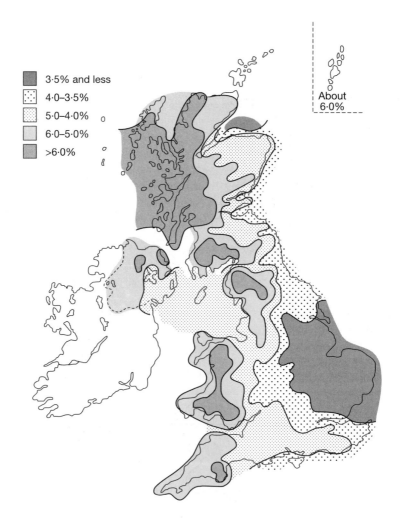

3·5% and less
4·0–3·5%
5·0–4·0%
6·0–5·0%
>6·0%

About 6·0%

Figure 8.1d   Rainfall on projects started in October.

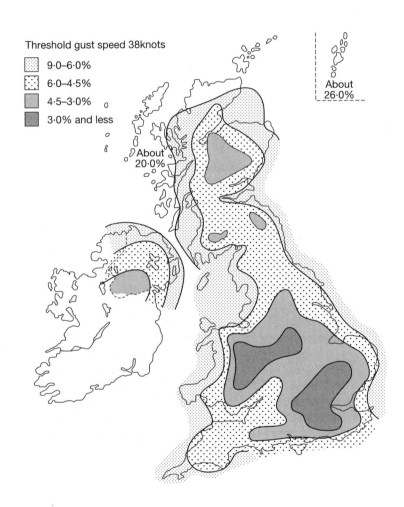

Figure 8.1e Wind gust effects on projects started in October.

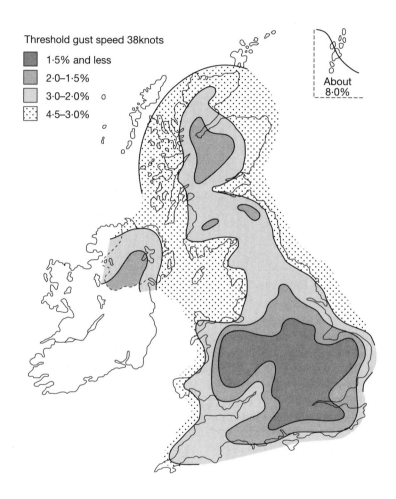

Threshold gust speed 38knots

- 1·5% and less
- 2·0–1·5%
- 3·0–2·0%
- 4·5–3·0%

About 8·0%

Figure 8.1f Wind gust effects on projects started in April.

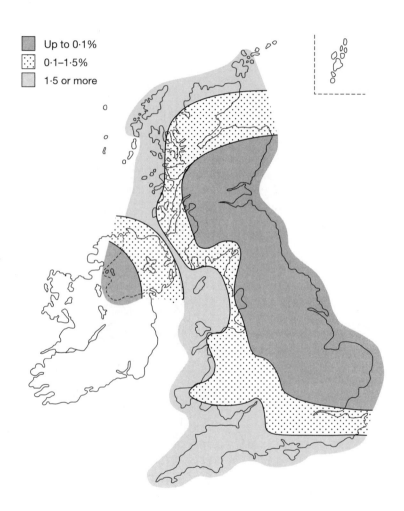

Figure 8.1g Windchill on projects started in October.

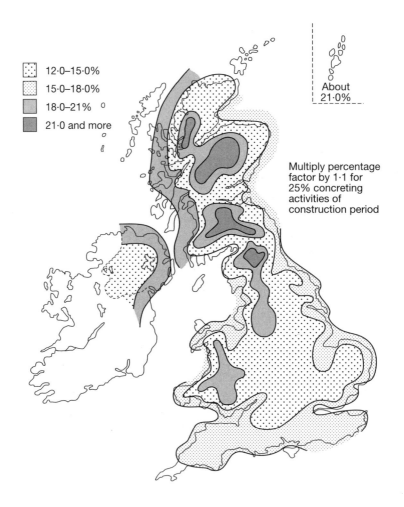

Figure 8.1h All weather effects on concrete-type projects started in October, concreting occupies 50% or more of construction period.

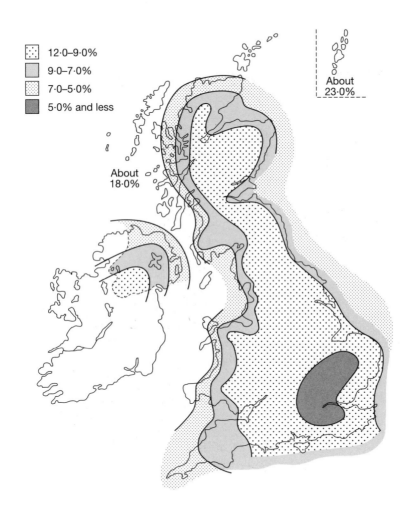

Figure 8.1i All weather effects on prefabricated-type structures started in October.

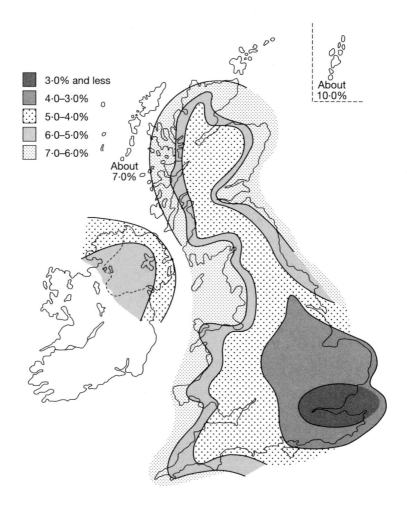

Figure 8.1j   All weather effects on projects started in April.

to determine the averages and standard deviation of delays to individual activities and overall project duration.

The modelling process operates by considering the three weather elements in turn and the project is examined for the influence of each by calculating the earliest finish time for each activity in the network. The activity is checked for sensitivity to the weather elements and the weather condition at the particular clock time compared to the threshold levels deemed likely to cause work stoppages when triggered. When the intensity of an element exceeds the threshold the activity is delayed by one hour and the weather at this updated time is now considered. The procedure is repeated until the activity has been completed. Any delay in the critical path extends the project duration, while float time is simply used up. In addition, activities involving the placing of concrete are tested during overnight frost conditions and postponed when frost damage will occur.

In practice some rescheduling of resources to alleviate the effects of weather may be possible and therefore the results from this particular model are worst-case scenarios. The results of simulations for various categories of construction work, started in October and April are shown in Figure 8.1a–j for a 20-year period.

8.3.2 Highway construction simulation model

Repetitive construction like highway pavements can be readily planned by line of balance methods. However, because of variations in daily productivity, strict adherence to the programme is seldom possible. The project manager then has to take corrective action to minimise the interference when some activities are delayed. The model described below simulates the effects of unpredictable productivity changes and allows the user to try to take corrective action by intelligent deployment of resources.

THE SIMULATION MODEL

The model simulates the construction of 10 km (6.2 miles) of road pavement, involving the following sequence of activities:

(1) Trim subgrade surface
(2) Lay sub-base
(3) Install road drainage
(4) Lay kerb foundations
(5) Lay concrete road base
(6) Lay wearing surface
(7) Install road finishes.

Each process is performed by a different subcontracted labour gang and equipment. The pre-contract plan is shown in Figure 8.2 and the cost estimate calculated from the information is given in Tables 8.1 and 8.2.

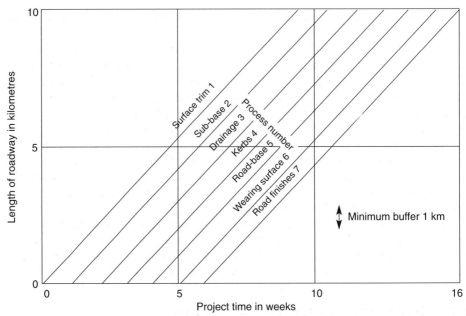

Figure 8.2 Planned programme for roadway construction.

Table 8.1 Planned resources for road construction.

| Process number and description | Resource type | | Number required | Code |
	Fixed	Variable		
(1) Surface trim		Bulldozer and scraper	3	M
(2) Sub-base	Bulldozer	Trucks	20	C
(3) Drainage		Excavator and gang	10	G
(4) Kerbs		Men	10	L
(5) Road base	Concrete paver	Trucks	10	C
(6) Wearing surface	Bitumen paver	Trucks	5	C
(7) Road finishes		Men	10	L

Source: Harris and Evans (1977).

Table 8.2 Other parameters used for estimating.

Parameter	Value
Rate of pay for worker	$4.00/hr
Overtime pay after 40 hr	$6.00/hr
Delivery charge for bringing any machine (except trucks) on-site	$500.00
Hire charge for machine (except trucks) excluding driver	$1000/week
Hire charge for truck excluding driver	$300/week
Overheads	$0.2 \times$ direct costs

Source: Harris and Evans (1977).

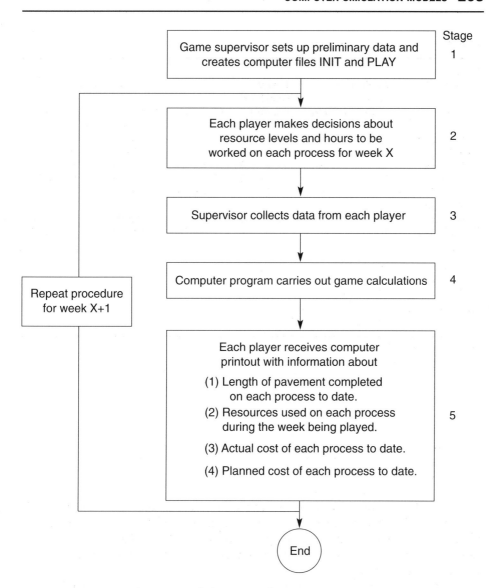

Figure 8.3 Sequence of decisions. *Source*: Harris and Evans (1977).

SIMULATION PRINCIPLES

The model simulates actual progress, with the user making decisions at the beginning of each new simulation round, about the size of labour gangs, rate of supply of materials, numbers and types of machines and equipment and hours to be worked, including overtime and weekend working (Figure 8.3).

Table 8.3 Computer progress information.

Player no. 11; Week no. 7 Process	Production units employed	Hours	Length completed (metres)	Cost ($)	Total cost to date ($) Actual	Planned
(1) Surface trim	2	40	10 000.00	4 640.00	75 960.00	72 600.00
(2) Sub-base	20	55	9 798.31	14 250.00	84 150.00	200 432.64
(3) Drainage	13	60	7 497.33	10 920.00	44 520.00	35 987.18
(4) Kerbs	12	60	6 497.33	3 360.00	14 840.00	10 395.72
(5) Road base	10	50	5 478.16	6 950.00	22 200.00	30 951.60
(6) Wearing surface	5	60	2 833.42	4 645.00	8 962.00	9 491.96
(7) Finishings	10	60	1 072.84	2 800.00	2 800.00	1 716.54

Cost for week 7
  Actual $47 570.00
  Overhead $4 313.74
Total $51 883.74

Total cost to date Actual $28 3628.68
                   Planned $29 1771.83

Source: Harris and Evans (1977).

The outcome is then simulated by randomly varying actual production in each activity to reflect bad weather, equipment breakdowns, inefficient materials supply, under- or over-achievement of work gangs and so on. Also, individual subcontracted work gangs have different underlying levels of production compared with pre-contract plans.

At the end of the simulation, actual progress and costs are produced for comparison with planned progress as shown in Table 8.3. The next simulation uses this information for further decision making and the process is continued until the project is complete.

RESULTS

The results of simulations shown in Figures 8.4 and 8.5 suggest that estimates are subject to error and that while managers can take corrective measures considerable variability compared to original targets is likely to be experienced.

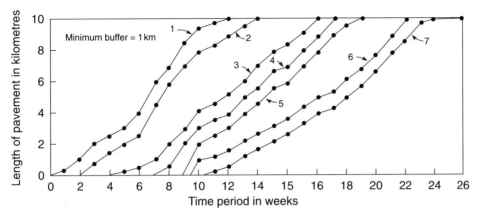

Figure 8.4 Road game – progress to completion. *Source*: Harris and Evans (1977).

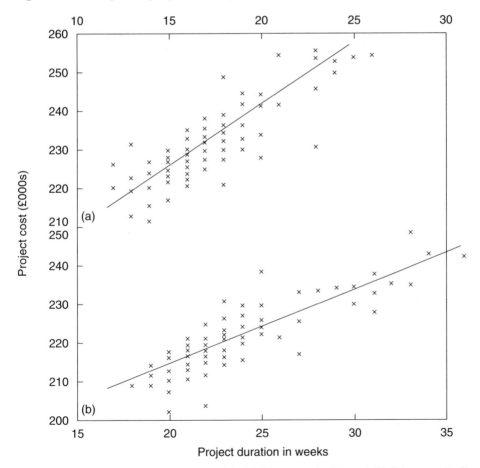

Figure 8.5 Simulation results. Players with (a) 1 km start buffer and (b) 2 km start buffer. *Source*: Harris and Evans (1977).

8.3.3 Truck-fleet composition for materials distribution

Balancing supply equipment with deliveries is a common problem requiring a solution for many aspects of construction, including earthmoving operations, concrete distribution (both site-mixed and ready-mixed), materials transport between depots, cranage, materials stock-pile layout and so on.

A key factor in achieving efficiency and economy is to operate the most suitable combination of trucks with respect to the supply equipment and thereby minimise operating costs and reduce wasted space. Several methods are commonly applied by practitioners in trying to solve such problems, from rudimentary estimates to full-scale simulation modelling.

SIMULATION MODELLING

The model simulates daily production to provide information on the percentage of empty space, total quantity of material transported and total number of trips that day, together with waiting time for trucks and supply machines.

The process is based on the daily routine of the trucks operating in a cycle beginning with loading, then delivering and finally returning to reload. The model is designed to investigate various fleet combinations and requires field data on radial distribution (Figure 8.6), journey time distribution (Figure 8.7) and load time/order size distribution (Figure 8.8).

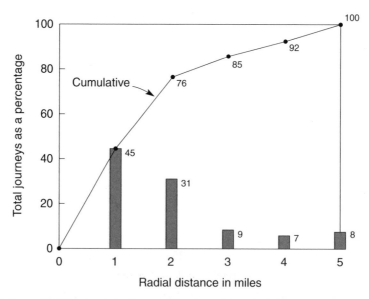

Figure 8.6 Radial distribution. *Source*: Woods and Harris (1980).

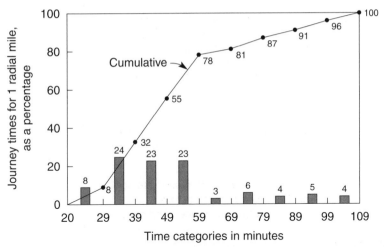

Figure 8.7   Journey time distribution for one radial mile. *Source*: Woods and Harris (1980).

Using random numbers in the range 0 to 99 allocated in proportion to the load time bandings (Table 8.4), the first truck in the fleet is selected and loaded. Similarly, the travel distance is selected and the travel time allocated. On arrival back at the supply equipment the truck joins the queue and the cycle is repeated, and so on until the end of the working day (Figures 8.9 and 8.10). Table 8.5 illustrates the kind of information that would be available from the simulation of a ready-mixed concrete plant, serving a fleet of trucks delivering over a region.

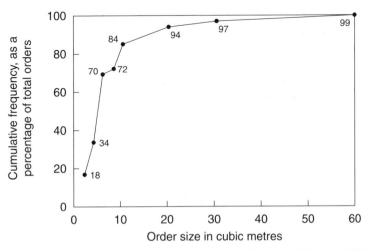

Figure 8.8   Cumulative order size distribution. *Source*: Woods and Harris (1980).

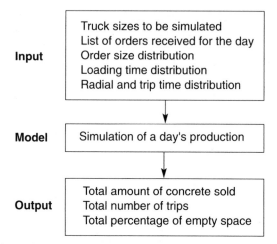

Figure 8.9   Basic model. *Source*: Woods and Harris (1980).

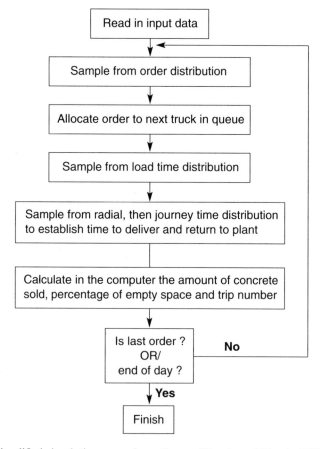

Figure 8.10   Simplified simulation procedure. *Source*: Woods and Harris (1980).

Table 8.4 Simulation of selection of orders.

Order size, in cubic yards (1)	Percentage of orders (2)	Random number (3)
1–2	18	00–17
3–4	16	18–33
5–6	36	34–69
7–8	2	70–71
9–10	12	72–83
11–20	10	84–93
21–30	3	94–96
31–60	2	97–98
> 60	1	99

Note: 1 cubic yard $= 0.765$ m^3. *Source*: Woods and Harris (1980).

Table 8.5 Typical range of truck composition alternatives for concrete production.

Plant	Fleet mix: number of trucks× size (yd^3)	Total average daily amount of concrete sold (yd^3)	Simulated daily number of trips	Total daily percentage of empty space	Annual cost ($)	Cost per cubic yard ($)
Toytown	8×5	95.44	22	12.96	40 657	1.584
	5×5, 3×4	94.32	22	11.11	44 627	1.759
	8×6	96.91	21	11.91	39 947	1.532
	8×4	80.31	27	13.77	37 848	1.752
	4×6, 4×4	80.25	21	10.79	44 030	2.039

Note: 1 cubic yard $= 0.76$ m^3. *Source*: Woods and Harris (1980).

8.3.4 Dynamic simulation applied to materials handling systems

While construction materials can be planned and timely procurement arranged, unfortunately achievements on-site seldom meet expectations for a variety of reasons, such as unpredictable breakdown of equipment, idle time, unanticipated demand for resources, operator inefficiency and non-availability of materials. Although unpredictable, their frequency of occurrence can be evaluated to establish behavioural patterns for such elements over a sufficient period of time to establish a statistical confidence level. The materials handling process can then be modelled using the principle of continuous simulation analogous to fluid flow in a pipe, involving elements akin to storage tanks and control values (Figure 8.11).

MODEL FRAMEWORK

The elements involved in the crane handling of different types of material – for example, concrete, bricks, form work and reinforcement – can be considered as

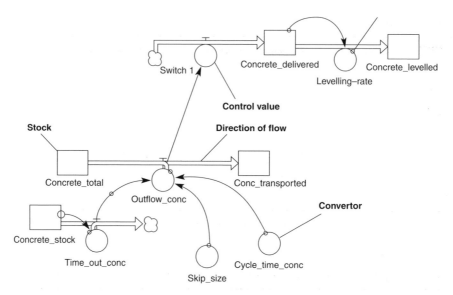

Figure 8.11 Sample system network using STELLA. Concrete_delivered, concrete delivered to point of placing; Concrete_levelled, total concrete in the shutters; Concrete_total, total quantity of concrete required to complete task; Conc_transported, total quantity of concrete transported; Concrete_stock, total time allocated for concreting; Levelling_rate, crew rate of handling concrete; Outflow_conc, rate of concrete delivered; Time_out_conc, rate of depletion of total time for concrete; Skip_size; concrete skip size; Cycle_time_conc, cycle time for handling concrete. *Source*: Wijesundera and Harris (1989).

portions of time in a continuous working cycle with each characterised by a distribution having a mean value, reflecting patterns of change in the quantity and order of materials handled, servicing time, breakdowns and idling. The whole process may be seen as a realistic flow of materials from stocks through the transport system to the user.

Experimentation with different distributions for a given material enables the effects of changing the size of work gangs and handling methods to be simulated. In simulating materials supply the work done to date with each material type is expressed as a percentage of the total quantity of materials of that type to be moved, as follows:

$$\text{New work done} = \text{Old work done} + \Delta t \times (\text{rate of work})$$

where start work done = 0 and Δt is the time interval considered. Work done starts at 0% and completes at 100%. The rate of work done is the percentage of total stock delivered in each cycle, divided by the time to load and deliver the material, this latter figure being selected from a distribution representing real data obtained from work study observation. The values are selected randomly. The system is shown diagrammatically in Figure 8.12.

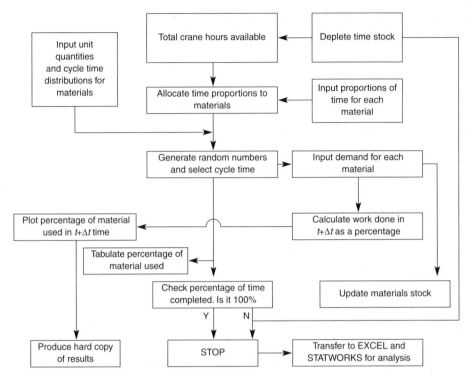

Figure 8.12 Flow chart of dynamic simulation applied to materials handling.
Source: Wijesundera and Harris (1989).

TIME PARAMETERS

The total available time, for example 9.00 a.m. to 5.00 p.m., and the incremental simulation time interval Δt are input, together with the quantity for each material type and the proportion taken up with this material in the cycle time. In the first cycle the proportions are decided by the user based on data typical for a particular project; thereafter they are determined automatically in the simulation to maintain balance in the cycle. However, logical sequences cannot be disturbed; that is, form work must precede concreting and so on.

OUTPUT

The output information consists of the percentage of each material used at any given time expressed either in tabular (Table 8.6) or graphical (Figure 8.13) form. By monitoring the performance of each type, the impact of making changes – for example gang size, rate of delivery and so on – can be examined.

Table 8.6 Percentage of material transported.

Time (hr)	Usage reinforcement (%)	Usage form work (%)	Usage concrete (%)	Usage bricks (%)
0	0	0	0	0
5	0	0.46	0	0
10	0.99	0.85	0	0
15	2.63	1.69	1.91	0
20	6.01	2.71	2.11	0
25	10.48	3.02	2.11	0.83
30	11.63	5.54	2.11	1.34
35	12.63	8.53	2.11	1.38
40	13.56	11.31	2.11	1.38
45	14.54	14.26	2.11	1.38
50	15.52	17.19	2.11	1.38
55	16.47	20.04	2.11	1.38
60	17.19	21.91	3.64	1.38
65	17.84	23.93	6.41	1.38
70	18.49	25.89	9.47	1.38
75	19.09	27.63	11.55	1.38
80	19.74	29.63	14.58	5.00
85	20.61	31.49	16.95	5.00
90	21.89	32.87	18.49	5.00
95	23.20	34.15	19.96	5.26
100	24.73	35.61	21.30	5.30

Source: Wijesundera and Harris (1989).

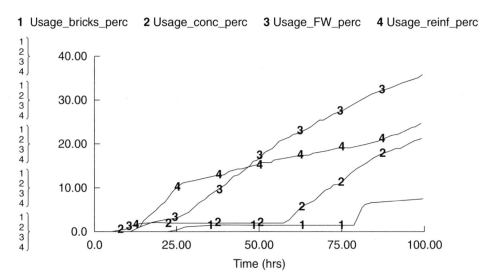

1 Usage_bricks_perc   **2** Usage_conc_perc   **3** Usage_FW_perc   **4** Usage_reinf_perc

Figure 8.13 Graph of percentage of materials transported (from STELLA).
Source: Wijesundera and Harris (1989).

8.4 LINEAR PROGRAMMING MODELS

Linear programming (LP) basically involves mathematical formulation of an objective function together with a set of associated constraints within which the objective should be achieved and solving the formulation to obtain an optimum solution. The objective function can be a maximisation problem – for example, the profit of a certain operation – or a minimisation problem – for example, cost of a project, distance travelled and so on. Some examples are described below.

8.4.1 Capital budgeting using a linear programming model

Construction clients and contractors alike make cash flow predictions to try to ensure a smooth flow of finance in meeting payments for work carried out on projects. While cash-flow forecasting is a relatively simple process requiring data for the value of work done and the timing of payments, in practice the task tends to be laborious without the use of computers and therefore is often neglected. Furthermore, the impacts of new projects and the timing of start dates also need careful attention if the costs of loans and borrowings are to be minimised. Linear programming can greatly assist in determining: (i) the optimum financing arrangement to meet the cash flow requirements of all the ongoing projects, and (ii)

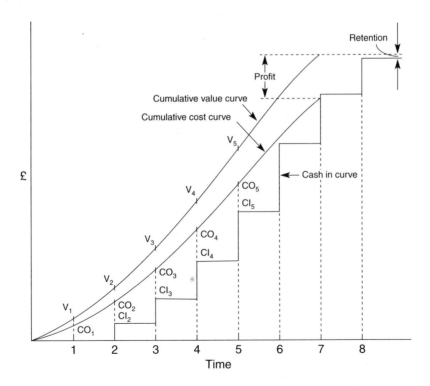

Figure 8.14 S curve representation. *Source* Wijeratne and Harris (1984).

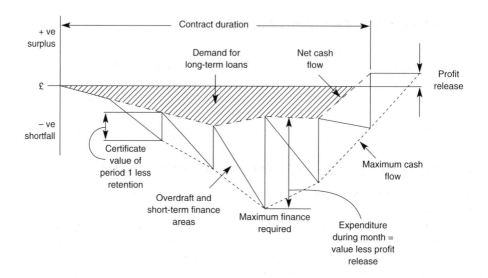

Figure 8.15 Cash flow curves. *Source*: Wijeratne and Harris (1984).

the most feasible financing arrangement to meet the additional cash flows of a new project.

CALCULATING CASH FLOW

Conventional methods simply apportion cash-out and cash-in according to the bar chart or network plan by taking into account payment delays and retention moneys to produce the project S curve as shown in Figure 8.14. However, where the S-shape tends to be uniform – that is, similar projects handled by a given client or contractor – then the S curve for all projects can be readily projected knowing only the end conditions. The method requires information on (i) percentage time and cost values to specify the standard curve, (ii) starting period and end date, and (iii) project/ contract sum. The cash flow diagram shown in Figure 8.15 can then be determined by the same procedures as in the conventional method.

THE LP MODEL TO MINIMISE THE NET PRESENT VALUE OF FINANCE

The following constraints are essential to include in the construction of the model for a practical demonstration:

(1) Periodic cash requirements of working capital
(2) Upper limit of borrowing from a source
(3) Upper limit on credit per period
(4) Minimum cash balance required per period
(5) Absolute upper limit of total borrowings based on the capital gearing ratio.

The full constraint linking all of the above elements can be expressed as:

Borrowings − Interest + Credit − Previous credit − Excess cash +
Previous excess cash = Cash for contracts + Dividends + Tax

or more conventionally as:

$$\sum L_{tk} - \sum I_k L_{(t-1)k} + C_t - C_{t-1} - EC_t + EC_{t-1} = CRQ_t + D + T$$

where L_{tk} is the amount borrowed from source k in time t, I_k is the interest rate for source k, $L_{(t-1)k}$ is the amount previously borrowed from source k, C_t is the trade credit available in this period, C_{t-1} is the trade credit obtained in the previous period, and to be settled in this period, EC_t is the excess cash in this period, EC_{t-1} is the excess cash from the last period, CRQ_t is the cash required in this period for projects/contracts, D is the dividend to be paid to shareholders and T is taxes payable.

SOLVING THE MODEL

The objective function to be minimised is the net present cost of finance for the planning period represented by:

$$\text{minimise} \sum L_{tj} N_{tj}$$

where N_{tj} is net present cost factor for loan L_{tj}; that is, the loan taken from source j in time t. The model can be solved using the Simplex method with the aid of a microcomputer and a suitable software package.

EXAMPLE

Company details

Financial planning period	= 24 months
Start of planning period	= 1
Number of financial sources	= 6
Borrowing limit based on debt/equity ratio	= £1 500 000
Minimum cash balance per period	= £2000
Annual overhead expenditure	= £36 000
Annual increase in overheads	= 6%
Tax rate on profits	= 52%
Percentage of profits to be paid as dividends	= 30%
Total number of contracts	= 3

Contract details

	Contract 1	Contract 2	Contract 3
Profits and overheads	= 9%	8.5%	10%
Delay in clients' payments	= 2 months	1 month	1 month

	Contract 1	Contract 2	Contract 3
Retention	= 10%	10%	10%
Limit of retention	= 5%	5%	5%
Maintenance period	= 6 months	6 months	6 months
Release of retention at practical completion	= 50%	50%	50%
Starting time of contract	= 0 months	3 months	6 months
Finishing time of contract	= 18 months	24 months	15 months
Value of contract	= £65 000	£1 000 000	£800 000

S curve for a typical contract

Time percentage:	0	20	40	60	80	100
Value percentage:	0	9	41	78	92	100

Trade credit parameters

	Percentage of total cost of a typical contract	Delay for payment in weeks
Labour wages	14	1
Plant hire	18	6
Material supplies	23	8
Subcontractors	45	8

Details of financial sources

		RE	OD	S1	S2	S3	S4
Repayment period in months	=	36	24	12	18	9	18
Annual percentage interest on borrowings	=	14	9	9.5	10	9	10.5
Interval of interest payments in months	=	–	1	1	3	1	3
Grace period in months at the start for interest payments	=	–	–	–	–	–	3
Number of instalments for repayment of loans	=	1	1	1	1	1	3
Upper limit on loan in £000s	=	750	300	50	150	25	700

Note: RE, retained earnings; OD, overdrafts; Sl–S4, loan sources 1–4; TC, trade credit per period = £7500.

It can be seen that three contracts are to be started within 6 months and the financial demands are to be analysed over a 24-month period. The results given in Table 8.7 using the above data illustrate the cash flow requirements in the financing of three projects over a 24-month period. Four loan sources were accessed plus trade credit and a bank overdraft. The net present cost of capital is shown at the foot of Table 8.7. Table 8.8 provides the schedule of repayments of interest and capital.

Table 8.7 Cash flow requirements to finance three projects.

Month	Retained earnings (£)	Overdraft (£)	Trade credit (£)	Loan 1 (£)	Loan 2 (£)	Loan 3 (£)	Loan 4 (£)	Loan 5 (£)	Loan 6 (£)	Loan 7 (£)	Loan 8 (£)	Loan 9 (£)
1	0	0	7500	12 408	0	0	0	0	0	0	0	0
2	0	0	7500	18 003	0	0	0	0	0	0	0	0
3	0	0	7500	0	0	18 140	0	0	0	0	0	0
4	0	12 189	7500	19 586	0	6859	0	0	0	0	0	0
5	0	61 779	7500	0	0	0	0	0	0	0	0	0
6	0	0	7500	0	0	0	42 939	0	0	0	0	0
7	0	64 353	7500	0	0	0	0	0	0	0	0	0
8	0	0	7500	0	107 993	0	0	0	0	0	0	0
9	0	0	7500	0	0	0	0	0	0	0	0	0
10	0	108 138	7500	0	0	0	197 760	0	0	0	0	0
11	0	55 277	7500	0	42 007	0	18 592	0	0	0	0	0
12	0	0	7500	0	0	0	0	0	0	0	0	0
13	0	0	7500	0	0	0	0	0	0	0	0	0
14	0	0	7500	0	0	0	0	0	0	0	0	0
15	0	0	7500	0	0	0	0	0	0	0	0	0
16	0	0	7500	0	0	0	0	0	0	0	0	0
17	0	0	7500	0	0	0	0	0	0	0	0	0
18	0	0	7500	0	0	0	0	0	0	0	0	0
19	0	0	7500	0	0	0	0	0	0	0	0	0
20	0	0	7500	0	0	0	0	0	0	0	0	0
21	0	0	7500	0	0	0	0	0	0	0	0	0
22	0	0	7500	0	0	0	0	0	0	0	0	0
23	0	0	7500	0	0	0	0	0	0	0	0	0
24	0	0	7500	0	0	0	0	0	0	0	0	0

Net present cost of finance for the period = £67 210.
Source: Wijeratne and Harris 1984.

Table 8.8 Schedule of repayments.

Month	Retained earnings (£)	Overdraft (£)	Trade credit (£)	Loan 1 (£)	Loan 2 (£)	Loan 3 (£)	Loan 4 (£)	Loan 5 (£)	Loan 6 (£)	Loan 7 (£)	Loan 8 (£)	Loan 9 (£)
1	0	0	0	0	0	0	0	0	0	0	0	0
2	0	0	7500	94	0	0	0	0	0	0	0	0
3	0	0	7500	231	0	0	0	0	0	0	0	0
4	0	0	7500	231	0	131	0	0	0	0	0	0
5	0	88	7500	380	0	180	0	0	0	0	0	0
6	0	533	7500	380	0	180	0	0	0	0	0	0
7	0	533	7500	380	0	180	0	0	0	0	0	0
8	0	997	7500	380	0	180	0	0	0	0	0	0
9	0	997	7500	380	2604	180	1085	0	0	0	0	0
10	0	997	7500	380	0	180	0	0	0	0	0	0
11	0	1776	7500	380	0	180	0	0	0	0	0	0
12	0	2175	7500	12 788	3617	18 320	6084	0	0	0	0	0
13	0	2175	7500	18 288	0	6909	479	0	0	0	0	0
14	0	2175	7500	149	0	0	0	0	0	0	0	0
15	0	2175	7500	19 735	3617	0	6084	0	0	0	0	0
16	0	2175	7500	0	0	0	470	0	0	0	0	0
17	0	2175	7500	0	0	0	0	0	0	0	0	0
18	0	2175	7500	0	3617	0	6084	0	0	0	0	0
19	0	2175	7500	0	0	0	470	0	0	0	0	0
20	0	2175	7500	0	0	0	0	0	0	0	0	0
21	0	2175	7500	0	3617	0	6084	0	0	0	0	0
22	0	2175	7500	0	0	0	470	0	0	0	0	0
23	0	2175	7500	0	0	0	0	0	0	0	0	0
24	0	2175	7500	0	1013	0	20 397	0	0	0	0	0

Source: Wijeratne and Harris (1984).

8.4.2 Earthmoving optimisation using LP

Planners and estimators customarily analyse large-scale earthmoving operations, such as roadworks, dams and so on, by means of the mass-haul diagram, where an assumed knowledge of the costs of transporting the material over the various distances involved is required.

Linear programming provides an alternative approach whereby an earthmoving system can be optimised by comparing alternative fleets (from available fleets) to provide the best material distribution and appropriate plant fleets to complete a project within the specified time. An equation of the following form is derived to optimise the total costs of the operation, subject to various constraints such as operating distance for items of equipment, capacity limits, quantities and so forth.

GENERAL MODEL OPTIMIZING FUNCTION

$$
\begin{aligned}
Min\ Z = & \sum_{i} \sum_{j} \sum_{n \in N_{i,j}} C(i, j, n) \cdot X(i, j, n) \\
& + \sum_{i} \sum_{k} \sum_{n \in N_{i,k}} C_D(i, k, n) \cdot X_D(i, k, n) \\
& + \sum_{p} \sum_{j} \sum_{n \in n_{p,j}} C_B(p, j, n) \cdot X_B(p, j, n) + \sum_{b=1}^{n_b} K_{SB}(b) \cdot Y_{SB}(b) \\
& + \sum_{b=1}^{n_b} \sum_{j} \sum_{n \in N_{b,j}} C_{SB}(b, j, n) \cdot X_{SB}(b, j, n) + \sum_{d=1}^{n_d} K_{SD}(d) \cdot Y_{SD}(d) \\
& + \sum_{i} \sum_{d=1}^{n_d} \sum_{n \in N_{i,d}} C_{SD}(i, d, n) \cdot X_{SD}(i, d, n)
\end{aligned}
$$

where Z is the total earthmoving cost; $C(i, j, n)$ is the unit cost of excavation, haul and compaction of material cut at section i to be filled in section j by fleet n; $X(i, j, n)$ is the quantity of material moved from cut section i to fill j by fleet n; $C_D(i, k, n)$ is the unit cost excavation, haul and disposal of material cut at section i to be disposed at disposal site k by fleet n; $X_D(i, k, n)$ is the quantity of material disposed from cut i to disposal site k by fleet n; $C_B(p, j, n)$ is the unit cost of excavation, haul and compaction of material cut at borrow pit p to be filled in section j by fleet n; $X_B(p, j, n)$ is the quantity of material borrowed from pit p to fill j by fleet n; $K_{SB}(b)$ is the set-up cost of borrow pit b; $Y_{SB}(b)$ is the binary variable for borrow pit b, which equals 1 if it is set up; $C_{SB}(b, j, n)$ is similar to $C_B(p, j, n)$ but for borrow pit b (to be set up); $X_{SB}(b, j, n)$, is similar to $X_B(p, j, n)$, but for borrow pit b (to be set up); $K_{SD}(d)$, $Y_{SD}(d)$, $C_{SD}(i, d, n)$ and $X_{SD}(i, d, n)$ have similar definitions to $K_{SB}(b)$, $Y_{SB}(b)$, $C_{SB}(b, j, n)$ and $X_{SB}(b, j, n)$ but for disposing material from cut section i to disposal site d (to be set up) by fleet n.

The above objective function can be expanded to include variation of soil strata, different degrees of compaction, project finish time and so on – all to a degree of detail generally not possible to analyse manually using other methods. Constraints can also be formulated using similar variables and may involve cut and fill quantities at different sections, capacity limitations of borrow pits and disposal sites and so on.

EXAMPLE

A length of roadway divided into six sections each 500 m long has access to two borrow pits and a disposal site (Figure 8.16). The cut and fill quantities are calculated from the drawing and are shown in Table 8.9. The contractor's available fleet is shown in Table 8.10 and can be used in the combinations given in Table 8.11.

Table 8.9 Cut/fill quantities and capacity limitations of borrow/disposal sites.

(1)	Section/location								
	1 (2)	2 (3)	3 (4)	4 (5)	5 (6)	6 (7)	B1 (8)	B2 (9)	D (10)
(a) Cut									
Strata 1	758	395	–	–	–	650	2500	1500	–
Strata 2	340	–	–	–	–	–	–	–	–
(b) Fill									
Subgrade	–	195	600	100	850	–	–	–	7500

Source: Jayawardane and Harris (1990).

Table 8.10 Equipment specifications.

Model (1)	Description (2)	Number (3)	Identification (4)
CAT 769C	Off highway trucks with 17.3 m³ struck capacity	8	T1–T8
CAT 773B	Off highway trucks with 26.0 m³ struck capacity	8	T9–T16
CAT D4H LGP	Bulldozer with straight blade with 2.17 m³ capacity	1	B1
CAT D6H	Bulldozer with straight blade with 3.35 m³ capacity	1	B2
CAT 980C	Wheel loader with 4.7 m³ bucket capacity	1	L1
CAT 988B	Wheel loader with 6.3 m³ bucket capacity	1	L2
CAT D3B LGP	Bulldozer equipped with push plate	1	B3
CAT 651E	Standard scraper with 24.5 m³ struck capacity	4	S1–S4
CAT 825C	Compactors	3	C1–C3
CAT 14G	Motor graders	2	G1–G2
CAT D4H	Dozer equipped with power angle and tilt blade	2	B4–B5

Source: Jaywardane and Harris (1990).

Table 8.11 Equipment fleet combinations.

Equipment combination (1)	Fleet identification (2)	Suitable haul distance (km) (3)
T1–T4, L1, B1, B4, C1, G1	1	0.40–0.65
T1–T5, L1, B1, B4, C1, G1	2	0.50–1.00
T1–T6, L1, B1, B4, C1, G1	3	0.90–1.50
T1–T6, L1, B1, B4, C1, G1	4	1.25–2.00
T1–T8, L1, B1, B4, C1, G1	5	1.75–2.50
T9–T12, L2, B2, B5, C2, G2	6	0.40–0.70
T9–T13, L2, B2, B5, C2, G2	7	0.60–0.95
T9–T14, L2, B2, B5, C2, G2	8	0.75–1.30
T9–T15, L2, B2, B5, C2, G2	9	1.20–1.80
T9–T16, L2, B2, B5, C2, G2	10	1.70–2.50
S1–S4, B3, C3	11	0.40–0.60

Source: Jayawardane and Harris (1990).

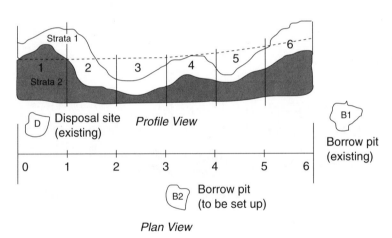

Figure 8.16 Plan and profile views of proposed highway. *Source*: Jayawardane and Harris (1990).

The unit costs, production, swell factor and fleet numbers together with these data were substituted into the appropriate equation in the LP model and solved with a suitable computer package. The optimum material distribution together with fleets used in the optimum solution are given in columns 1 and 4 of Figure 8.17 and depicted in Figure 8.18, where broken and solid lines represent cheaper and more expensive fleets, respectively. The model explored completion time from 10 days to 60 days using the more expensive fleet combinations.

Variable (1)	Quantity (100m³) (2)	Strata (3)	Fleet no. (4)	Duration (days)																	
				1	2	3	4	5	6	7	8	9	10	11	12	13	14	15	16	17	18
X(B1,4)	45.39	S1	4	▓																	
X(2,2)	195.57	S1	11	▓	▓																
X(B1,5)	92.58	S1	3		▓	▓															
X(2,3)	178.33	S1	11				▓	▓	▓												
X(2,2)	21.09	S1	1				▓														
X(B1,5)	201.85	S1	8					▓	▓	▓											
X(1,D)	571.72	S1	1							▓	▓	▓	▓	▓	▓	▓	▓	▓	▓	▓	▓
X(6,5)	650.00	S1	11						▓	▓	▓	▓	▓	▓	▓						
X(1,3)	176.27	S1	8									▓	▓	▓							
X(1,3)	206.74	S2	8												▓	▓	▓	▓			
X(1,4)	59.14	S2	9																▓	▓	
X(1,3)	74.11	S2	2																	▓	▓

Figure 8.17 Optimum material distribution schedule in bar chart form. *Source*: Jayawardane and Harris (1990).

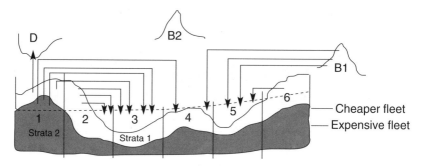

Figure 8.18 Material distribution of example problem. *Source*: Jayawardane and Harris (1990).

8.5 EXAMPLES OF EXPERT SYSTEMS

An expert system (ES) consists of a knowledge base structured logically and stored in a computer. This knowledge can be accessed by the computer program, called the shell, posing a series of questions in everyday English to be answered by the user, typically in the format Yes, No or Don't Know (Figure 8.19).

The program (shell) then locates the applicable rules either by forward or backward chaining through the logic tree and produces a decision giving likely solutions to the problem in hand. In a comprehensive shell program many options may be available, the most useful being an explanation facility to provide reasons behind the analysis, integration with external programs, data sources and so forth.

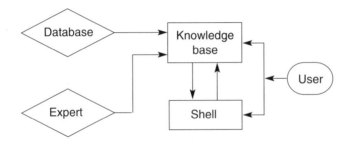

Figure 8.19 Simplified concept of an expert system. *Source*: Wijesundera and Harris (1986).

Other features may include the ability to deal with uncertainty; for example, positive to negative answers to a question can be spread across a range of values, such as +5 to −5, with −5 perhaps being definitely 'no' and +5 definitely 'yes'. Replies in between would lead to different pathways through the analysis. Similarly, probability factors could be included and calculations made on the likely outcome for proceeding through the logic.

KNOWLEDGE ACQUISITION

Designing an ES requires a good understanding of the way decisions are made by practitioners in the particular domain. In many instances 'rules of thumb' feature strongly and need to be interpreted into everyday English and located realistically in the logic tree. An example is shown in Table 8.12 for cranage equipment selection. The best results are generally obtained by building up a sound relationship between the ES designer and the practitioner. However, this relationship will vary with individuals and may require several meetings before suspicion of the interviewee's intentions can be overcome. Eventually a free exchange of information usually evolves. The methods proved suitable are informal conversations, questionnaires, posing examples to the practitioner and observations.

VALIDATION

Absolute validation of the model is generally not possible because of the open-ended nature of the problems usually requiring solutions. However, by a process of trial and error – that is, changing and modifying rules as more information becomes available – the solution can be confirmed or otherwise by the expert or practitioners.

EXAMPLES

Expert systems are constantly being developed as more individuals and enterprises understand the concept and see the advantages. Typical examples under trial by

Table 8.12 'Rules of thumb' example for crane selection.

Classification	Explanation	Tower crane (T/C) type	Mobile crane type
Conventional r/c frame or a mixture of r/c and p/c.	Long and narrow structure or a square floor area. No access to centre.	Tower crane commonly with radius (40 to 50) metres. A travelling T/C on tracks or several T/Cs.	Mobile crane possible with a fly jib capability to reach building. Access roads may be needed at each side of building.
	As above but with the access to the centre possible.	A large radius T/C (dependent on the dimensions of the building) at the centre could provide reach required.	
Tall building with r/c core (slip formed) and r/c or steel frame r/c floor.	Shape generally irrelevant as the crane positioned inside core.	T/C may be used for slip formed core and the floor or only for the construction of the floor. More support of T/C to be considered if free standing height is exceeded.	Height usually rules out the possibility of using mobile cranes.
Physical obstructions.	Other building in the vicinity. Overhead lines, oversailing other property and client-imposed restrictions.	Options: Several small radius T/Cs. Luffing jib T/C. Articulated jib T/C. Use of self erecting T/C where the jib can be lowered at night.	Mobile cranes usually avoided.
	Ground conditions and levels.	Heavy crane or poor ground will require expensive foundations. Sloping ground may preclude the use of travelling T/Cs.	Adequate foundations required for crane stabilising pads.
	Proximity of crane foundations to other buildings and services.	Surcharging of retaining wall, foundations near open excavations and underground services may need careful examination prior to erecting T/Cs.	
	Access for erection and dismantling.	Erection and dismantling of large radius T/Cs demand the use of a 100–200 T mobile crane. These are very expensive to hire and in certain circumstances public roads may also have to be closed.	Generally not a problem for mobile cranes.
Period of use.	Only required for a short period or intermittent use.	Conventional T/C not normally suitable for short durations due to the cost of foundations, erection and dismantling. Self erecting saddle back may be suitable.	Lorry mounted crane with a strut jib or tower and luffing jib configuration.
Safe working load.	Radius and load to be determined.	T/Cs are normally used as general-purpose machines for lifting form work, concrete reinforcement etc.	Mobile cranes do similar duties as T/Cs but are available with much higher capacities. Travelling under load usually avoided. Outreach poor.
	Height.	Free standing height is dependent on the type of base section of the tower, wind effects etc. (1) Strengthen sections to take the height. (2) Tie the building under construction. Care has to be taken to ensure that the structure can withstand the tie forces.	Mobile cranes limited by relatively short jib length.

Source: Wijesundera and Harris (1986).

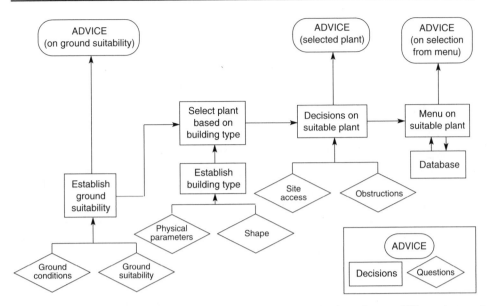

Figure 8.20 Expert system example flow chart for crane selection. *Source*: Wijesundera and Harris (1986).

construction industry users include (i) cranage selection (Figures 8.20 and 8.21), (ii) claims analysis (Figures 8.22–8.23) and (iii) earthmoving equipment selection (Figures 8.24 and 8.25; Tables 8.12–8.15).

While textbooks and other published material can provide important and valuable information, they rarely contain heuristic knowledge, thereby limiting the ability to understand real and dynamic problems. ES to some extent overcomes this disadvantage. Furthermore, the knowledge of practitioners is recorded and therefore available for others to improve upon, augment and so forth.

Furthermore as computer technology and programs are improved, development of more versatile systems may become possible, with CAD, 3D graphics and virtual reality software in particular offering potential benefit in the analysis of construction problems such as site layout planning, activity sequencing etc. Finally and importantly, the knowledge of practitioners is permanently recorded in an Expert System and therefore available for others to improve upon, augment and modify as new experience is gained.

. . . . . WELCOME TO CONPLANT . . . . .

The expert system for plant selection in multi storey construction

Can you tell me whether you are familiar with CONPLANT
(Y..:..N or an option) Y
You seem to have used CONPLANT before. Remember the help facility can be invoked
by pressing 'h' if you get stuck.
   We shall now start the consultation on plant selection.
I am now trying to find the suitability of the ground to take the loading of equipment. The
questions presented to you are intended to find out:
   — the internal structure of the soil
   — external factors affecting the soil....
(I am currently trying to find out the ground conditions in relation to its......soil properties
   The ground conditions of the site have to be investigated to find out if the ground can
take the loading of heavy equipment.
   If you are in an office and have not visited the site it may be difficult to answer this
question. Try to get details of the soil investigation which might help you to answer this question.
   Does the ground consist of:
      1) — soil or
      2) — thin soil bed overlaying rock bed
   enter a number and remember that an answer '!' shall be taken as unknown
(1..2. : if not known or an option) 1
(I am currently trying to find out the ground conditions in relation to its .... soil properties
   The soil bed can be of four types, and the characteristics of each layer will affect the
foundations required for plant. Can you tell me the soil description of your site. A soil classification
chart is provided with this question.
   Enter your choice:
      1) gravel
      2) sand
      3) silt
      4) clay
Do you want to see more (Y,N) ? N
(1..4. : if not known or an option) 1
(I am currently trying to find out the ground conditions in relation to its .... soil properties
   When a site is located in built up areas it is quite common to have open excavations
protected and unprotected which may have been unforeseen during feasibility studies. It is
important for me to check on this before advising on plant to be used. Can you tell me whether
there are such open excavations outside the site boundary.
   Answer:
      −5 if there are unprotected excavations
      −3 if there are partially protected excavations
       0 if you are uncertain
      +3 if there are excavations but protected
      +5 if there are no excavations around site.
(−5..0..5 or an option) 3
   Now I have completed the questions on ground conditions. Do you wish to see a
sub-report or simply carry on with the consultation.
   Please enter your choice:
      1 — to see the report
      2 — to carry on with the consultation
(1..2 or an option) 1
The report is:—
   The evaluation of the ground condition is now complete and my assessment is that....
   The ground should be able to take the load of heavy plant.

Figure 8.21 Crane selection dialogue by CONPLANT expert system. *Source*: Wijersundera
and Harris (1986).

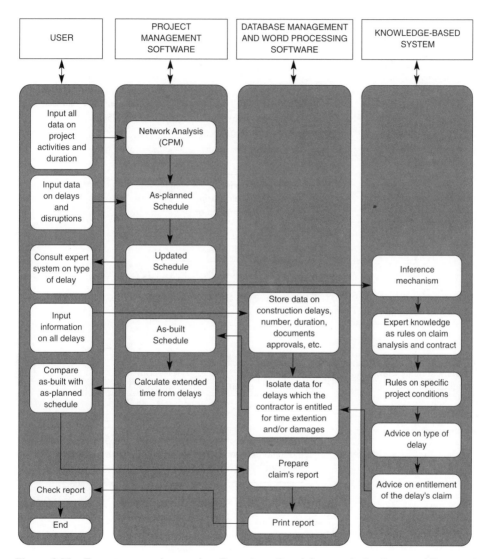

Figure 8.22 Expert system integration flow chart for claims analysis. *Source*: Alkass and Harris (1991a).

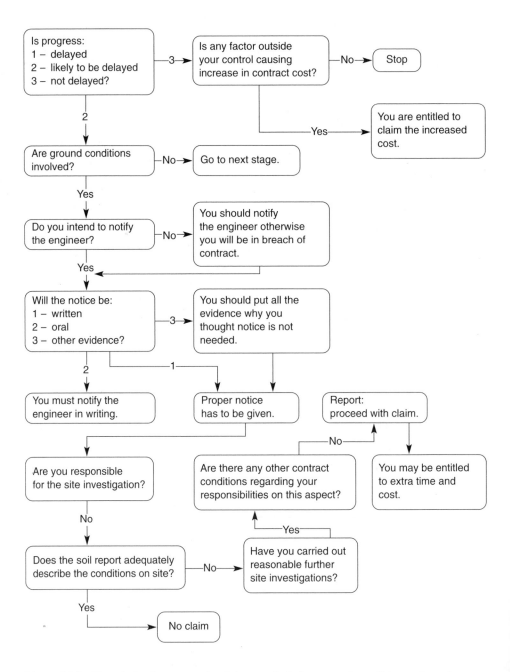

Figure 8.23 Knowledge base route in claims analysis for ground conditions where the progress is likely to be delayed. *Source*: Alkass and Harris (1991a).

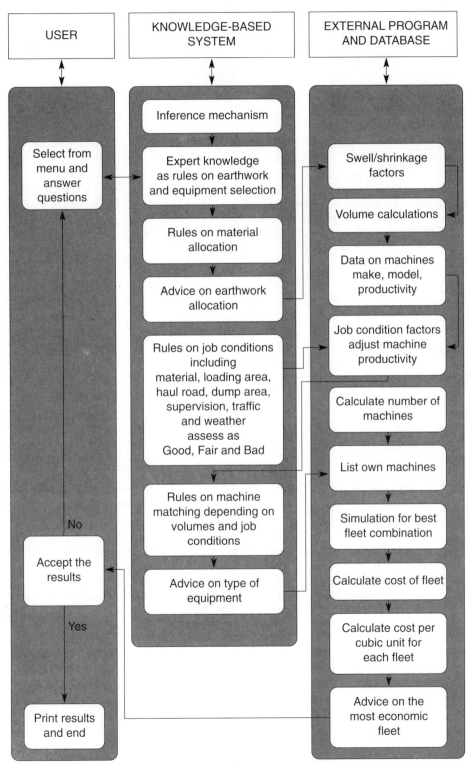

Figure 8.24 Expert system integration flow chart for earthmoving equipment selection. *Source*: Alkass and Harris (1991b).

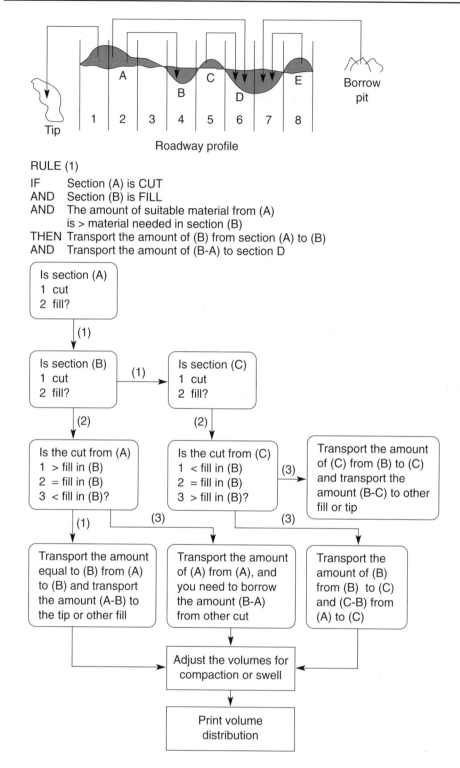

RULE (1)

IF   Section (A) is CUT
AND Section (B) is FILL
AND The amount of suitable material from (A)
         is > material needed in section (B)
THEN Transport the amount of (B) from section (A) to (B)
AND Transport the amount of (B-A) to section D

Figure 8.25 Rules for earthwork allocation. *Source*: Alkass and Harris (1991b).

Table 8.13 Material allocation from cut sections.

Do you want to view the material ALLOCATION between CUT and FILL sections in:
(1) All in a TABLE form?
(2) Each section individually (1. .2, 1 if not known or an option) 1

You need to transfer the amount of material from CUT SECTIONS to FILL SECTIONS as shown below:

Section no:	Amount (cubic metres)	Amount transported	To section
1	139 066		
		21 579	2
		117 487	4
3	8111		
		8111	4
5	0		
7	136 552		
		136 552	6
9	0		
11	161 385		
		61 421	10
		56 422	3
		43 542	6
13	315 105		
		21 295	14
		282 834	12
		10 974	16
15	608		
		608	16

Source: Alkass and Harris (1991b).

Table 8.14 Type of equipment suggested by the system.

To transport material from:

SECTION 1 to SECTION 2   SECTION 13 to SECTION 14
SECTION 3 to SECTION 4   SECTION 13 to SECTION 12
SECTION 7 to SECTION 6   SECTION 13 to SECTION 16
SECTION 11 to SECTION 10   SECTION 15 to SECTION 16

*** Single engine conventional SCRAPER is recommended.

   Because the task is mass excavation, material size is between 12 and 18 inches, the soil moisture is less than 30%, THE HAUL DISTANCE IS LESS THAN ONE KILOMETRE, the grade when empty is less than 12% and job conditions are good. If any of these assumptions are wrong please run the program again.

To transport material from:

SECTION 1 to SECTION 4
SECTION 11 to SECTION 8
SECTION 11 to SECTION 6

***Hydraulic EXCAVATOR and DUMP TRUCKS are recommended.

   Because the task is mass excavation, material size is between 12 and 18 inches, the soil moisture is less than 30%, THE HAUL DISTANCE IS MORE THAN ONE KILOMETRE, the grade when empty is less than 12% and job conditions are good. If any of these assumptions are wrong please run the program again.

Source: Alkass and Harris (1991b).

Table 8.15 Material allocation, equipment selection and durations suggested by the system.

Section no.	Amount (cubic metres)	Amount transported (cubic metres)	To section	Haul distances (metres)	Equipment type	No.	Time (days)
1	139 066	21 579	2	705	(a) Single engined scraper 16 cm	4	50
					(b) Single engined scraper 24 cm	2	50
		117 487	4	1905	Hyd. excavator and 24 cm trucks	2 13	50
3	8111	8111	4	695	(a) Single engined scraper 16 cm	4	10
					(b) Single engined scraper 24 cm	2	10
5	0						
7	136 552	136 552	6	750	(a) Single engined scraper 16 cm	10	50
					(b) Single engined scraper 24 cm	6	50
9	0						
11	161 385	61 421	10	598	(a) Single engined scraper 16 cm	4	14
					(b) Single engined scraper 24 cm	2	14
		56 422	8	1198	Hyd. excavator and 20 cm trucks	1 4	14 14
		43 542	6	2714	Hyd. excavator and 20 cm trucks	1 8	14 14
13	315 103	21 295	14	600	(a) Single engined scraper 16 cm	5	14
					(b) Single engined scraper 24 cm	2	14
		282 834	12	780	(a) Single engined scraper 16 cm	6	120
					(b) Single engined scraper 16 cm	10	90
					(c) Single engined scraper 24 cm	10	70
		10 974	16	1585	(a) Single engined scraper 16 cm	6	10
					(b) Single engined scraper 24 cm	4	10
15	608	608	16	638	Single engined scraper 16 cm	3	3

Source: Alkass and Harris (1991b).

8.6 OTHER OPTIMISATION MODELS

8.6.1 Bankruptcy prediction

The construction industry suffers more failures than any other sector of industry. While accountants have developed some measures to monitor financial performance of companies, such as balance sheet and profit and loss account information for application in ratio analysis, a robust general model has not been available. Multivariate discriminant analysis (MVDA) provides a useful statistical method of addressing this problem by producing a Z score value of performance for a particular company, which can then be compared to values for failed and solvent companies.

Z SCORE ANALYSIS

The model is constructed from a number of discriminating variables derived from published accounts which reflect the characteristics of solvent and failed firms. The data are mathematically combined using the MVDA technique to produce a single value at the point of separation of the two groups of companies along a scale of solvency (Figure 8.26). The function is of the form:

$$Z = C_0 + C_1 R_1 + \cdots + C_n R_n$$

Using recent data for 20 solvent and 11 failed companies, the following model has been developed using the concept in Table 8.16.

$$Z = 14.6 + 82V_1 - 14.5V_2 + 2.5V_3 - 1.2V_4 + 3.55V_5 - 3.55V_6 - 3V_7$$

V_1 is the ratio of earnings after tax and interest charge to net capital employed, V_2 is the ratio of current assets to net assets, V_3 is the ratio of turnover to net assets, V_4 is the ratio of short-term loans to earnings before tax and interest charges, V_5 is the tax trend, V_6 is earnings after tax and V_7 is the short-term loan trend. A Z value of approximately zero denotes the separation of the two groups.

The model was also developed using data up to four years prior to failure to produce a trend path to insolvency as an aid in identifying companies at risk (Figure 8.27, Table 8.17). Remedial action can then, hopefully, be instituted in good time.

8.6.2 Evaluating the performance of designers and contractors

The important factors affecting the outcome of construction projects are manifold and might typically be represented by the different attributes of the design firms and contractors involved. Some are likely to be more significant than others, resulting in some projects being finished to time and cost with better quality than others. By separating out the two categories of performance, for example, good and bad, multivariate discriminant analysis can be used to develop a Z function of attribute values similar to that described in bankruptcy prediction. In this manner potential performance on a particular project could be predicted from a knowledge of the attributes of the firms involved. Results from a pilot research study indicate that a Z score can be statistically determined with confidence using a function involving the following six important variables:

- V_1: complexity of the project
- V_2: quality of the management team, professional qualifications
- V_3: project leader's experience
- V_4: contractor's past performance
- V_5: origin of the contractor – local or national
- V_6: supervision and control by architects/engineers or clients of the quality and progress of the work.

A function derived from 40 sample projects of the type given below produced a good indication of performance.

$$Z = -1.14 - 0.56V_1 + 11.9V_2 + 0.095V_3 + 1.78V_4 + 0.82V_5 + 1.04V_6$$

A further five variables were shown to be significantly influential in a unidimensional scaling model, namely (i) staff training programme, (ii) contractors' experience in the

Figure 8.26 Histogram of Z scores of failed and solvent companies. *Source*: Mason and Harris (1979).

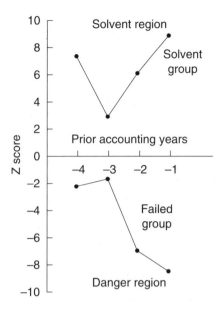

Figure 8.27 The path to failure. *Source*: Mason and Harris (1979).

type of job, (iii) listing on the stock market, (iv) decision making centralised or decentralised from head office, and (v) architects'/engineers' past performance.

8.6.3 A database/spreadsheet application for equipment selection

As an aid to equipment selection, adoption of the Kepner and Tregoe method can be of value. The procedure involves identifying and ranking the desirable features of a piece of equipment, then subsequently rating alternative makes against the features to provide a weighted score of each for comparison purposes. The analysis can be carried out on a computer by assembling elements such as machine performance and quality, costs and prices and so on in a computer file and subsequently performing the selection process on each alternative machine with a spreadsheet.

Table 8.16 Classification of solvent and failed companies.

Group	Percentage classified by the model as failed	Percentage classified by the model as solvent
Failed	100	0
Solvent	0	100

Source: Mason and Harris (1979).

Table 8.17 Prior year's classification for 31 failed firms.

	Prior accounting year			
	−4	−3	−2	Last
Percentage classified as failed	58	55	68	87

Source: Mason and Harris (1979).

EXAMPLE

A site manager decides that a loader–excavator is required to carry out a trench-digging task along a public road for drain-laying and also to unload the pipes when delivered and backfill after the operation. On advice from the company accountant and purchasing officer a new purchase has been justified on the basis of rate of return calculations. The task is now to select the best buy from many similar alternatives.

The manager insists that the following criteria *must* be obtainable:

(1) Total unit weight must be under 9000 kg.
(2) A road travel speed of at least 28 kph is required.
(3) The trench is 3.5 m deep and hence the excavator arm must be capable of reaching 4 m deep.
(4) To unload from a truck, the load-over height must be at least 3.5 m.
(5) The excavating arm must be able to achieve an offset of at least 630 mm to operate along the line of the road without holding up traffic.
(6) To achieve the desired productivity, a bucket capacity of at least 0.22 m^3 is required.
(7) The excavating arm must be able to turn 180° or more to tip material by the side of the trench.
(8) A breakout force of at least 4000 kgf is needed to dig the compact material.
(9) A loader shovel reach of at least 0.9 m is required to facilitate easy positioning while backfilling.

THE COMPUTER PROGRAM

The program draws on data held on file (Table 8.18 shows an extract for several different makes of machine) and the analysis of selection is performed interactively by the user following the series of steps given below.

(1) *Introduction:* a series of self-explanatory instructions are shown on the screen on how the criteria entry form should be filled in.
(2) *Open database:* the complete loader–excavator database file is retrieved and the criteria entry form created.
(3) *Enter criteria:* the program halts to let the user fill in the criteria for selection. For example, the 'want' objectives shown in Table 8.19 were chosen for the backhoe.
(4) *Criteria correct?:* the user now has a choice to proceed, re-enter the criteria or

exit from the system through a menu in the control panel. Instructions are entered by means of a window occupying a limited area on the screen.

(5) *Matching:* the matching procedure is a standard function in the software which seeks out the records (that is, machine details) in the database that fit the criteria.

(6) *List possible choices:* the user, at this point, can choose to view the preliminary choices in: (i) the sheet environment where the choices are highlighted in a list of all records similar in format to Table 8.18 or (ii) the form environment where the choices are viewed individually in their record entry forms, or the user can proceed straight to step 9 (analysis). Any machines not complying with the criteria are eliminated at this stage and the offending information highlighted.

(7) *Continue:* after viewing the alternatives, the user either proceeds to the next step, enters new criteria back into step 3 (especially when no matching records are found) or exits the system (for example, halt the system to allow the user to change ranking and rating entries when only one match is found). The user is then given brief instructions on how to carry out Kepner and Tregoe analysis.

Table 8.18   Database extracts of records and fields.

Manufacturer	Model	Engine	Flywheel (kW)	Governed RPM	Front tyre size	Rear tyre size
A	BEN 2000 PSB UniDT	Perkins 4248	61	2500	13.0×24	13.0×24
A	BEN 2000 PSB Un2RM	Perkins 4248	61	2500	11.0×16	15.5×25
A	BEN 1800	Deutz F4L912	60	2800	9.0×20	16.9×30
A	BEN 1900	Deutz F4L912	60	2800	9.0×20	16.9×30
B	10 534	Fiat 8061	81	2400	12.5×18 16pr	17.5×25
B	7531	Fiat 8045	58	2500	12.0×18 12pr	14.9×28 10pr
B	9531	Fiat 8051	53	2400	12.0×18 12pr	15.5×25
B	8531	Fiat 8041	53	2400	12.0×18 12pr	15.5×25
B	1.35 Artic	Fiat 8041	51	2300	16.5×20	16.5×20
B	1.25 Artic	Fiat 8031	41	2400	14.5×20	14.5×20
B	1.15 Artic	Fiat 8035	34	2600	12.5×18	12.5×18
B	1.05 Artic	Fiat 2.5	24	2100	10.5×18	10.5×18
C	655 4WD	Ford Diesel	57.4	2400	10.5×18 10ply	16.9/14×28 10ply
C	655	Ford Diesel	57.4	2400	9.0×16 10ply	16.9/14×28 10ply
C	555 4WD	Ford Diesel	50.3	2400	10.5×18 8ply	14.28 10ply R1
C	555	Ford Diesel	50.3	2400	9.0×16 10ply 3r	14×28 10ply R1
D	56F4	Ford 3-cycl. Diesel	44	2200	9.0×16 10ply 3r	14×28 8ply
E	Centremount	4C Turbo	61	2000	10.5×18 12pr	18.4×26 12pr
E	3CCX 4WD	Perkins	56	2000	10.5−18 10pr	18.4−26 12pr
E	3CX	Perkins	56	2000	10.5−18 10pr	18.4−26 12pr
E	3D	Perkins	54	2000	10.5−18 10pr	18.4−26 8pr
E	3CC	Perkins	54	2000	9.0×16 10pr	16.9×28 pr

Source: Chan and Harris (1989).

(8) *Read choices to spreadsheet (Table 8.19):* the program now prepares a table on the screen for the subsequent ranking of the 'want' criteria and rating of a viable model (that is, Kepner and Tregoe analysis) with the headings: 'want' criteria, ranking, model information, rating and weighted score. The field names in the database input at step 3 are then copied to the column under 'want' criteria and the user is asked to fill in the ranking column.

(9) *Analysis:* thereafter all the information needed for analysis is copied to the corresponding model information column and the user rates the models' performance against each 'want'. The weighted score is automatically worked out, as the multiple of the ranking and rating values; the total score is calculated and recorded in a blank area of the work sheet. While ranking and rating are being executed, the headings are held on the screen even when the columns are scrolling. This helps to maintain a clear order of the worksheet for the user's convenience.

(10) *Any more alternatives?:* the alternatives are analysed one at a time until all have been examined. However, the program can be halted to allow the user to change ranking and rating entries.

(11) *Compare totals:* after each new total score is obtained, it is compared to the previous one. If it is greater, it replaces the old one, otherwise the previous one is retained in memory. A hard copy of the analysis sheet is automatically made after each model for record and later reference.

(12) *Suggest best choice:* when all possible choices have been analysed, the make and model of the choice with the highest score is suggested as the most suitable choice from the database for the criteria entered.

(13) *End:* after making a note of the choice, the user can exit the system. The completed analysis is shown in Table 8.19, resulting in the best choice machine 3CX.

FURTHER POINTS ON THE METHOD OF ANALYSIS

To fully benefit from a systematic selection approach, the top few alternatives should always be investigated further to include economic criteria, manufacturers' current status, services and discounts. If possible, site tests and demonstrations should also be arranged to investigate the suitability of the alternative with reference to compatibility, robustness, ergonomics and standard accessories, including opinions of operators, associated staff and the maintenance team. Many of these can, of course, be included in the computer analysis.

Finally, the consideration of adverse consequences resulting from the analysis must not be overlooked. Experience indicates that this phase is best left for subjective evaluation outside the computerised system.

8.6.4 A model for determining optimum crane position

The consideration of site layout from an operational point of view is an indivisible part of construction planning, as the physical factors of a site often have a direct

Table 8.19 Plant selection analyses for (a) 9531 model and (b) 3CX model.

'Want' criteria	Ranking of 'wants'	Model information	Rating of model performance	Weighted score (=ranking and rating)
(a)				
Manufacturer	6	B	6	36
Model	–	9531	–	–
Engine	5	Fiat 8051	7	35
Flywheel (kW)	7	53	5	35
Governed RPM	5	2400	6	30
Front tyre size	5	12.00×18 12pr	5	25
Rear tyre size	5	15.5×25 12pr	5	25
Number of driven wheels	8	4	9	72
Ground clearance (mm)	7	240	7	49
Total unit weight (kg)	10	8000	8	80
Road travel speed (kph)	10	29.5	7	70
Turn radius (m)	8	7.2	5	40
Hydraulic pump output (lpm)	8	128	5	40
Hydraulic system pressure (log p cm^2)	8	150	5	40
Backhoe				
Digging depth (m)	10	4.1	2	20
Load over height (m)	10	3.5	5	50
Reach at ground (m)	8	6	9	72
Bucket capacity (m^3)	10	0.3	7	70
Bucket rotation (deg)	5	190	9	45
Slewing arc (deg)	10	180 (just)	7	70
Max. offset (mm)	10	795	9	90
Max. digging force (kgf)	10	5800	9	90
Shovel				
Lift capacity to (kg)	4	2000	6	24
Bucket capacity (m^3)	6	1.05	8	48
Discharge height (m)	10	2.9	6	60
Forward reach (m)	10	1.2	7	70
Dump angle (deg)	3	45	4	12
Crowd angle (deg)	3	41	5	15
Max. breakout force (kgf)	5	7000	9	45
Special feature 1	1	N/A		0
Special feature 2	1	N/A		0
Special feature 3	1	N/A		0
				1358
(b)				
Manufacturer	6	C	8	48
Model	–	3CX	–	–
Engine	5	Perkins	7	35
Flywheel (kW)	7	56	8	56
Governed RPM	5	2000	5	25
Front tyre size	5	10.5–18 10pr	6	30
Rear tyre size	5	18.4–26 12pr	6	30
Number of driven wheels	8	2	5	40
Ground clearance (mm)	7	280	8	56

Table 8.19 — *continued*

'Want' criteria	Ranking of 'wants'	Model information	Rating of model performance	Weighted score (=ranking and rating)
Total unit weight (kg)	10	7160	10	100
Road travel speed (kph)	10	31.3	9	90
Turn radius (m)	8	4.95	8	64
Hydraulic pump output (lpm)	8	109	4	32
Hydraulic system pressure (kgpcm^2)	8	207	6	48
Backhoe				
Digging depth (m)	10	4.67	6	60
Load over height (m)	10	4.06	6	60
Reach at ground (m)	8	5.29	7	56
Bucket capacity (m^3)	10	0.3	7	70
Bucket rotation (deg)	5	201	9	45
Slewing arc (deg)	10	180	9	90
Max. offset (mm)	10	630	5	50
Max. digging force (kgf)	10	4437	6	60
Shovel				
Lift capacity to (kg)	4	2219	7	28
Bucket capacity (m^3)	6	0.9	7	42
Discharge height (m)	10	2.67	4	40
Forward reach (m)	10	1.56	9	90
Dump angle (deg)	3	53	5	15
Crowd angle (deg)	3	45	5	15
Max. breakout force (kgf)	5	4267	4	20
Special feature 1	1	Extending option	5	5
Special feature 2	1	6 in 1 bucket	9	9
Special feature 3	1	ROPS/FOPS cab	8	8
				1417

Source: Chan and Harris (1989).

bearing on the method, sequence and duration of every site activity. Tower crane location in particular is critically important in this respect, and can be mathematically modelled to determine the most suitable position, by minimising transport costs in terms of crane operating time with respect to positions requiring crane services.

THE MODEL

When a crane operates, its hook has to move to and from the facilities. For movement between two points (Figure 8.28), the travel time associated with the movement is the maximum of:

(1) $\quad \dfrac{\text{Radial distance travelled}}{\text{Radial velocity}} = \dfrac{(r_1 - r_2)}{\text{CRV}}$

(2) $\quad \dfrac{\text{Angular distance travelled}}{\text{Angular velocity}} = \dfrac{A(\theta\theta_j)}{\text{CRV}}$

As the angular movement can be carried out in either the clockwise or anti-clockwise direction the angular travel time movement can be given mathematically as:

$$\max\left(\frac{A(\theta\theta_j)}{\text{CAV}}, \frac{(r_1 - r_2)}{\text{CRV}}\right)$$

In order to determine the total frequency of movement between two facilities, the total amount of load to be lifted and the average size of load are required.

EXAMPLE

The construction of a building (Figure 8.29) involves four facilities: form work workshop, steel yard, lifting platform and the building. The average economic lifts of steel and form work are 2 T and 1 T, respectively, and quantities and frequencies of movement are as follows:

Form work workshop (Fl) to building (F3)	100 T/1 T	= 100 times
Lifting platform (F2) to building (F3)	500 T/1 T	= 500 times
Lifting platform (F2) to form work workshop (F1)	100 T/1 T	= 100 times
Steel yard (F4) to building (F3)	1000 T/2 T	= 500 times

The weightings of movement frequencies are thus:

Origin and destination	Frequency	Interfacilities weighting (ITFW) (%)
F1 to F3	100	8.3
F2 to F3	500	41.7
F2 to F1	100	8.3
F4 to F3	500	41.7
Total		100.0

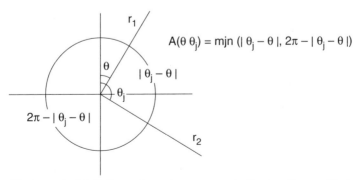

$A(\theta\,\theta_j) = \mathrm{mjn}\,(|\,\theta_j - \theta\,|,\, 2\pi - |\,\theta_j - \theta\,|)$

Figure 8.28 Mathematical definition of angular movement of crane. *Source*: Choi and Harris (1990).

Since every lifting movement requires a return move for reloading, the total transportation time is:

$$2\left[\sum_{i=1}^{n}\sum_{j=1}^{n} \text{ITFW}_{ij} \times \max\left(\frac{A(\theta_i\theta_j)}{\text{CAV}}, \frac{(r_i - r_j)}{\text{CRV}}\right)\right]$$

where i represents origin and j represents destination.

CASE STUDY

This equation is used in analysing the site layout shown in Figure 8.30. Seven facilities are involved requiring lifting capacities as follows:

Concrete (including skip)	1.25 T
Steel reinforcement	2.2 T
Form work	1.0 T
Sundry items	1.0 T

The frequencies of interfacility movements (Figure 8.31) are given in Table 8.20 and the weightings in Table 8.21. Four possible crane positions were investigated based on practitioner advice (Figure 8.30), which produced the transportation costs given in Table 8.22. Position C3 is the optimal position.

The model could be further developed to embrace three-dimensional considerations, for application in high-rise construction. Also, the inclusion of more than one crane and the effects of interaction would be of interest to planners.

8.6.5 Equipment selection by computer graphics

Excavating equipment, cranes and similar machines are generally selected by 'rule of thumb' methods (Table 8.23) or outline sketches prepared where precise checks are needed in assessing clearance dimensions, safe working loads, reach and so forth.

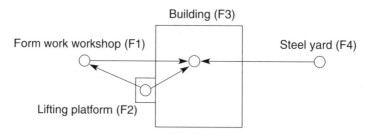

Figure 8.29 Facilities involved in construction of building. *Source*: Choi and Harris (1990).

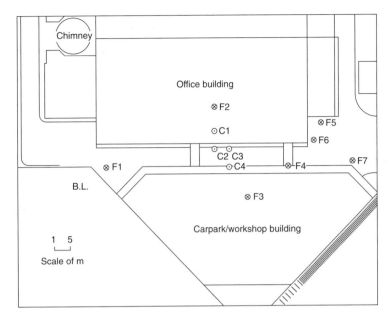

Figure 8.30 Four possible crane positions (C1–C4). *Source*: Choi and Harris (1990).

Increasingly, however, computer software, particularly computer aided drafting packages, are being developed to assist the process. As an aid to demonstrating the potential of computer aided drafting a bespoke computer program was written to evaluate the on-site configuration of a backhoe used on specific trench excavating tasks.

THE MODEL

The model selects the appropriate machine from a file of alternatives, containing machine specification details. The computer program uses stored information on the trench excavation dimensions, type of soil, ground conditions and total volume of work with associated details such as bulking factor, angle of soil repose, operating factors for angle of swing, machine type for task in hand and so on, together with the required rate of production. A search is then made in the machine file for a unit of sufficient size to satisfy the parameters of the job. The selection is subsequently represented graphically (Figure 8.32) and the boom, arm and bucket movements drawn from enveloping curves stored for the particular machine (that is, the curves provided in manufacturers' catalogues and encaptured by means of a digitiser. Alternatively, an algorithm can be derived to reproduce an approximation of the curve trace).

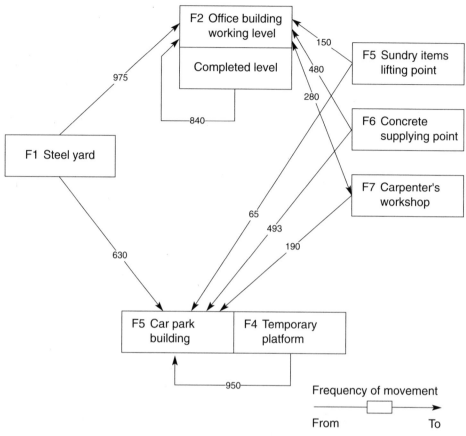

Figure 8.31 Activity relationship diagram. *Source*: Choi and Harris (1990).

Table 8.20 Frequencies of interfacility movements.

To	F1	F2	F3	From F4	F5	F6	F7
F1							
F2	975				150	480	280
F3	630			950	65	493	190
F4							
F5							
F6							
F7		280	290				

Source: Choi and Harris (1990).

Table 8.21 Reduced interfacility weightings.

To	F1(%)	F2(%)	F3(%)	F4(%)	F5(%)	F6(%)	F7(%)	Total(%)
				From				
F1								
F2	21				3	10	6	40
F3	14			20	1	11	4	50
F4								
F5								
F6								
F7		6	4					

Source: Choi and Harris (1990).

SELECTION RULE

Matching of the curve and trench configuration is considered acceptable if the machine is able to be moved along the line of the excavation in 2 m steps (shorter distances involve too many moves for practical purposes).

Much of the data, particularly on the equipment specifications, is already available from manufacturers and could in theory be provided on computer disks. Other information, such as machine performance in specific soils and job conditions, would have to be obtained from work study or similar methods. Finally, as standard drafting software continues to be improved the kind of graphical analysis described using bespoke software could become a more commonplace feature.

8.7 COMPUTERISED COLLECTION OF WORK STUDY DATA

Numerous investigations have shown that on average about 50% of the working day is lost on construction sites, with only about a quarter of firms achieving the practical optimum of about 80% maximum production. A significant proportion of this lost time can be allocated to ineffective management and shoddy work, where typically equipment breakdowns, redoing work, and workers taking extended breaks and moving about can account for up to 90% of lost time.

The common work study techniques such as method study, activity sampling and work measurement, discussed previously, can be adapted to pinpoint specific problems. As a 'rule of thumb', improvements of about 10% increase in production can on average be demonstrated. The remainder generally relates to ineffective management. However, the vagaries of construction work associated with open sites, inclement weather, one-off activities and gang-based working practices have made the collection of work study data very difficult and prone to mis-recording. Computerising the process can eliminate much error and also facilitate the transfer of data between different forms of software, such as planning, estimating, quantity surveying and cost control packages. Indeed, a reliable source of such data should provide the foundation of good planning and estimating from which firm monitoring and managerial control ought ultimately to lead to improved efficiency.

Table 8.22 Results of case study.

Project title=Ap Lei Chau power station
Crane selected=BPR GT 217B2

(1) Jib length (m)=50	(3) Angular velocity (deg min)=360
(2) Under hook height (m)=50	(4) Radial velocity (m/min)=30

Facility	1	2	3	4
(1) Title	Steel yard	Office	Carpark	Platform
(2) Co-ord. X (m)	28	63	74	88
Y (m)	44	63	34	44
(3) Weighting of positive movement	34	6	4	20
(4) Average load to be lifted	2	2	2	1

Facility	5	6	7
(1) Title	Sundries	Concrete	Carpentry
(2) Co-ord. X (m)	98	96	108
Y (m)	58	52	46
(3) Weighting of positive movement	5	21	10
(4) Average load to be lifted	1	1.5	1

Interfacility weighting

1−2 = 21	3−4 = 20
1−3 = 14	3−5 = 1
1−4 = 0	3−6 = 11
1−5 = 0	3−7 = 8
1−6 = 0	4−5 = 0
1−7 = 0	4−6 = 0
2−3 = 0	4−7 = 0
2−4 = 0	5−6 = 0
2−5 = 3	5−7 = 0
2−6 = 10	6−7 = 0
2−7 = 12	

	Crane positions		*Transportation cost*
X	Y		Total
68	49	C3	119.8894
68	43	C4	122.2651
63	49	C2	123.5516
63	55	C1	129.8307

Source: Choi and Harris (1990).

COMPUTER METHODS

The system basically comprises a hand-held portable computer which can later be connected to more sophisticated equipment. The device typically requires the following features:

Table 8.23 Equipment selection by rule of thumb.

Application	Machine type
(1) All ground conditions except on finished surfaces	Tracked hydraulic backhoe excavator Maximum dig depth 26 metres Bucket capacity 0.05–33 m^3
(2) Good ground and weather conditions and wherever frequent movement of machine is needed	Wheeled hydraulic excavator Dig depth up to 7.8 m Bucket capacity 0.05–1.7 m^3
(3) Excavation of shallow trenches	Small hydraulic excavator Tracked: dig depth up to 4 m Bucket capacity 0.03–0.37 m^3 Wheeled: dig depth up to 3.5 m Bucket capacity 0.05–0.67 m^3
(4) Good ground and weather conditions and also for material transport, quick filling	Digger loader centre post type Dig depth up to 6.1 m Bucket capacity 0.05–0.67 m^3
(5) Where trenches are adjoining buildings	Digger loader offset type Dig depth up to 4.7 m Bucket capacity 0.06–0.4 m^3

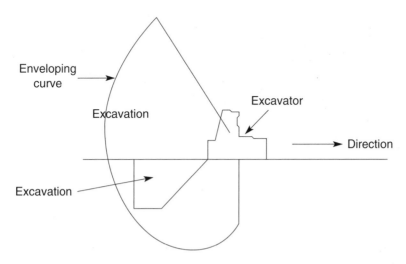

Figure 8.32 Equipment envelope for selection by computer graphics. *Source*: Kirupanather and Harris (1986).

(1) Rechargeable battery with at least 20 hours operating time.
(2) Internal clock to prompt the user and record the beginning and end of recorded events.
(3) Built-in LCD display to assist the user in inputting the required information for recording.
(4) Micro-cassette tape or disk to store the program and recorded data.
(5) Random access memory (RAM) which maintains data on file even when the machine is switched off.
(6) Interfacing with a printer and other peripheral devices.

ACTIVITY SAMPLING PROGRAM

The computer program simply reflects the procedures and data collection processes normally carried out in the manual method of activity sampling, as shown in Figure 8.33. Each element of activity and work-piece coding must be pre-input because of the need to record instantly the work in progress. Typing in long descriptions would clearly be impractical. Examples of the common activities and their respective code numbers are shown in Figure 8.34. The work-piece codes are used to identify the particular work-pieces being worked on.

The Activity Sampling Program
The Activity Sampling Program is based on a series of menus which allow the user to select one of the options available at any one time

---

Data (use format 12-12-83)? **10-7-84**
Weather? **SUNNY BUT COLD**
Site description? **LEISURE CENTRE**
Location? **WOLVERHAMPTON**
Main contractor? **SCORPION CONSTRUCTION**
Sub-contractor? **MERILLION LTD.**
Job description? **STRUCTURAL STEEL ERECTION**
Any other comments? **NO**

Activity Sampling Program Site Details

Enter details when prompted.
Use 'E' to exit from system
Details must NOT exceed 20 characters.
Do NOT use commas.
Details
Man 1
Details? **Foreman steel erector**

Figure 8.33 Activity sampling program, entering of operative details. *Source*: Emsley and Harris (1986).

1. Break	12. Carry
2. Away	13. Search
3. Walk	14. Instruction (look at drawings)
4. Talk (discuss)	15. Redo work
5. Recover	16. Act as banksman
6. Wait (external inference)	17. Fasten/unfasten chains
7. General	18. Guide piece with hand/rope
8. Other work	19. Move up and down ladder
9. Interference (internal)	12. Position and bolt
10. Prepare work area	21. Final tightening of bolts
11. Clear up	

Example of Activity Code Details Structural Steel Erectors

Time 13:16:23 **1**

Man 1
Details foreman steel erector
Activity code? **3**
Work-piece code? **2**
Rate? **100**

Man 2
Details steel erector
Activity code? **18**
Work-piece code? **2**
Rate? **100**

Figure 8.34 Activity sampling program prompts to enter activity sampling data. *Source*: Emsley and Harris (1986).

The Time Study Program
The Time Study Program follows similar principles to the Activity Sampling program and is again based on a series of menus.

Machine type 1? **Lorry**
Lorry details

Lorry 1
Details? **123**

Lorry 2
Details? **133**

Lorry 3
Details **E**

Machine type 2? **Excavator**
Excavator details

Excavator 1
Details? **Demag**

Figure 8.35 Time study program, entering of machine details. *Source*: Emsley and Harris (1986).

TIME STUDY PROGRAM

The time study program follows similar principles to the activity sampling program as indicated in Figure 8.35, which shows the coding for equipment used in a machine-type activity. Cycle breakpoints are entered by the user as they occur in the cycle of events (Table 8.24).

DATA ANALYSIS

The analysis requires calculating basic times and site factors for the activities observed, the latter being determined on a daily/weekly/monthly and so on basis, and representing the proportion of time wasted on that type of activity. The information is subsequently used to construct a multiple activity chart for all the observed activities and production output rates are then ascertained.

VIDEO METHODS

The application of computers has tended to highlight one of the main perceived disadvantages of work study, namely the disputing of collected data and their interpretation. Video can help to overcome some of the criticism by providing the opportunity to recreate the picture and thereby demonstrate work in progress accompanied by all the attendant delays and inefficiencies. Subsequently the film can be viewed, and in conjunction with the computer programs for activity sampling and/or time study, full analysis of the data can be carried out to construct the multiple activity chart in the conventional manner. However, to avoid the need for constant filming of an operation, the camera can be operated to simulate the time-lapse method, whereby short periods of filming are undertaken on an activity sampling basis, and the data then analysed by the usual activity sampling theoretical method. See Section 5.4 for a detailed description of video methods.

Table 8.24 Description of cycle breakpoints and cycle elements.

Element	Basic time (min)
Wait	1.19
Load	1.23
Haul	2.14
Tip	1.16
Return	2.72
Cycle time	8.44

Source: Emsley and Harris (1986).

8.8 AUTOMATION TECHNOLOGY IN PRODUCTIVITY IMPROVEMENT

While computer models have greatly assisted the planning and production processes, the application of automation technology in construction has proved more difficult to introduce with solid evidence of success, largely because the hostile environment on-site and the uniqueness of each project present too much variability for installing regular systems and robotised equipment. However, a number of manufacturers are investing in equipment improvements, some even being routinely accepted, notably sensor devices on excavating machinery mechanisms, for control of bucket lifting height, digging depth and so on. Laser controlled equipment such as tunnelling borers, road pavers, pipeline breakers and micro-bore systems are also now quite familiar, with many of these devices seemingly finding ready suitability in ground-related work. Furthermore, the Global Positioning System (GPS) satellite, based on hardware set up by the US military, is able to locate positions anywhere on the Earth's surface to within 20 mm accuracy. An example of construction use of GPS is setting out in major bridgework. Trials have also demonstrated applications in automatically locating and controlling excavators and dump trucks on large-scale earth moving operations with driverless cabs, although the system is yet to be proven commercially. The method uses an on-board computer, initially taught by a driver to follow the operation cycle of load, haul, unload and return, combined with parameters of speed, direction and so on and thereafter remotely monitored and controlled by laser pole beacons, located along the route covering a range of about 100 m and coupled to the GPS. Secondary pressure sensors operate close contact work, with supersonic sensors used for control up to 15 m.

Building works are also beginning to see developments of sensor applications, with leading tower crane manufacturers demonstrating prototype systems for monitoring and controlling resource pick-ups and delivery. Ultimately it may be possible to automate complete resource flow through computer planning software, thereby optimising delivery patterns and the location points of material stores, crane positions, and the numbers and type of auxiliary equipment needed, such as concrete pumps, hoists and so on.

No doubt other examples will emerge and perhaps be incorporated into routine tasks such as spray painting, bricklaying, cladding fixing and so forth. More likely, however, will be increasing use of off-site assembly to utilise the efficiency of tried and trusted factory assembly systems, for bridge fabrication and toilet pods in high-rise buildings, for example, and more precast concrete applications as the most likely trends.

8.9 SUMMARY

This chapter provided vanguard examples of applications of mathematical modelling and operational research techniques aimed at encouraging planners, estimators and managers in general to give more consideration to the balancing of equipment, labour and financial resources, with a view to improving productivity.

Application of computers in solving such models was highlighted. A realistic determination of the most appropriate mix of resources can in most cases only be evaluated with the aid of computer modelling based on field data and information. Examples of expert systems in production planning were presented, and computerised collection of work study data and automation technology in productivity improvement were discussed.

REFERENCES AND BIBLIOGRAPHY

Abidali M. and Harris F.C. (1995). A methodology for predicting failure in the construction industry. *Construction Management and Economics*, **13**, 189–196

Alkass S. and Harris F.C. (1988). Expert system for earthmoving equipment selection in road construction. *Journal of Construction Engineering and Management ASCE*, **114**(3), 426–440

Alkass S. and Harris F.C. (1991a). Expert system for construction contractors claims analysis. *Building Research and Information*, **19**(1), 56–64

Alkass S. and Harris F.C. (1991b). Development of an integrated system for planning earthwork operations in road construction. *Construction Management and Economics*, **9**, 263–289

Broomfield J.R., Price A.D. and Harris F.C. (1984). Production analysis applied to work improvement. In *Proc. ICE, Part 2*, September.

Chan C.M.R. and Harris F.C. (1989). A database/spreadsheet application for equipment selection. *Construction Management and Economics*, **7**, 235–247

Choi C.W. and Harris F.C. (1990). A model for determining optimum crane position. In *Proc. ICE, Part 1*, June 1990

Clifton H.T. and Sutcliffe A.G. (1994). *Business Information Systems*. Englewood Cliffs, NJ: Prentice Hall

Curwin J. and Slater R. (1991). *Quantitative Methods for Business Decisions* 3rd edn. London: Chapman & Hall

Daellenbach H.G. and John A. (1978). *Introduction to Operational Research Techniques*. London: Allyn and Bacon

Emsley M.W. and Harris F.C. (1986). Work study is important to construction–computer applications. *Building Technology and Management CIOB*, April, 10–15

Harris F.C. and Evans J.B. (1977). Road construction – simulation game for site managers. *Journal of the Construction Division ASCE*, **113**(CO3), 405–414

Harris F.C. and McCaffer R. (1975). Evaluating the effects of adverse weather. *Building Technology and Management. CIOB*, October, 8–13

Hillier F. and Lieberman G. (1995). *Introduction to Operations Research* 5th edn. New York: McGraw-Hill

Holt G.D., Olomolaiye P.O. and Harris F.C. (1994). Factors influencing UK construction clients' choice of contractor. *Building and Environment*, **29**(2), 241–248

Jayawardene A.K.W. and Harris F.C. (1990). Further development of integer programming in earthwork optimisation. *Journal of Construction Engineering and Management ASCE*, **116**(1), 18–34

Jayawardane A.K.W. and Price A.D.F. (1994). A new approach for optimising earthmoving operations: Part 1. In *Proc. ICE Transp.*, **105**, 195–207

Jayawardane A.K.W. and Price A.D.F. (1994). A new approach for optimising earthmoving operations: Part 2. In *Proc. ICE Transp.*, **105**, 249–258

Kirupananther S. and Harris F.C. (1986). Plant selection for trenching work by computer graphics. *International Journal for Construction Management and Technology*, **1**(1), 68–72

Levin R.I. and Ki C.A. (1992). *Quantitative Approaches to Management* 8th edn. New York: McGraw-Hill

Littlechild S.C. (1977). *Operational Research for Managers*. London: Philip Allan

Mason R. J. and Harris F.C. (1979). Predicting company failures in the construction industry. In *Proc. ICE Part 1*, May 1979

Tam C.M. and Harris F.C. (1996). Model for assessing building contractors' project performance. *Engineering Construction and Architectural Management*, **3**(3), 187–203

Wijeratne N.N. and Harris F.C. (1984). Capital budgeting using a linear programming model. *International Journal of Operations and Production Management*, **4**(2), 49–64

Wijesundera D.A. and Harris F.C. (1986). The integration of an expert system into the construction planning process. In *Proc. of the 2nd International Conference Civil and Structural Engineering Computing, ICE, Vol. 2*, September 1986

Wijesundera D.A. and Harris F.C. (1987). Video and computer applications in production analysis. In *Proc. of 5th International Symposium, CIB W-65*, September 1987

Wijesundera D.A. and Harris F.C. (1989). The selection of materials handling methods in construction by simulation. *Construction Managment and Economics*, **7**, 95–102

Wilkes M. (1989). *Operational Research – Analysis and Apllications*. New York: McGraw-Hill

Woods D.G. and Harris F.C. (1980). Truck allocation model for concrete distribution. *Journal of the Construction Division ASCE*, **16**(CO2), 131–139

Zhang P., Harris F.C. and Olomolaiye P.O. (1996). A computer-based model for optimising the location of a tower crane. *Building Research and Information*, **24**(2), 113–123

9

MANAGING CONSTRUCTION PROJECTS FOR IMPROVED PRODUCTIVITY

9.1 INTRODUCTION

Throughout the previous chapters productivity principles, tools, techniques, models and procedures applied to production management in construction were discussed. Just to recapitulate, these included: (i) definitions and importance of productivity and its influencing factors; (ii) nature of construction activities, the workforce and diagnosing failing productivity; (iii) method study and other production analysis techniques to pinpoint the problem areas and effect improvement; (iv) work measurement techniques mainly aimed at establishing planning and controlling data; (v) on-site data capturing methods and diagnostic tools to identify poor productivity; (vi) planning and controlling techniques explaining how the established data are actually used in preplanning, together with project planning, monitoring, progressing, expediting and controlling during actual construction; (vii) workforce motivation principles and techniques aimed at maintaining a satisfied and efficient workforce; and (viii) computer applications for fast and efficient processing of data for the above applications and computer models for assisting some of the associated functions.

This last chapter presents several other approaches for overall performance improvement towards long-term excellence in the construction industry, starting with a brief description of goal setting – a further motivation technique. It then discusses quality management, covering quality control, quality assurance and total quality management, followed by benchmarking – a performance comparison technique; breakthrough approaches – for overcoming productivity barriers and introducing innovations; and lean construction – a new production philosophy. Finally, a global productivity improvement system is presented, with the emphasis on labour productivity integrating all the related productivity enhancement approaches.

9.2 GOAL SETTING

Money alone is not always sufficient to motivate workers for higher performance, as seen in Maslow's hierarchy of needs in Chapter 7. In addition to regular income and financial incentives, other incentives – such as participation in decision making, job enrichment, behaviour modification, organisational development, and recognition – have been tried, with varying degrees of success. It has been repeatedly shown, however, that *goal setting*, which is a straightforward motivational technique, is not only more effective than alternative methods but also the major mechanism by which the other incentives affect motivation (Locke and Latham 1990).

The goal-setting concept, which involves assigning employees a specific amount of work to be accomplished – for example, a specific task, a quota, an output standard, an objective or even a deadline for a certain task – is not new. The task concept supported by time and motion study and incentive pay was the principle of scientific management founded by F.W. Taylor nearly a century ago to motivate blue-collar workers. The same concept when designed for managers is more widely known today as *management by objectives* (MBO). Recent studies have shown that programmatic use of goal setting and feedback can increase productivity by up to 20% (Locke and Latham 1990). If properly applied, it also reduces absenteeism, encourages competition, increases enthusiasm and prevents boredom. As discussed under financial incentives, targets often tied with income are frequently used in the construction industry, even today, but research indicates that goal setting significantly improves performance even when goal accomplishment is not financially rewarded.

9.2.1 Goal types

Classification of goal types may depend on the standpoint of their application. The three main ones are (i) time span, (ii) objective and (iii) approach.

From the standpoint of the time span, goal types may include (i) distal goals, (ii) proximal goals and (iii) sub-goals. *Distal goals* are long-term or end goals; for example, goals set to achieve within the next six months, next year or even five years. *Proximal goals* are short term; for example, goals set to achieve within a day, a week or sometimes even a month. *Sub-goals* are established by dividing a distal goal into logical components so that each sub-goal is attained in a fraction of the time required to achieve the distal goal. Sub-goals facilitate performance improvement by operating as a feedback device. They also serve to maintain effort over long periods but have the possibility of limiting performance if they are treated as performance ceilings. The optimum time span for a goal depends on the situation.

From the standpoint of the objective, goal types may include (i) personal goals, (ii) organisational goals and (iii) performance improvement (or productivity) goals. *Personal goals* are generally long term and established for career development; examples include the number of research papers to be published within the next year in the case of an academic, or the time frame to achieve the next promotion. They are considered to be an essential component in career advancement. *Organisational goals* have similar objectives; for example, student intake to be increased by 20%

within the next year in the case of an academic institution, or the best contractor award to be obtained within the next five years, or even to setting a certain profit level. They are also considered to be an essential component in the long-term development and survival of an organisation. *Productivity goals*, on the other hand, are set to achieve a certain output level in a construction situation, for example, and are generally proximal goals. These goals may be influenced by organisational goals since they are generally set in line with the latter.

From the standpoint of approach, goal types may include (i) assigned, (ii) participative and (iii) team goals. The *assigned goals* are set by the supervisor, and the workers are expected to comply. For example, an output target is set by a trade supervisor for a gang without consulting the gang members. On the other hand, *participative goals* are set by the superiors in consultation with the workers. The third type, *team goals*, are set by a team generally consisting of superiors, subordinates, peers or even external consultants after detailed discussions, negotiations, evaluations, brainstorming and so forth, a typical example being organisational goals. See Ryan and Sebastianelli (1987) for a good example. Indeed, different approaches work best under different circumstances.

9.2.2 How to make goal setting work better

Like all other motivational techniques, goal setting will not yield higher performance unless properly applied. The following are some tested guidelines to obtain the maximum benefits from this technique, with the emphasis on productivity goal setting:

(1) Set specific goals rather than vague goals. For example, lay 500 bricks within a day or complete this activity by tomorrow, rather than 'do your best'.
(2) Set hard or difficult goals rather than moderate or easy ones because high goals lead to higher performance, if accepted.
(3) When circumstances allow, let the workers themselves set goals. This encourages commitment, leads to setting of higher goals and ensures acceptance of and commitment to set goals.
(4) When assigned goals are in operation, do not criticise workers for failure to attain goals. Lower the goal if warranted, investigate and remove the cause, for example, by providing necessary training, and then raise the goal gradually. This provides a feeling of accomplishment and increases morale for the higher attempt. The supervisor's role should be as helper and goal facilitator.
(5) Provide precise feedback to workers to assess their performance and to adjust their effort or the strategy accordingly. A useful way of doing this is by maintaining graphs or charts indicating performance over time.
(6) Once a goal is set (either assigned or participative) every attempt should be taken to prevent goal blockage or external interruptions.
(7) Make sure that the goal is properly conveyed and understood since very often workers tend to report that 'this is the first time I knew what my supervisor expected of me on this job'.

(8) Set challenging but achievable goals. Set more easily achievable goals for employees with low confidence or ability. Scientific work measurement is the best method to decide goals (see also Section 9.7.1).

(9) Design goals to maximise accomplishment and group cooperation by weighting the advantages and disadvantages of individual and group goals depending on the circumstances.

(10) Ensure goal commitment. Simple instruction backed by positive management support, supervisory presence and absence of threats and punishment is generally sufficient in most cases. Ensure fairness and build up trust so that workers do not feel that they are being exploited.

(11) Do not encourage formal competition if it leads the employees to place individual goals ahead of organisational goals. The emphasis should be accomplishment of the task and not on 'beating each other'.

(12) Overcome employee resistance to assigned goals by additional training, making participative goals, deciding on the goal level or even a reward in the form of incentives or otherwise.

(13) Provide support elements with adequate resources, money, instructions, equipment and necessary authority or freedom after making sure that the individual or group has sufficient ability and knowledge to achieve the set goal. Asking them to prepare an action plan for reaching the goal, as in the case of MBO, will help to judge the required ability.

(14) Always set proximal goals. If long-term goals are necessary set sub-goals; research indicates that long-term goals are ineffective without sub-goals.

(15) Guard against poor quality, safety aspects and short-term advantages since worker behaviour may change when working under goals.

As with financial incentives, goal setting is not a substitute for poor management although it can be applied in its own right without necessarily being part of a wider management system. Supplemented with good management and the strategies mentioned above, goal setting yields remarkable productivity improvement. This applies irrespective of whether the goals are assigned or set participatively; whether the accomplishment is sufficiently rewarded or not; or whether it is applied to unionised construction or open shop although the level of goals and the extent of productivity improvement may vary under these factors. Furthermore, proper goal setting compels management to better preplan and tends to produce long-term changes in the employees' attitudes, not only in productivity but in every other aspect of their performance. This change of attitude embraces the habit of thinking of new ways for continuous improvement of job performance. As will be seen in the next section, goal setting is therefore an integral part of total quality management.

9.3 QUALITY MANAGEMENT

Quality and productivity are complementary. It has been shown many times that programmes that attempt to improve both simultaneously are the most successful. All too often, projects fail to satisfy clients' requirements technically, financially, contractually, functionally, aesthetically or any combination of these, due to faults in concept, design, procurement, estimating, planning, materials or workmanship. Limiting our discussion to contractors, the main causes of these problems stem from poor management, poor supervision, lack of planning, lack of skilled operatives, poor communication, insufficient training and inadequate procedures to ensure that materials and workmanship meet the specified requirements.

As in manufacturing, where the customer does not see the production process but is often provided with a guaranteed product, for example an automobile, modern construction clients cannot afford their time and effort to solve the problems of others or to get involved in the associated risks. This has compelled contractors to carry out quality management by themselves to try to guarantee a quality end product. Such an assurance is becoming increasingly important today for survival in the industry, as more and more clients tend to consider quality an important parameter in contractor selection.

The word 'quality' used in the industry today does not, however, mean the excellence traditionally attached to it, but rather it has an engineering sense to convey compliance with a defined measurement, value for money, fitness for the purpose, or customer satisfaction. In this sense, a luxurious hotel and a thatched cottage will have the same quality if they satisfy the functional and other requirements and provide the owners with an equal feeling of satisfaction for the money spent.

The concept of quality used in the construction industry today is considered to have evolved through several stages over many years. They include: (i) quality inspection to check that the produced item is what is required, usually done at the end of the operation or project; (ii) quality control to ensure that workmanship conforms to the specified standard through regular inspection and sample testing; (iii) quality assurance to enhance clients' confidence in the contractor's performance; and (iv) total quality management to achieve long-term excellence. The last three stages are discussed in a little more detail in the following subsections.

9.3.1 Quality control

Quality control (QC) involves the operational techniques and activities that are used to fulfil requirements for quality at various stages of construction and is the simplest form of quality management. Effective QC programmes ensure conformity with specifications, reduce clients' complaints, improve product reliability, increase clients' confidence and reduce production cost. Quality control is primarily concerned with defect detection, mainly by inspection, statistical methods or final testing to ensure that the work produced and materials used are within the specified tolerances.

Clearly, inspection includes such activities as checking line, level, verticality and dimensions, which are non-subjective, and those subject to the inspector's judgement, such as cleanliness, tolerances and visual checks. These activities are usually carried out at the end of each operation or sub-operation. Statistical methods are usually employed to control the quality of construction materials such as bricks, aggregates or cube testing of concrete. Final tests include such things as pressure testing of a pipe network before commissioning.

The main disadvantage of QC is the creation of an inspection mentality, which leads to contractors' staff setting their standards to just satisfy the inspector. It may also lead to expensive rework in situations where approval cannot be obtained, creating adversarial relationships or even corrupt practices. This, together with contractors' failure in other aspects such as meeting schedules and reducing waste, has led to quality assurance, discussed below.

9.3.2 Quality assurance

Quality assurance (QA) is a major step beyond QC, emphasising defect prevention once the item is constructed as against defect detection in QC. It is a structured approach to production and construction management processes and procedures to ensure that the quality is built into the production process. The ultimate objective is to provide the client with a quality product that meets the agreed specified requirements completely, without the need for the client checking during the production process.

Quality assurance is achieved by adopting a system that documents what processes are followed and how they are accomplished by self-checking that each process is completed satisfactorily and finally recording and certifying that fact. Quality assurance evolved to remedy the subjectivity of QC, which is practised with no standard controls, resulting in vast differences in performance between organisations practising QC. Quality assurance, on the other hand, ensures 'fit for the purpose', 'right first time' concepts by operating within the international quality standard ISO 9000, which provides a universal framework for quality assurance. Many clients in the construction industry today consider contractors' certification as operating to ISO 9000 standards as a prerequisite for entry into contracts or retention of their names in the bidders list.

QUALITY ASSURANCE STANDARDS

ISO 9000, introduced in 1987 by the International Organization for Standardization, is the universally recognised quality standard applicable to any industry in developing QA systems. It consists of five parts, ISO 9000 to ISO 9004. ISO 9000 and ISO 9004 are guidance documents while ISO 9001–ISO 9003 are quality system specifications, supplemented by ISO 8402 for quality vocabulary. The UK equivalent of ISO 9000 is BS 5750, which consists of four parts, BS 5750 Parts 1–3 being quality system specifications equivalent to ISO 9001–ISO 9003, and BS 5750 Part 4 being guidelines to the use of Parts 1–3 supplemented by the BS 4778 quality vocabulary. BS 5750 has now been accepted as an international standard equivalent to ISO 9000.

ISO 9001 (or BS 5750 Part 1) is the highest level of QA and is the only one which covers the design process. Any organisation involved in design, such as design and build contractors, design consultants and architects, would therefore set up a QA system to meet this standard. ISO 9002 is the next level of QA applicable to manufacturing, installation or construction organisations, and demands process control during production. It applies to many construction contractors, where evidence of inspections and tests carried out during construction has to be given to the client. ISO 9003 is the lowest level of QA, which relies on setting up management systems to control the activities and requires demonstration to the client of the adequacy of the product by final inspection or test. It does not require a well-documented system and applies to any simple building process, such as building of a non-load-bearing brick wall or even laying of roof tiles.

DEVELOPING AND IMPLEMENTING A SYSTEM

There are four stages common to development and implementation of any QA system: (i) create awareness, (ii) develop quality manuals, (iii) system introduction and (iv) system evaluation.

Stage 1: Create awareness This is where the requirement of a QA system is established by the top management, in most cases because of external pressures for the organisation to remain competitive. With top management's full commitment, the requirement of a QA system and its benefits should be communicated to all levels of management to create a positive and quality culture in the organisation. This can best be achieved by a short training course in QA.

Stage 2: Develop quality manuals The quality manual is where the system is documented and is the basis for any QA system. A quality manual usually contains:

(1) Company profile, to introduce the company and its activities;
(2) Amendments record, to list any modifications to the previous version of the quality manual for quick reappraisal of the current status;
(3) Policy statement, to state simply the company's commitment to undertake business in accordance with a QA standard;
(4) Quality standards, to describe briefly how the company's QA system satisfies the quality standard (ISO 9000) with which it is intended to comply;
(5) Organisational structure and responsibilities, to indicate the organisational relationships, various functions, and roles and responsibilities of those who work under each function to facilitate easy identification of individuals or groups responsible for specific tasks;
(6) Procedures, to define the what, where, when, how and who of each key function of the organisation;
(7) Work instructions, to provide detailed work instructions for the procedures identified above for individual tasks and to define how each task should be completed.

Stage 3: System introduction When the draft manual has been prepared it should be introduced initially on a progressive trial basis with the trial period lasting between three and six months to generate an understanding of QA and to test and debug the system. Serious problems often identified by the employees should receive immediate rectification while others can be incorporated in the refined system. After the trial period the refined system can be introduced formally by providing quality manuals to section managers, who will in turn implement QA system within their own work areas.

Stage 4: System evaluation   Regular system evaluation is usually carried out by (i) management review, where managers formally and periodically review the success of the QA system within their own areas to ensure continuing adequacy of the system, or (ii) internal audits, where the performance of the QA system is reviewed by an independent internal auditor who reports directly to management about any inadequacies, suitable corrective actions, persons responsible for corrective actions and their timing. The system can then be upgraded.

When the QA system is fully operational, companies can apply for third-party accreditation, for example, Lloyd's Register or BSI in the UK, to be certified that the company's quality management system meets the requirements of ISO 9000 (or BS 5750). This involves submission of the quality management system and documentation for scrutiny and involves external auditing of the system. However, Hellard (1993) argues that this kind of third-party accreditation has little value in the construction industry due to its own peculiarities and the non-repetitive nature of its products, and encourages second-party (or client) auditing on a project by project basis before entering into contracts.

As far as a contractor is concerned, the QA system should include detailed procedures for all operations commencing with the receipt of the tender, through tender submission, setting up of site team, preparation and obtaining approval for a project quality plan, placing suppliers and subcontractors under the QA system, execution of production under the project quality plan and so forth, to the preparation of handover packages and submission. The reader is referred to Duncan *et al.* (1990) for a more detailed discussion of these aspects. Hughes and Williams (1991) provide a case study in developing a QA system for an interested contractor to use as a framework to build on.

9.3.3   Total quality management

Total quality management (TQM) is a step beyond QA which, in addition to ensuring that the ultimate product meets the complete satisfaction of the client, extends the philosophy of continuous improvement of products, services or processes towards excellence. It is a management-led, company-wide process with the participation of all employees, which creates a quality culture in the entire organisation with continuous improvement considered as a part of normal business. Thus, TQM can be considered as a journey rather than a destination. Indeed, it incorporates QA, and provides principles, tools and techniques for continuous improvement to meet the needs and satisfaction of both employees within the organisation and customers and clients outside. The TQM approach is now considered essential to long-term survival of any business, including construction, and is further emphasised by the recently issued BS 7850 (British Standards Institution 1992).

PRINCIPLES AND ATTRIBUTES OF TOTAL QUALITY

The fundamental goals of TQM are *customer satisfaction* and *continuous improvement*, and are therefore the principles on which it is based.

Customer satisfaction demands monitoring of performance in meeting or exceeding customer requirements, with customers considered as clients receiving the completed facility and also the internal staff and operatives. Similar to a production line, construction staff and operatives work in a process where each person or a group can be regarded as an internal customer to the previous supplier, who provides a product in the form of plans, specifications, instructions, inspections, approvals, materials or part of a completed product, but also as a supplier to the next person or the operative down the line. Thus, every party in a process has three roles: supplier, processor and customer. This is identified as the 'triple role' concept by Juran (1989). These three roles are carried out at every level of the construction process, whether it is by a company, division, department, subcontractor, working gang on-site or even an individual. This chain of suppliers or chain of quality demands everyone's contribution to quality satisfying internal customers and ultimately leading to the external client.

The second principle, *continuous improvement*, involves efforts to maintain and incrementally improve current methods and procedures through process control and direct efforts to achieve major technological advances in the construction process through innovation. Process control emphasises the necessity of controlling production throughout the construction process on a regular basis for increased efficiency and effectiveness. Regular application of production planning, production analysis, method study and the related techniques discussed throughout this book is therefore an essential part of TQM.

The second aspect of continuous improvement is through innovation or breakthrough by which major shifts of performance can be obtained; for example, the use of a concrete pump instead of a crane and skip or the use of laser-controlled screed laying instead of old techniques (see Section 9.5 for more details about breakthrough). In this way, once targets are met, new ones are set, aiming for even higher levels of efficiency, so that a real competitive edge can be developed by steadily widening the advantages over static or slowly changing competitors.

To fulfil these two goals, *customer satisfaction* and *continuous improvement*, any successful TQM programme should have the following attributes:

(1) Committed leadership of the highest standard throughout the lifetime of the organisation because TQM is a culture and philosophy that must permeate as *the* method of management.
(2) Training targeted to every level of management and employees because TQM uses a participative, disciplined and organised approach to problem identification and solution.

(3) Teamwork, because TQM requires extensive involvement of all employees and harnessing to the maximum extent the qualities and capabilities of everyone.

(4) Supplier involvement, because TQM cannot succeed without the involvement of material suppliers and subcontractors.

(5) Upstream preventive management which shifts emphasis from past-event inspection to pre-event planning. This requires seeking out potential problems (or improvement opportunities) and not merely waiting for a failure to happen before effecting improvement.

(6) Ongoing preventive action requiring the need to attack constantly the real root causes of problems or potential problems by the combined efforts of management, staff and operatives to minimise panic management or 'fire fighting'.

(7) Improved communication to make sure that all required information is supplied at the correct level, at the correct time and to the required degree of detail by driving out fear of reporting at all levels and breaking down communication barriers.

(8) Clearly identified vision, mission and goals; TQM cannot be steered to continuous improvement without them.

(9) Focus on employees to include carrier development plans, profit sharing, enhanced training, employee involvement and recognition; employee satisfaction is indispensable in TQM.

The reader interested in further details of these aspects and how they apply to the construction industry is referred to Burati *et al.* (1991, 1992) and Chase (1993).

DEVELOPMENT OF TQM IN A CONSTRUCTION COMPANY

Once the principles and attributes of TQM are known, a management framework or model can be formulated to establish quality culture in the organisation for continuous improvement. There are no fixed models suitable for a particular type of organisation but the right model for a company culture is the one that incorporates the overall company goal. A number of general models exist. For example, Deming (1988) provides a list of 14 points to establish TQM; Oakland (1989) provides a pictorial multi-step programme for TQM suitable for training purposes; Peratec (1994) provides six key elements of a management framework for TQM.

The International Council for Building Research and Documentation (CIB W88) has developed two guides, one for professional consultants and the other for contractors, to assist the implementation of TQM in the construction industry. Burati and Oswald (1993) also provide detailed guidelines on how to implement TQM in engineering and construction, and Deffenbaugh (1993) describes how to implement TQM on construction sites. Furthermore, the European Construction Institute (ECI 1991b) has produced a matrix to benchmark the degree to which a company operates under TQM together with guidelines for improvement. Hellard (1993) provides a similar benchmarking system. The reader interested in this particular aspect of TQM is encouraged to follow up these literature sources.

TOOLS OF TQM

Indeed, all of the production analysis, problem identification, data recording and method study techniques, and the planning and control procedures we have been discussing throughout the book are part of the TQM toolbox. In addition, there are statistical techniques required specifically for sample testing of materials, known as the 'seven statistical tools'. These are: histograms, cause-and-effect diagrams, check sheets, Pareto diagrams, graphs, control charts and scatter diagrams. See Imai (1986) and Hensey (1993) for further details of statistical tools.

PRESENT SITUATION AND FUTURE TRENDS IN TQM IN CONSTRUCTION

Despite the early arguments that TQM will not work in construction because of the fragmented nature of the industry, Japanese construction companies, for example, after benefiting from the experience of manufacturing industry, embraced TQM during the 1970s. Since then, three Japanese contractors have been awarded the prestigious Deming prize for quality improvement (Deming 1988), indicating that the concepts of TQM can be applied to construction. Furthermore, Burati *et al.* (1991) indicate that TQM has been actively applied by both owners and contractors in the US private construction sector. Indications are that the application of TQM in the construction industry in the UK and Europe is growing quickly. Thus, it is no longer a question of whether TQM is a possibility but a question of how long it will be before all owners, designers, architects, contractors and suppliers, at least in the industrial construction market, have their own TQM programmes. However, the question of a transient craft workforce, and the traditional practice of awarding contracts to the lowest bid, especially in the public sector, are some constraints facing the full implementation of TQM. As more and more organisations embrace the TQM philosophy and new procuring techniques which encourage all-party cooperation, such as 'partnering', gain more and more acceptance in the industry, these constraints will no longer be hurdles in the near future.

9.4 BENCHMARKING

Benchmarking is a recently developed management tool, originating in the manufacturing industry, although its principles were applied as early as in the 19th century by F.W. Taylor. It is a well-formalised technique in the present context and is defined by its originator, Xerox, in the USA as 'the search for industry best practices that lead to superior performance' (Camp 1989). After identifying the shrinking market share of photocopiers to Japanese competitors, Xerox applied the technique for the first time in the Western world to compare its performance in a structured way with superiors, resulting in vast performance improvements to regain market share. Since then benchmarking has captured the interest of many businesses, executives and managers in both the manufacturing and service sectors, especially in North America, as a powerful performance improvement tool in all aspects of organisation activities. In Europe, too, application of benchmarking is growing rapidly.

With its wide-ranging applications, benchmarking is now defined in a more refined form as 'a systematic and continuous measurement process; a process of continuously measuring and comparing an organisation's business process against business leaders anywhere in the world to gain information which will help the organisation to take action to improve its performance' (APQC 1992). The following discussion is aimed at describing the technique in a little more detail and identifying its applications in performance improvement in the construction industry.

9.4.1 Benchmarking types

According to the definition of benchmarking, its ultimate aim is to achieve superior performance in all of the activities of the organisation by comparing them with the world's best. Indeed, it is not always possible, except market giants, to compare with the world's best and act to achieve superior performance in all situations due to constraints such as size of organisation, time, resource requirements, difficulty in finding the world's best and large performance gaps. This has led to many different types of benchmarking. Although there seems to be no consensus about the typology in the literature, the following three identified by Karlof and Ostblom (1993) broadly incorporate all of the categories:

(1) *Internal benchmarking:* benchmarking carried out with similar business units within the same organisation, for example, between different branches, geographically scattered subsidiaries, divisions, service groups and so forth, is called internal benchmarking. Clearly, internal benchmarking requires less time and resources, provides accurate information and is usually the first step in any benchmarking study. It very often reveals ample opportunities for performance improvement, narrowing the performance gap between different divisions of the same organisation and satisfying both clients and employees alike.

(2) *External benchmarking:* this is when benchmarking is carried out with similar or identical organisations elsewhere, the salient point being the high degree of comparability between organisations. They may be direct competitors or similar organisations in other countries serving different markets but the approach will be considerably different depending on the partner's market. Benchmarking with direct competitors can be very fruitful but conditional upon one being able to establish a dialogue. The risk is that it tends to focus on competition factors rather than performance, and one should embark on it after identifying a clear framework by detailed negotiations. This problem is much less significant when the partners serve different markets.

(3) *Functional benchmarking:* this is the comparison of various functions of the organisation with those of the best companies regardless of their businesses with the objective of identifying the best performance wherever it may be found. A banking group, for example, may decide to benchmark its over-the-counter services against an organisation excellent in this area, perhaps an airline. Taking some examples in the construction industry, a contractor may decide to benchmark material

management policies in the central stores with those of a reputed automobile producer practising just-in-time (JIT), or may even compare form work fabrication and erection with a very specialised firm carrying out similar work. Indeed, one cannot make aggregate comparisons when benchmarking with different industries; the emphasis here is on the individual activities or functions and not the overall aspects. Functional benchmarking utilises the full potential of benchmarking and is the type that offers opportunities for moving up into world class.

9.4.2 Benchmarking process and focus

There is no specific procedure or model to carry out benchmarking and the approach will depend on the individual situation. The literature indicates several models adopted for specific situations. For example, Watson (1993) uses the Deming cycle as the basis; Shetty (1993) uses five stages; the Xerox model (Karsnia 1991) has ten stages, and so on. Again, the core of the process can be divided into five broad stages, as follows (Karlof and Ostblom 1993), although the detailed steps can be quite complex:

(1) Decide what to benchmark
(2) Identify benchmarking partners
(3) Gather information
(4) Analyse
(5) Implement for effect.

The focus of benchmarking can vary depending on the objective. For example, the objective may be to achieve world class in (i) quality of the end product or the customer perceived value for money, (ii) productivity or the least cost from the producer's viewpoint, or (iii) offering prompt service with minimum lead time. It is, however, practically difficult to separate the focus during a benchmarking exercise. The TQM discussed earlier embraces all three aspects. As TQM becomes part of the organisation's management philosophy, external and internal benchmarking become part of the process as a means of setting goals and identifying best practices. The value of benchmarking in TQM is the exposure of all activities in the organisation, including internal supplier–customer relationships where normal market mechanisms are totally absent. Benchmarking is therefore an integral and essential aspect of TQM.

9.4.3 Potential of benchmarking in construction and future trends

In manufacturing, benchmarking has gone a long way, leading to the establishment of a code of conduct making it more acceptable as a formal management tool (Watson 1993), the formation of benchmarking clubs in which partners (or even competitors) offer to learn from each other (Main 1992) and the establishment of the International Benchmarking Centre in the UK in 1993 as a 'dating agency' with the objective of coordinating benchmarking efforts (Costanzo 1993). In the construction industry, however, there is at present only limited application of benchmarking in its true sense, except in those companies practising TQM.

The concept as applied in the construction industry today includes benchmarking with 'artificial' benchmarks set by industry development groups rather than an approach initiated by individual contracting organisations. For example, the ECI productivity task force (ECI 1994) has identified best practices in the industry through a comprehensive study, and its recommendations for best practices have been given in the form of a benchmarking questionnaire where organisations can identify their own status in the journey to TQM. Another report developed for the same purpose is given by Hellard (1993). However, with the increasing acceptance of TQM concepts in construction organisations and enthusiasm of industry practitioners, academics and policy makers, benchmarking has great potential in performance improvement in the construction industry.

9.5 BREAKTHROUGH APPROACHES TO PRODUCTIVITY

Most of the principles, tools, techniques and procedures that we have been advocating throughout the book for productivity improvement attempt to analyse the existing set-up, identify inefficiencies and effect systematic improvement. They can therefore be considered to have a *control* approach. However, many organisations fail to improve productivity this way beyond a certain limit due to inherent bureaucratic procedures, rigid rules and regulations, old-fashioned attitudes, and use of yesterday's technology. Furthermore, no contractor can gain a competitive advantage while cheating on quality and slipping completion dates with various excuses. In these situations, organisations should pursue a breakthrough or innovative approach to overcome these barriers and break out to retain competitive advantage. In the following sections, an attempt is made to differentiate the two approaches, *control* and *breakthrough*, and explain the application of breakthrough approaches for productivity improvement in construction.

9.5.1 Breakthrough and control

Control means no change, staying on course and adherence to standards or norms. In construction these standards can be considered as specifications, budgets, schedules, targets, standard outputs and so on. Any departure from these standards in the wrong direction leads to a crisis requiring management attention. These departures often happen in construction due to such causes as unforeseen ground conditions, inclement weather, variation orders, material shortages, poor workmanship, poor quality of materials, inefficient methods, worker absenteeism, shortages of skilled workers and so on. While some of these departures can justify changing standards, the others require management attention for rectification. As mentioned earlier, these can be rectified by diligent application of productivity measurement, production analysis and method study procedures, together with planning and other control techniques discussed previously.

Breakthrough means change in the right direction, a dynamic, enterprising or decisive movement to a new, higher level of performance. Such changes are necessary in any business to find new markets, to reduce costs and accidents, and to increase outputs, quality and profits. Breakthrough can be aggressive or defensive. Aggressive breakthrough includes such things as shifting to a new market opportunity; for example, production of ready-mixed concrete in addition to construction or a policy to offer internal equipment for outside hiring to avoid plant division eating up a company's profits. Defensive breakthrough may include such things as introduction of a quality assurance system, purchasing a project management software package and so on after learning that competitors have introduced such systems.

Breakthrough is therefore the creation of good or necessary changes generally for long-term benefits and can be considered as productivity drives or breakouts. Control is prevention of bad changes, 'fire fighting' and getting back on target, and is carried out as a short-term activity. Both are necessary for the survival and health of a company and can be in operation at the same time. The effects of control activities and breakthrough activities on performance are depicted in Figure 9.1.

Management's approaches to control and breakthrough are remarkably different. For example, in control the managerial attitude is that the present level of performance is good enough, or if not, cannot be improved (in other words, it is a fate, not a problem). The objective is to maintain the current level of performance through control and eliminate sporadic departures from the usual practice. On the other hand, in breakthrough, the attitude should be that the present level of performance is not good enough, that something can be done to improve it (in other words, it is a problem, not a fate). The objective is to achieve better performance through breakthrough procedures by eliminating chronic obstacles to better performance. Indeed, the data for control activities are relatively simple, collected regularly, often without formality, and collected by line managers. Action is taken by line managers themselves. In breakthrough, the data is usually complex and collected rarely; data collection and interpretation are done by special task forces and actions are usually taken by higher management.

9.5.2 Applications of breakthrough approaches in construction

Breakthrough can be industry-wide or limited to a particular organisation. Industry-wide breakthroughs are generally the result of continued research, for example, the introduction of pre-stressed concrete, which revolutionised the design of long-span concrete structures, or legislation enacted by governments or controlling bodies such as British Standards, conditions of contracts, procuring methods, safety regulations or even the recommendations of special industry-wide task forces. Limiting our discussion to contractor organisations, breakthroughs can be drastic changes which affect the whole company or changes in one area of company activities. For example, approaches such as the introduction of a QA system or launching a TQM system, discussed earlier, or reorganisation of the company management structure, are company-wide breakthroughs and are normally carried out to retain or improve competitive advantage in the market. In addition, the application of concepts such

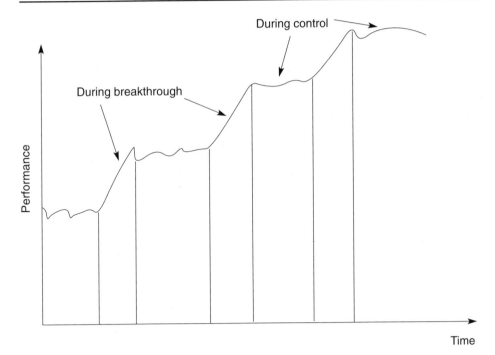

Figure 9.1 Effect of control and breakthrough on performance.

as concurrent engineering, just-in-time management, business process, re-engineering or benchmarking are further breakthrough techniques. All of these techniques are widely applied in manufacturing industry. Construction, which is becoming a manufacturing process, with more and more assembling rather than craftsmanship, is increasingly accepting these techniques, some of which have already been consolidated into a coherent theory, termed *lean construction*, which is explained later in the chapter.

Changes such as the introduction of a computerised project management system or the purchase of a versatile piece of equipment, for example, affect only one area of company activities. At a much smaller scale, breakthrough may include changing a site management structure, introduction of a site cost control system, installation of a site computer for data transfer or even application of a new construction method which saves a considerable amount of money.

Whatever the degree of breakthrough, the respective managers should identify opportunities and act diligently in addition to regular control procedures. A prerequisite to this is a drastic change of the present practice of contract managers from crisis management to smooth running of projects through preplanning, considering all realistic constraints and thereby releasing their time and energy for strategic breakthrough approaches. Otherwise they become preoccupied with meeting targets but fail to challenge the target itself. In the absence of such breakthrough the rest of the world just walks away from the static company and enters into new opportunities with competitors.

9.6 LEAN CONSTRUCTION

Lean construction is a new production philosophy that originated in the manufacturing industry in Japan and is still in the very early stages in its application in the construction industry. Lean production has created a profound impact on productivity in the manufacturing industry in the recent past, especially in the motor vehicles and electronics sectors. Koskela (1997) claims that the new philosophy applied to construction will be far-reaching and broad and that pioneering organisations have shown that substantial and sometimes dramatic improvements are realisable in a few years after the shift to the new philosophy. The following subsections briefly introduce the concept of lean construction, its tools and potential benefits in productivity improvement in construction (Alarcon 1997).

9.6.1 Concepts and principles of lean production

The lean concept is considered to have evolved through three stages: (i) as a tool such as quality circles, (ii) as a production method, such as just-in-time and (iii) as a general management philosophy (Koskela 1997). The lean philosophy considers that any production process consists of two aspects: (i) conversion activities which add value to the material or piece of information being transformed into a product, and (ii) flow (or non-value-adding) activities such as inspection, waiting and moving, through which the conversion activities are bound together (Koskela 1997). The primary concern of lean philosophy is the improvement of flows by either reducing or eliminating them while making conversion activities more efficient. This is in contrast to the traditional management approach, which usually does not differentiate between conversions and flows and considers all activities as value adding, even if attention to improvement is directed only to conversion activities. Materials and information flows, which are characterised by time, cost and value, are therefore the basic unit of analysis in the lean philosophy.

Koskela summarises lean production principles as follows:

(1) Reduce the share of non-value-adding activities
(2) Increase output value through systematic consideration of customer requirements
(3) Reduce variability
(4) Reduce cycle times
(5) Simplify by minimising the number of steps, parts and linkages
(6) Increase output flexibility
(7) Increase process transparency
(8) Focus control on the complete process
(9) Build continuous improvement into the process
(10) Balance flow improvement with conversion improvement
(11) Benchmark.

The above principles are universal; that is, they apply for total flow processes or sub-processes and physical production processes such as building, and for informational production processes such as design.

9.6.2 Methodologies and tools for lean production

As seen earlier, dramatic improvements witnessed in the manufacturing industry through the lean concept have not been due to radical or sharp changes in technology but rather are a result of the new lean philosophy. It does not include new management techniques but combines existing techniques and principles in a new dimension for productivity improvement and cost reduction by stimulating employees (Melles 1997). Among the methodologies and tools used for attaining lean production, the following are the most important (Koskela 1997; Melles 1997):

(1) Just-in-time (JIT)
(2) Total quality management (TQM)
(3) Time-based completion (TBM)
(4) Concurrent engineering
(5) Process redesign (or re-engineering)
(6) Value-based management
(7) Visual management
(8) Total productive maintenance
(9) Employee involvement
(10) Multi-functional task groups.

All of the above approaches have emerged in manufacturing industry since the 1970s and some have appeared in construction industry rather recently. They mainly look at the production process from a particular angle and are therefore partial approaches to productivity, although they have a common core concept. Lean philosophy generalises all of these partial approaches. For example, JIT looks at good flow control and reduction of stocks, TQM looks at quality and continuous improvement, TBM looks at reducing cycle times, concurrent engineering attempts to reduce overall project time by integrating design and construction and so on. Indeed, some of these methodologies are more important than others, depending on the situation or the industry to which they are applied, and therefore different authors have given different emphases. Various tools and techniques have been developed within the framework of these approaches; for example, quality circles and the seven statistical tools in the case of TQM.

9.6.3 Lean production applied to construction

The full potential of lean philosophy seems to be difficult to harness in the construction industry due to its inherent peculiarities and fragmented nature. However, initiatives like the 'sequential procedure' in France, the 'open building system' in the Netherlands, and the 'new construction mode' in Finland are directed at alleviating related problems. For example, the one-off nature of the sector is reduced through standardisation, modular coordination and widened role of contractors and suppliers; site production difficulties are reduced by increased use of prefabrication, temporal decoupling and through specialised or multi-functional teams; and the number of temporary linkages between organisations through long-term strategic alliances (Koskela 1997). In addition, QA and TQM, which are partial approaches to lean production, are increasingly being practised in the construction industry, as mentioned previously. Concepts similar to JIT have also been applied to construction, especially in the field of component manufacturing and prefabrication.

Under these circumstances, pioneering researchers in lean construction (Koskela 1997; Howell and Ballard 1997) indicate that there is tremendous potential in the application of lean philosophy in construction toward productivity improvement, and its successful application may result in a complete change in the way in which the construction industry operates at the present juncture. Researchers, however, caution that the construction industry must develop its own approaches to managing construction flows due to its inherent uncertainties rather than borrowing tools and techniques developed in manufacturing industry.

One of the prerequisites for the successful application of lean philosophy is to bring stability to the work environment by proper preplanning, not simply by the critical path methods currently in operation, which consider only conversion activities under very uncertain conditions, but by detailed consideration of reality according to the available data. To this end, several implementation strategies and techniques have already been proposed, for example, reducing inflow variation (Howell and Ballard 1997) and stabilising work flow (Ballard and Howell 1997). Indeed, for lean construction to be successful there should be a complete attitudinal change in all employees in an organisation. This is an essential component of the TQM previously discussed, hence TQM provides the necessary environment to introduce other lean concepts. Total quality management is therefore the integrator of lean concepts, without which all other partial approaches will fail in the long run.

Although there is a strong need for a complete new philosophy for the construction industry to reverse its continuing productivity decline and the ever-increasing gap between construction and manufacturing productivity, it is too early to predict the possible extent of the application of lean philosophy in construction compared to that practised in manufacturing. As Howell and Ballard point out, there should be substantial modification of at least some of the manufacturing lean production tools if they are to be realistic in the construction industry. Lean construction has attracted considerable attention from researchers in recent years, especially after the formation of the International Group on Lean Construction, and lean philosophy may perhaps be what the industry is waiting for to reverse its declining productivity. The interested reader is referred to Alarcon (1997) for a comprehensive discussion of lean concepts, implementation strategies, applications, tools and research areas.

9.7 A GLOBAL PRODUCTIVITY IMPROVEMENT SYSTEM

The situations where the productivity improvement principles, tools, techniques, models and procedures presented throughout the book should be applied were indicated when they were described. However, a clear understanding of the concepts, their integration and the sequence of application is necessary in order to obtain the maximum benefit of productivity improvement. This can be achieved by viewing the entire process of production as a global productivity improvement system (Figure 9.2). Indeed, a comprehensive system will include integration of all factors affecting productivity, covering inception to commissioning from the client's perspective and pre-tender planning to completion from the contractor's perspective. Figure 9.2 has been deliberately simplified with the emphasis on site labour productivity since it is through the operatives that the ultimate culmination of the efforts of all the parties end up in the completed product.

As discussed earlier, this system demands that the contractor should embrace the lean philosophy for maximum productivity and should practise TQM as *the* management system, which acts as the integrator and facilitator for the application of lean production principles and techniques. As can be seen, the productivity improvement principles, tools, techniques, models and procedures that were discussed previously are regularly applied both for the contractor organisation as a whole and for individual projects while operating within the framework of a project quality plan. The project quality plan emphasises the need for accurate preplanning and proper organisation at all stages of project execution as the most important activities in productivity improvement. Once these realistic plans are available, the system then shows the stages that should be followed to maximise on-site labour productivity through operative drive. These stages are described in detail in the following subsections, but first let us revisit standard output and capacity determination, which is the most important prerequisite for such productivity drives.

9.7.1 Standard output and capacity determination

As discussed in Chapter 4, *standard output* or *capacity* is basically the output of a properly motivated worker or gang carrying out a construction operation in a well-organised site, under satisfactory working conditions using efficient methods and is established by work measurement techniques. Clearly, these data form the basis for any productivity improvement effort because without a basis there is no target to achieve and no way of identifying how far the actual output is from that of the capacity. Thus, standard output or capacity determination is indeed the focal point in any mission towards on-site productivity improvement.

As suggested earlier, the best and most economic way to maintain such data, as done in some European countries, is for the construction industry authorities in individual countries to develop them centrally. They should be available for all main construction operations under different local conditions in the country. This reduces the cost of separate studies by individual organisations and the hoarding of scientific data by larger firms. Stored on a computer, data could be accessed on line by subscribing firms – a simple exercise today with the ever-advancing information transmission efficiency. Indeed, individual organisations can, and in fact should, maintain a supplementary standard data bank on activities specific to themselves to enhance their utilisation.

As discussed in Chapter 2, construction operations involve a significant proportion of contributory activities, which vary from trade to trade as well as type

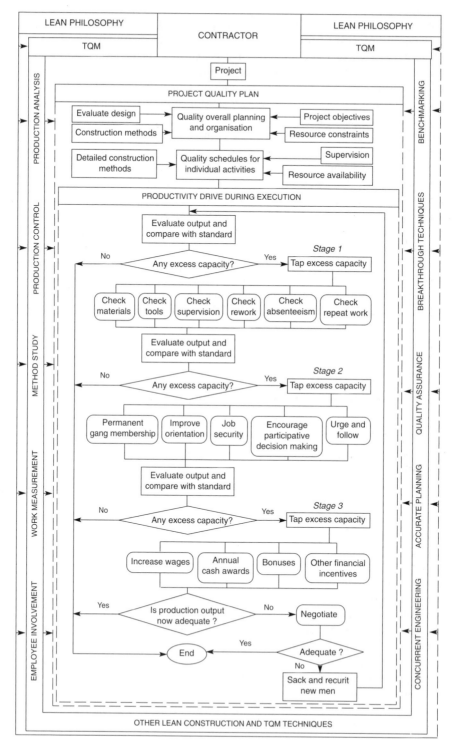

Figure 9.2 A global productivity improvement system.

of work within a trade. In addition to maintaining properly developed standard output values, it is also necessary to keep a record of the proportions of these contributory activities. Any unfavourable deviations can then be compared quickly with productivity ratings or activity sampling studies during construction.

9.7.2 Construction operative drive

Once the standard outputs or the capacities are known the productivity drive can commence. Clearly, attempts to improve productivity by concentrating only on the gang without removing production bottlenecks will not produce the desired results. Recent research (Olomolaiye 1989) indicates that motivation explains only 25% of the productive time; that is 75% is controlled by management actions, and on-site problems are more important than operative influences. The construction organisation's drive to improve operatives' productivity should therefore recognise the potential hierarchy of necessary management actions in approaching productivity. In other words, it is essential that management removes 'boulders' from its own eyes before the 'dust' in the operatives'. Lean construction still being in its experimental stages and the application of TQM also being relatively new, there are still ample opportunities for productivity improvement through rectification of management shortcomings. See Figure 2.2 for some of these shortcomings. A productivity drive should therefore follow from top management to operatives, as suggested in Figure 9.2 and explained below.

9.7.3 Tapping excess capacity

Excess capacity is the difference between standard output and observed output. It is always more productive to use optimistic standard output values for targets in any productivity drive, as seen in goal setting, although perhaps more realistic times modified by site factors, as discussed in Chapter 4, may be used for planning purposes to keep the productivity drive active all the time. Output values can be obtained during production by applying any of the production analysis tools described in the book but the most widely used – and the recommended technique – is activity sampling. This will help to identify causes of poor productivity, quantify unproductive times under each cause, and also indicate the need for further investigations.

  If there is excess capacity, which is most likely the case, Stage 1 of the productivity drive can start, in which excess capacity is reduced by removing production problems and inefficiencies within the control of management. For example, Table 9.1 shows the results of a production analysis study carried out on seven construction sites covering three trades, namely, joinery, bricklaying and steel fixing, using activity sampling. As can be seen, the mean percentages of working time are very low, indicating a lot of excess capacity in every trade. Clearly, a similar analysis can be carried out for a single project.

STAGE 1: REMOVAL OF MANAGEMENT SHORTCOMINGS

Management's general responsibilities for productivity include: (i) selection of the most productive construction methods based on a cost effective analysis of safety, cost, time, productivity, quality and availability and utilisation of resources; (ii) planning and organisation for timely project completion and to make sure that the workplaces are ready for uninterrupted progress of work; (iii) assignment of work to skilled and qualified workers and provision of training where required; and (iv) fostering of conditions where high motivation and willingness to cooperate naturally flourish.

By the time actual construction starts, selection of appropriate construction methods and overall planning should be at least partly complete. What remain in the hands of site management are: production planning and organisation, workload distribution, and continuous improvement of work-face activities using production analysis and method study techniques. Recent research indicates that more than 50% of the unproductive time of work-face activities is due to management shortcomings, hence it is a futile exercise to attempt any productivity drive without first addressing these problems.

The first step in tapping the excess capacity of workers should therefore be proper production planning and organisation, especially in drawing up weekly and daily work plans. The key here is to make *reliable* and *quality* plans for actual execution by considering the proper sequence of operations, and identifying the right

Table 9.1 Time utilisation by construction operatives in the key trades.

Trades/activities	Percentage of attendance time per site							
	Mean	A	B	C	D	E	F	G
Joinery								
Working	44	52	61	37	46	38	43	29
Idle	37	33	23	39	31	47	29	54
Taking instructions	13	7	11	13	21	9	19	13
Waiting	6	8	5	11	2	6	9	4
Bricklaying								
Working	51	53	72	50	22	56	54	48
Idle	27	24	14	35	39	27	28	20
Taking instructions	6	6	8	6	9	4	6	4
Waiting	16	17	6	9	30	13	12	28
Steel fixing								
Working	56	67	77	64	65	21	47	51
Idle	36	22	16	32	34	71	41	34
Taking instructions	5	8	6	3	1	7	4	4
Waiting	3	3	1	1	0	1	8	9

These are activity sampling results at 95% confidence level. Two typical craftsmen were chosen in each trade for the observations, with slight differences in the tasks performed from site to site (Olomolaiye *et al.* 1987).

quantity of work and the practicability of actual completion using available resources. Recent research has shown that reliable production planning is one of the key factors in productivity improvement (Ballard and Howell 1997) because (i) it ensures that the workplaces are ready for the gangs to continue work uninterrupted; (ii) gangs doing subsequent work receive a predictable flow of work, enabling advance planning and reduced unproductive time; (iii) buffer times can be reduced, enabling higher throughput; (iv) more time and energy are released to better match labour to work flow and to improve working methods; and (v) it removes workforce demotivators due to management shortcomings.

Problems arising out of unreliable production planning and organisation by management and their severity can be identified by production analysis techniques such as SDS and WQ, as discussed previously. For example, Table 9.2 shows the rank order of management shortcomings influencing site productivity on the same seven construction sites revealed by a worker questionnaire survey carried out at the same time as activity sampling (Olomolaiye and Ogunlana 1988). Some of these major problems are the ones shown in Figure 9.2 in the first stage of tapping excess capacity. Indeed, the severity of these problems may vary from contractor to contractor or from site to site, or depending on the employment conditions or even the effectiveness of site management. This should be investigated prior to taking action using a suitable technique such as SDS or WQ as in this example, where operatives were employed directly under a main contractor (Olomolaiye et al., 1987).

Lack of materials may be due to lack of proper financial planning and inadequate work scheduling. Making materials available involves materials planning with adequate scheduling of deliveries, checking all the deliveries to ensure that improper materials are not delivered, maintaining good storage space to ensure safe keeping of materials, a requisition system devoid of bottlenecks in getting materials to the workers, and a suitable on-site material transporting system both vertically and horizontally.

Making available proper tools and equipment will involve reliable scheduling and a good maintenance programme for existing tools, and purchase and safe keeping of an adequate number of good quality tools. Poor instructions from supervisors, misinterpretation of plans and design changes are some of the causes of repeat work, which is completely unproductive. Although reducing design changes is not directly within the control of the contractor, other causes can be overcome by proper involvement of supervisors in making short-term plans and getting such plans checked by site management for accuracy and reliability before actual execution. Absenteeism may be controlled by relating it to employment, making workers conscious of the possibility of dismissal in the event of unjustifiable absenteeism.

A further area of management shortcoming would be the inefficiencies of construction methods. This should be overcome by constant application of method study techniques, depending again on the severity of the problem identified from production analysis tools. After these management 'corrections' have been effected, a check should be made on the output of workers compared with established standards. If all excess capacities have been removed, the system should be

Table 9.2 Rank order of problems influencing operatives' productivity.

| Problem | Point total for ordering demotivators | | | | Relative index= point total/3×sample size | | | |
	Joiners	Brick-layers	Fixers	Totals	Joiners	Brick-layers	Fixers	Totals
Unavailability of materials	65	54	81	200	0.45	0.49	0.75	0.55
Unavailability of tools	49	30	38	117	0.34	0.27	0.35	0.32
Repeat work	55	75	49	179	0.38	0.68	0.45	0.49
Instruction delays	26	39	42	107	0.18	0.35	0.39	0.29
Inspection delays	33	56	21	110	0.23	0.50	0.19	0.30
Absenteeism	16	13	25	54	0.11	0.12	0.23	0.15
Supervisors' incompetence	26	32	22	80	0.18	0.29	0.20	0.22
Changing gang members	10	19	13	42	0.07	0.17	0.12	0.12

Sample size, 121; sample distribution: 48 joiners, 37 bricklayers and 36 steel fixers (Olomolaiye *et al.* 1987).

maintained by periodic productivity reviews. If there is still excess capacity, the drive can proceed to the second stage.

STAGE 2: WORKFORCE MOTIVATION WITHOUT FINANCIAL INCENTIVES

At this stage, operative motivators should be introduced in their rank order and demotivators should be systematically removed by a concerted management effort. These motivators and demotivators can also be identified by a similar production analysis technique such as SDS or WQ. For example, the rank order of operatives' motivators and demotivators revealed by WQ on the same seven sites are shown in Tables 9.3 and 9.4, respectively. Some of the motivators can be conveniently introduced while some demotivating conditions can be corrected easily. For example, provision of enough labourers, good safety standards and regular payment of wages can be corrected easily since they are discernible. However, other issues such as making tasks interesting, encouraging participative decision making and fostering good relationships with other workers require some management ingenuity.

Workers are generally interested in jobs that test their skill and imagination, which should be explored by supervisors when allocating work. When a task is challenging worker concentration is bound to increase, as seen in goal setting, and overcoming challenging tasks should always attract commendation from supervisors. A feeling of recognition is thereby aroused, leading to even better performance. Workers should be treated as part of the team and not just as instruments to be used and discarded after the project. Their views should be sought and they should be allowed to participate in the decision making process but not to the extent of giving them the upper hand, which may create a feeling in them that they are indispensable. Relationships among workers and understanding can be

Table 9.3 Rank order of operatives' motivators.

Motivator	Point total for ordering motivators				Relative index= point total/3×sample size			
	Joiners	Brick-layers	Fixers	Totals	Joiners	Brick-layers	Fixers	Totals
Fringe benefits	77	69	60	206	0.80	0.88	0.80	0.83
Good relationship with other workers	68	66	52	186	0.71	0.85	0.69	0.75
Challenging task	60	56	49	165	0.63	0.72	0.65	0.66
Job security	58	54	48	160	0.60	0.69	0.64	0.64
Recognition on the job	62	44	48	154	0.65	0.56	0.64	0.62
Good safety provision	57	44	47	148	0.59	0.56	0.63	0.59
Participating in decision making	58	35	47	140	0.60	0.45	0.63	0.56
Good orientation programme	58	32	46	130	0.60	0.41	0.61	0.55
Reduction in changing instructions	55	42	40	137	0.57	0.54	0.53	0.55

Sample size, 83; sample distribution: 32 joiners, 26 bricklayers and 25 steel fixers (Olomolaiye and Ogunlana 1988).

improved by reducing changing gang members, as this is one of the most important motivators (see Table 9.3).

When management urges higher productivity, it should be backed up with positive action rather than maintaining a nonchalant attitude. The literature indicates that motivators have a greater influence on productivity than demotivators (Herzberg 1968; Borcherding and Oglesby 1974; Olomolaiye et al. 1987) so management should concentrate more on motivational aspects. When the motivational situation has been rectified, another check should be conducted on the output. If no excess capacity is apparent, the productivity level should be maintained by regular reviews. If there is still excess capacity, the productivity drive continues to its final stage.

STAGE 3: INTRODUCTION OF FINANCIAL INCENTIVES

At this stage, financial incentives tied to performance should be introduced to boost workers' outputs. It should be emphasised that these financial incentives should be no more than a reasonable wage for a fair day's work. Excess capacity remaining up to this stage may mean that workers are being underpaid. Efforts should be made to give them a fair price for their input but care is necessary because an increase in income without a corresponding increase in output will mean lower productivity. It may therefore be necessary for some bargaining to be done before there is any increase in wages or bonuses. After introducing financial incentives, another check should be made on the output to check its adequacy. If it is inadequate an attempt

Table 9.4 Rank order of operatives' demotivators.

| Demotivator | Point total for ordering demotivators | | | | Relative index= point total/3×sample size | | | |
	Joiners	Brick-layers	Fixers	Totals	Joiners	Brick-layers	Fixers	Totals
Bad treatment by the supervisors	64	73	51	188	0.67	0.94	0.68	0.76
Lack of recognition of effort	53	67	65	185	0.55	0.86	0.87	0.74
Productivity urged but no one cares	80	40	48	176	0.92	0.51	0.64	0.71
Reducing work	77	52	40	169	0.80	0.67	0.53	0.68
Incompetence of gang members	59	59	47	165	0.61	0.76	0.63	0.66
Lack of communication	73	45	38	156	0.76	0.58	0.51	0.63
Underutilisation of skill	46	33	53	132	0.48	0.42	0.71	0.53
Lack of participation in decision making	55	38	39	132	0.57	0.49	0.52	0.53
Unsafe conditions	60	30	43	133	0.63	0.38	0.57	0.53
Poor inspection and supervision	52	41	29	122	0.54	0.53	0.39	0.49
Little accomplishment	50	37	34	118	0.52	0.47	0.45	0.47

Sample size, 83; sample distribution: 32 joiners, 26 bricklayers and 25 steel fixers (Olomolaiye and Ogunlana 1988).

should be made to renegotiate with the workers. If there is no sufficient improvement after negotiations, it may be assumed that workers are restricting output and a staggered system of dismissal should be adopted while new workers are being recruited. This will ensure continuity of work and at the same time much needed reorganisation. For this system to work, the sequential order of tests and analysis should be followed. The usual temptation to jump to the financial incentives stage should be avoided because research has proved that they are mere 'movements' and do not lead to higher productivity if improperly applied (Herzberg 1968; Neal 1979; Oxley 1978).

9.7.4 The concept of break-even and hyper-productivity

When the observed worker output is equal to the established worker capacity there is a break-even relationship between the site and the industry and both the site and the worker can be described as 'break-even' or typical. If management is satisfied with this output, it should be maintained as the break-even productivity. If the observed output is greater than the established capacity then there is a positive variance, which means getting more from the workers than what the industry expects them to give. This is construed as hyper-productivity, a rare phenomenon in the construction industry. See Figure 9.3 for the conceptual frame. It may be counterproductive if not applied carefully. However, as a cup is not full until it is filled to overflowing, productivity will not be optimised until this realm of hyper-productivity is reached. After the optimal level is reached (a very challenging management task in real life) there is a need for management to be careful that the 'overdrive' level is not reached, because this will be counterproductive.

The standard capacity of construction workers will reflect the general level of skill in particular trades and activities. If worker performance improves with more training, technological growth and as a result of the breakthrough approaches discussed previously, the standard capacity will have to be adjusted. If this is not done, the industry or the contractor may be under an illusion of overdrive when, in fact, there is none.

This concept can be moulded into an expert system package for monitoring and improving productivity in construction operatives. Such a system can be aggregated into a congenial expert system incorporating all aspects of operative productivity improvement and updated with skill variations and technological changes as an effective management tool for improved productivity.

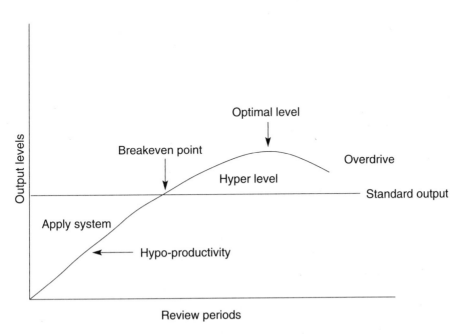

Figure 9.3 A conceptual frame of construction hyper-productivity.

9.8 SUMMARY

The first part of this chapter discussed goal setting with special emphasis on its application for maximising labour productivity. It then described several other concepts and methodologies, namely, quality management, benchmarking, breakthrough approaches and lean construction, as overall performance enhancing approaches for long-term excellence in the construction industry. Finally, a global productivity improvement system was presented with the emphasis on labour productivity, integrating all of the related productivity enhancement approaches.

REFERENCES AND BIBLIOGRAPHY

Alarcon L., ed. (1997). *Lean Construction*. Rotterdam: A.A. Balkema

APQC (1992). *Planning, Organising and Managing Benchmarking Activities: User's Guide*. Houston, TX: APQC

Ashford J.L. (1989). *The Management of Quality in Construction*. London: E&FN Spon

Ballard G. and Howell G. (1997). Implementing lean construction: stabilising work flow. In *Lean Construction* (Alarcon L., ed.), pp. 101–110. Rotterdam: A.A Balkema

Borcherding J.D. and Oglesby C.H. (1974). Construction productivity and job satisfaction. *Journal of the Construction Division ASCE*, **100**(CO3), 413–431

British Standards Institution (1992). *Total Quality Management (BS 7850)* London: BSI

Burati J.L. and Oswald T.H. (1993). Implementing TQM in engineering and construction. *Journal of Management in Engineering ASCE*, **9**(4), 456–471

Burati J.L., Matthews M.F. and Kalidindi, S.N. (1991). Quality management in construction industry. *Journal of Construction Engineering and Management ASCE*, **117**(2), 341–359

Burati J.L., Matthews M.F. and Kalidindi S.N. (1992). Quality management organisations and techniques. *Journal of Construction Engineering and Management ASCE*, **118**(1), 112–128

Camp R.C. (1989). *Benchmarking: The Search for Industry Best Practices that Lead to Superior Performance*. American Society of Quality Control. Quality Press

Caplen R.H. (1988). *A Practical Approach to Quality Control* 5th edn. Business Books

Chase G.W. (1993). Effective total quality management (TQM) process for construction. *Journal of Management in Engineering ASCE*, **9**(4), 433–443

Costanzo L. (1993). Benchmarking: top of the class. *Engineering*, **233**(8), 27

Culp G., Smith A. and Abbott, J. (1993). Implementing TQM in consulting engineering firm. *Journal of Management in Engineering ASCE*, **9**(4), 340–356

Deffenbaugh R.L. (1993). Total quality management at construction job sites. *Journal of Management in Engineering ASCE*, **9**(4), 382–389

Deming W.E. (1988). *Out of Crisis*. Cambridge, MA: MIT Press

Demski S. (1993). Resistance to change: why your TQM efforts may fail. *Journal of Management in Engineering. ASCE*, **9**(4), 326–332

Duncan J., Thorpe B. and Sumner P. (1990). *Quality Assurance in Construction*. London: Gower

ECI (1991a). *Report on the total quality management task force – stage 1*. European Construction Institute, Loughborough University, UK

ECI (1991b). *Total quality in construction – measurement matrix and guidelines for improvement*. European Construction Institute, Loughborough University, UK

ECI (1991c). *Total quality in construction – stage 2*. European Construction Institute, Loughborough University, UK

ECI (1994). *Total productivity management: guidelines for the construction phase*, Productivity Task Force, European Construction Institute, Loughborough University, UK

Federle M.O. and Chase G.W. (1993). Applying total quality management to design and construction. *Journal of Management in Engineering ASCE*, **9**(4), 357–364

Fletcher S. (1993). *Quality and Competence – Integrating Competence and Quality Initiatives*. New York: Kogan Page

Graves R. (1993). Total quality – does it work in engineering management? *Journal of Management in Engineering ASCE*, **9**(4), 444–455

Hadavi A. and Krizek R.J. (1993). Short-term goal setting for construction. *Journal of Construction Engineering and Management ASCE*, **119**, 622–630

Hellard R.B. (1993). *Total Quality in Construction Projects*. London: Thomas Telford

Hensey, M. (1993). Essential tools for total quality management. *Journal of Management in Enginnering ASCE*, **9**(4), 329–339

Herzberg F. (1968). One more time – how do you motivate employees? *Harvard Business Review*, **46**(1), 53–62

Howell G. and Ballard G. (1997). Implementing lean construction: reducing inflow variation. In *Lean Construction* (Alarcon L., ed.), pp. 93–100. Rotterdam: A. A. Balkema

Hughes T. and Williams T. (1991). *Quality Assurance – A framework to Build on*. Oxford: Blackwell Science

Imai M. (1986). *Kaizen, the Key to Japan's Competitive Success*. New York: Random House

Ishikawa K. (1990). *Introduction to Quality Control*. London: Chapman & Hall

Juran J.M. (1989). *Juran on Leadership for Quality*. New York: Macmillan

Karlof B. and Ostblom S. (1993). *Benchmarking: A Signpost to Excellence in Quality and Productivity*. Chichester: John Wiley & Sons

Karsnia A.L. (1991). Toward world class development: benchmarking to improve project management practices. In *Seminar Proc.*, pp. 1–9, Project Management Institute, Dallas, Texas

Koskela L. (1997). Lean production in construction. In *Lean Construction* (Alarcon L., ed.), pp. 1–10. Rotterdam: A.A. Balkema

Latham G.P. and Locke E.A. (1979). Goal setting – a motivational technique that works. *Organisational Dynamics*, **8**(2), 68–80

Laufer A. and Howell G. (1993). Construction planning: revising the paradigm, *Project Management Journal*, **24**(3), 83–90

Lema N.M. and Price A.D.F. (1994). Benchmarking: performance, improvement towards competitive advantage. *Journal of Management in Engineering ASCE*, **11**(1), 28–36

Locke E.A. and Latham G.P. (1990). *A Theory of Goal Setting and Task Performance*. Englewood Cliffs, NJ: Prentice Hall

Main M. (1992). How to steal the best ideas around. *Fortune International*, **126**(8), 86–89

Mefford R.N. (1991). Quality and productivity: the linkage. *International Journal of Production Economics*, **24**, 137–145

Melles B. (1997). What do we mean by lean production in construction? In *Lean Construction* (Alarcon L., ed.), pp. 11–16. Rotterdam: A.A. Balkema

Neal R.H. (1979). Motivation of construction workers – theory and practice. *CIOB Site Management Information Service*, no. 78

Oakland J.S. (1989). *Total Quality Management*. London: Butterworth-Heinemann

Olomolaiye P.O. (1989). A review of construction operative motivation. *Building and Environment*, **24**(3), 279–287

Olomolaiye P.O. and Ogunlana S.O. (1988). A survey of construction operative motivation on selected sites in Nigeria. *Building and Environment*, **23**((3), 179–185

Olomolaiye P.O. and Ogunlana S.O. (1989). A system for monitoring and improving operative productivity in Nigeria. *Construction Management and Economics,* **7**, 175–186

Olomolaiye P.O., Wahab K.A. and Price A.D.F. (1987). Problems influencing craftsmen's productivity in Nigeria. *Building and Environment*, **22**(4), 317–323

Oxley R. (1978), Incentives in the construction industry – effects on earnings and costs. *CIOB Site Management Information Service*, no. 74

Peratec (1994). *Total Quality Management: The Key to Business Improvment*. London: Chapman & Hall

Ryan M.M. and Sebastianelli S.R. (1987). Team goal setting-key to sucessful productivity effort. *Journal of Management in Engineering ASCE*, **3**(4), 325–334

Shetty Y.K. (1993). Aiming high: competitive benchmarking for superior performance. *Long Range Planning*, **26**(1), 39–44

Stevens J.D. (1996). Blueprint for measuring project quality. *Journal of Management in Engineering ASCE*, **12**(2), 34–39

Strange P.S. and Vaughan G.D. (1993). TQM: A view from the playing field: *Journal of Management in Engineering ASCE*, **9**(4), 390–398

Walker J. and Allen D. (1993). *The Quality Management Manual*. New York: Kogan Page

Watson G.H. (1993). *Strategic Benchmarking: How to Rate Your Company's Performance against the World's Best*. New York: John Wiley & Sons

INDEX